WRITING IN TIME

A POLITICAL CHRONICLE

Also by the author:

The Village of Ben Suc

The Military Half

The Time of Illusion

The Fate of the Earth

The Abolition

History in Sherman Park

The Real War

Observing the Nixon Years

WRITING IN TIME

A POLITICAL CHRONICLE

by Jonathan Schell

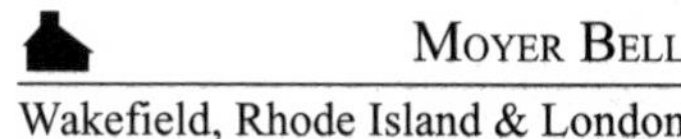
Moyer Bell
Wakefield, Rhode Island & London

Published by Moyer Bell

Jacket design: Darcy Magratten Design

First Edition

LIBRARY OF CONGRESS
CATALOGING IN PUBLICATION DATA

Schell, Jonathan
Writing in time: a political chronicle

p. cm.

Columns published in Newsday between 1990 and 1996.
1. United States-Foreign relations-1989–1993 2. United States-Politics and government-1989–1993 3. United States-Foreign relations-1993– 4. United States-Politics and government-1993–
I. Title
E881.S34 1997
973.928—dc20 96-8516
ISBN 1-55921-177-6 cloth CIP

Printed in the United States of America.
Distributed in North America by Publishers Group West,
P.O. Box 8843, Emeryville, CA 94662, 800-788-3123
(in California 510-658-3453)

For Niccolò Tucci, whose work and conversation
remind me again and again what it is
that a writer and writing should be

ACKNOWLEDGMENTS

All but one of the pieces collected in this book were written for *Newsday* and *New York Newsday* (which, alas, is no more), or both. The other piece was written for *The Atlantic Monthly.* It was my great and rare good fortune to work at the two *Newsdays* with a series of wonderful editors–Ben Gerson, Ken Emerson, Noel Rubinton, Ernest Tollerson and Chris Lehmann, all of whom worked, in turn, under the direction of the thoughtful and beneficent editor of *Newsday*'s editorial page, Jim Klurfeld. I am deeply grateful to them. But my special thanks must go to Ben Gerson, who invited me to write for the papers. His delicate, meticulous editing, discernment, and inspired editorial judgment are anonymously present everywhere in this book.

CONTENTS

INTRODUCTION

IN SEPTEMBER OF 1990, I BEGAN WRITING A COLUMN for *Newsday* and its sister paper in New York City, the late *New York Newsday*, which was folded by its parent company, The Los Angeles Times Company, in the summer of 1995. I was returning to a form of writing—the short, timely, political commentary—that I had given up two years before, when I had left *The New Yorker*, for which, during the better part of the previous two decades, I had been the principal writer for the "Notes and Comment" section of "The Talk of the Town." In those years, the dominant, overarching political drama, in which most other events had their place and acquired their meaning, was, of course, the Cold War. Certainly, almost all of the main issues that I had written about for *The New Yorker*—the Vietnam war, the constitutional crisis that came to a head in the Watergate scandal, the anti-communist rebellions in Eastern Europe, the nuclear confrontation between the Soviet Union and the United States—were subplots of that half-century-long struggle. In the fall of 1990, however, the Cold War was on its last legs. Within the year, it would formally end, with the wholly unexpected dissolution not just of the conflict between the Soviet Union and the United States but of the Soviet Union itself. The abruptness of the Union's disintegration left the world dumbfounded. No thought had been given to the shape of the post-Cold-War world because almost no one—and certainly not those in charge of American foreign policy—had anticipated living in that world. The principal stakes in the Cold War struggle—human freedom on the one hand, human survival on the other—were immense, and they were clear to almost everyone. But what was at stake in the new era? What was its character? We embarked on a shapeless, themeless, foggy period—a season of hesitations, failed predictions, irresolute initiatives, false starts, and dumb inertia. Looking back, one is struck by how much sheer silliness was taken seriously—by the number of short-lived global "visions" that came and went in the oratory of the period, of "defining moments" that turned out to define nothing, of "historical realignments" and "revolutions" that lasted but a day.

Like all journalism, the columns I wrote for the two *Newsdays* were attempts to write in time. By writing in time, I mean, in the first place, simply writing and publishing quickly enough to be of service to citizens and other actors as they make their decisions. If reporters give citizens the facts they need to carry out their responsibilities, columnists round out the picture by trying to make sense of the facts. You could do worse than describe a columnist as a citizen who has been given the privilege of devoting all his working time to the duties of citizenship. An ideal columnist would be an ideal citizen. By writing in time, I mean, in the second place, writing with an eye cast forward to the future as well as backward upon the past. For whatever a column's immediate subject matter may be, present or past, it always, in addition, addresses the future. Most columnists are respectful enough of the mischievous gods of history, who love nothing better than upending conventional wisdom (viz., the unforeseen collapse of the Soviet Union), to resist the temptation of making flat predictions. (The lists of predictions that some columnists go in for at the beginning of each year are the playful exceptions to the rule.) But the fact is that every column is a wager that the future will take one shape or another—a bet, for instance, that some peril or opportunity is real, and perhaps growing, while others are dwindling, or imaginary. They say of the owl that symbolizes wisdom that it flies at dusk—that all wisdom is retrospective. But such wisdom can hardly satisfy in a political column, which, like a weather report, is worthless if it does not also manage, however obliquely, to shed some light forward into the future. Thus does it happen that every column is put, sooner or later, to an exacting test—the test of future events, which can render political commentary ridiculous in dismayingly short order. Such, for example, was the fate of the commentators who, in the 1930s, advised that Hitler could be appeased by concessions; or of those who, in the 1960s, said that there was light at the end of the tunnel in Vietnam; or those who, in the 1980s, said that Gorbachev's *perestroika* was a mere smokescreen to conceal a mighty Soviet Union's stepped-up timetable for world domination.

A column is also put to a further, and, in some respects harsher test—the test of the ethical opinions of posterity. For example, the defenders of slavery in the United States in the 1850s, of Stalin and Hitler in the 1930s, or of racial segregation in the United States in the 1950s all face the settled disapprobation of majority opinion today. The question what weight to attach to the judgments of posterity is a deep and difficult one, for each posterity will, after all, be succeeded by further posterities, who may arrive at different judgments. Perhaps slavery, the rule of Stalin and Hitler, and racial segregation will be smiled upon by future generations, though we may doubt it. Suffice it to say that writers who, like newspaper columnists, form their opinions on the cusp of moment, not in order to make sense of action after the fact but to precede and inspire it, run an abnormally high risk of making instant fools of themselves.

None of this is meant to strike a self-pitying note or to claim any heroic virtues for the column-writing tribe. There is no doubt that a lot that is written by us columnists richly deserves the oblivion into which it instantly falls. One may even wonder whether columns, whose very nature it is to be written in and for the present, ever deserve the second look that collection in a book affords. One justification, it seems to me, lies precisely in the fact that at the time they were written the future, in all its menace, hope, and unfathomable uncertainty, still lay open. Historians, no matter how careful they may be, risk a sort of falsification by hindsight. Bent as they are on explaining *why* things happened as they did, they are in danger of overlooking the open-endedness of events and the inevitability and importance of individual choice, which is to say the importance of freedom. Such temptations are not placed in the way of columnists who, in their unequal wrestling match with time, scarcely dare predict anything at all, much less declare something inevitable. A column, unlike a work of history, is written from the anxious, unsettled, and unsettling position in which each and every one of us, as we go through life, stands, and will forever stand, in relation to the future.

In the interest of brevity or coherence, I have restricted the present volume to columns that addressed, directly or indirectly, a single running theme. I believed while I was writing the column—and believe now—that the most important event of the period was something that did *not* happen. I mean a bi-partisan, multi-national undertaking by the Western nations and like-minded allies and friends around the world to seize the God-given opportunity presented by the end of the Cold War to offer their former antagonists in the East an ambitious plan for economic aid, political cooperation, and radical disarmament (the Marshall plan at the end of the Second World War is the obvious precedent), including especially nuclear disarmament, all of which together might have created the foundation for a lasting, durable peace. However, there are only so many times that one can bewail a non-event. In this book, I have retained two of several columns in which I made the complaint. There was, however, another thread that ran through the columns, which ended in 1996, with a year-long series of longer pieces on the 1996 election. This was a many-sided change in the American political system that gathered momentum in these years. I hesitate, in the aftermath of so many evanescent "revolutions," to use that word. Let us, a little more modestly, call it a systemic transformation. Its apparent cause is the virtual takeover of politics by the burgeoning techniques of communication (those used to measure opinion as well as those used to influence opinion); its broad effect has been to move the system away from its formal representative character toward a kind of informal, passive plebiscitary system; and the danger it poses is a radical reduction in the role of judgment and deliberation by the people's representatives in the formation of policy. But since these developments are the matter of this book, I'll say no more about them here.

In short pieces that follow the twists and turns of a single story, reiterations of the tale so far are bound to be frequent. Since in a book presenting all the pieces together such passages become repetitions, I have deleted them wherever possible. I was on leave for 1995, so no columns appear for that year. I have included an article that appeared in *The Atlantic Monthly* in August of 1996. I have not deleted any columns or parts of columns because, in hindsight, I thought I had made a mistake. Such deletions would be out of keeping with the spirit of the enterprise, which is to risk rendering judgments on events as they happen, and hazard the knowing smiles of a wiser posterity.

I
ELECTION

JANUARY 19, 1992

THIS COLUMN IS NOT ABOUT BILL CLINTON, THE governor of Arkansas, who is running for the Democratic nomination for the presidency. It is about something that has happened to Clinton as the primaries draw near. He has become the "front-runner" in the Democratic race. We know he has become the front-runner because the most important newspapers and television stations have said so. *The New York Times* has referred to his "front-runner" status. Morton Kondracke, of *The New Republic*, has said on "The McLaughlin Group" on NBC, "I assume Clinton's the front-runner." *Time* has called him "the front-runner by default." Even foreign news organizations have picked up the refrain. "Arkansas Gov. Bill Clinton has emerged as the clear front-runner to represent the Democratic Party," *Agence France-Presse* has bluntly informed its readers. Some go a step further and ask, with Joe Klein, of *New York* magazine, whether Clinton may not be on the verge of locking up the nomination in the season's first primary in New Hampshire.

But just what, we may ask, is a front-runner? How can you tell who is one and who isn't? Who confers this honor, and what does it mean? If someone is crowned king, I know what has happened. If he shouts "Off with his head!," some poor wretch's head is going to roll. If someone is elected president, I know what that means, too. I even have some idea of what it means if someone wins the Democratic primary in New Hampshire. But what can it mean for someone to be "anointed" (as they say) front-runner in a political contest before a single vote has been cast? The general meaning of the word is clear enough. A front-runner is the person deemed likeliest to win a race or contest. It's surprising, therefore, to find that many of those who maintain that Clinton is the front-runner tell us in their very next breath that this by no means guarantees Clinton an advantage over his rivals. On the contrary, being the front-runner, they cagily warn, may actually be a drawback. "Front-runners . . . ," the *Times* quickly reminds its readers, "are often bleeders, particularly front-runners who acquire that status with no input from the voters . . ." By this reckoning, then, front-runners in presidential races may be candidates who have acquired a significant handicap in their run for the presidency. From this, we might draw the following conclusion: Front-runners in political races are those who have fallen behind the other candidates. After all, our interest is to know who is likely to be the nominee, and if "front-runner status" is a harbinger of failure, then the phrase must in this case signify the very opposite of what the words plainly mean. That such paradoxical speculations are not idle can be shown by many examples, including that of Sen. Edmund S. Muskie of Maine, who in 1972 was widely designated the Democratic front-runner in the months before the primaries but went down to rapid defeat as soon as the voting began.

The elaborate business of front-runnership becomes more elaborate still when we remember that the principal (though not the only) evidence that someone is the front-runner is the fact that he is reported to be one. To be fully accurate, articles reporting that someone is a front-runner ought to cite those very same articles as evidence of the fact. The *Washington Post*, indeed, recently followed a procedure close to this one. One article, which seemed almost self-consciously to avoid calling Clinton the "front-runner" (it called him "the attention-getter in January, 1992" instead), reported his growing "success" among political professionals. Another article the same day reported that the press had bestowed "front-runner status" on Clinton, and mentioned one of the paper's own columnists as someone who had participated in the deed.

The impression that being a front-runner is a sort of curse is only strengthened when we read that the candidates thus labeled often strenuously shun the honor, as Clinton did recently in New Hampshire. His aides claim that former Democratic Sen. Paul Tsongas, who does in fact lead in the polls in New Hampshire, is the front-runner. Candidates, it seems, fear having to live up to the high expectations imposed on a front-runner, and live in dread of the sudden deflation of a candidacy that can occur when a supposed front-runner is dethroned from his position by some minor reversal. They know that the very pressures that caused the press and others to puff up the doubtful bubble of front-runnership may drive them shortly to burst it. They know, too, that voters may resent the preemption of the people's will by reporters and political professionals, and vote out of spite for someone less celebrated, who then, in the full and true sense of the word, will be the front-runner.

FEBRUARY 16, 1992

IN THE LAST DAYS OF THE PRESIDENTIAL PRIMARY IN New Hampshire, Gov. Bill Clinton of Arkansas has taken to running against the press, which, he says, has unfairly harmed his candidacy in recent weeks. He urges the people to take politics back from "the tabloids." He is right to do so. American politics is in the grip of a pathology that needlessly harms or destroys candidates for public office. Just as the freedom of the press is weakened whenever a publication is lost, so the people's right to choose their own government is weakened whenever a political candidate is unjustly driven out of political life. There is no such thing as political choice when there is no field of candidates among whom to choose. In defending himself, therefore, Clinton protects the political process, which is the country's principal instrument for dealing with the problems it faces in what promise to be rough times ahead.

At the heart of the pathology is the grotesquely disproportionate coverage given to accusations that are either unproven or are irrelevant to the choices before the voters. The destruction of people's reputations by false charges is an old story, as readers of history, including the history of the McCarthy period, are well aware. Today's version of the old story, however, has some new twists, and it is important to try to understand exactly what is going on. The accusations that have threatened Clinton's candidacy are, as everyone knows by now, those by Gennifer Flowers that he had an extramarital affair with her, and the press reports that he improperly secured a deferment from the draft for three months in 1969, while the Vietnam War was raging.

Each story is, in its way, empty of substance. Clinton, who has admitted to "difficulties" in his marriage, flatly denies Flowers's charge, and no independent source has confirmed it. This story has remained just that—a tale, though now known to the whole country, that is untethered to any reliable facts. The draft story is more complex. In 1968, Clinton's draft board in Arkansas temporarily exempted him from the draft, so that he could study at Oxford University, in England. When he returned to the United States, in the summer of 1969, he understood that the deferment would end. He thereupon signed up with the Reserve Officer

Training Corps, which entitled him to a further deferment (but required him to serve as an officer at a later date). A few months later, he told ROTC that he was withdrawing from the program—thereby putting an end to his deferment and leaving him open to be drafted. However, two months later, in December, 1969, the draft lottery was instituted. Clinton received a high number and was never called up.

Unlike the Flowers story, this one has the advantage of being based on certain ascertainable facts. The difficulty comes when one tries to figure out what, if anything, it means. After all, as Clinton has pointed out, his decision to leave ROTC ended a deferment and made him available for the draft. To put the very worst construction on his actions, one might say that by signing up for ROTC, he kept himself out of the draft pool during two months in which he might have been somewhat more likely to be drafted than he was under the lottery that he volunteered for. All in all, the story would seem to be more to his credit than otherwise.

Why, then, has so much coverage been given to the two stories? The most common explanation is that, whether true or false, relevant to Clinton's fitness or not, they have damaged his "electability." And since electability, in this view, has always been one of Clinton's primary claims on the Democratic voters' allegiance, the stories were politically significant. Few in the news business say to themselves, "I believe that Governor Clinton had this affair, and I judge that this unfits him for the presidency; therefore, I will report the story." But many say, "Others may believe the story, and others may judge that it unfits him for the presidency, thereby destroying his electability; and that is news, so I will report it." In a curious displacement of the role of judgment in democratic political life, no one in this process consults his own opinions. All busy themselves asking what someone else's opinion might be. Thus do stories that are pointless, unconfirmed or simply untrue sweep like tornados through the political scene.

When that happens, the stories, though empty, acquire an undeniable, derivative importance, for they begin to shape the fortunes of the United States. Then everyone—voters, candidates and the press alike—must concern themselves with them, if only to urge that the press begin to act on its own judgment of what is important, leaving the voters to decide on election day who is electable and who is not.

MARCH 15, 1992

FINDING MYSELF BEWILDERED IN SOME NEW WAY about my reaction to the presidential campaign, I turned introspective for a moment. In a presidential election, the civics books tell us, the voters choose the person they think will be the best president. Yet as the campaign proceeds I discover that I am doing something considerably more elaborate. I am looking at each candidate with two sets of eyes. One set is my own pair: I am asking myself who I think will make the best president, just as the civics books say I should. The other set belongs to all the other voters. Once I have looked at the candidates in these two ways, a process of dickering and horse-trading starts up within me, as if a miniature political convention has convened right within my own mind.

Let me give an example. Using my own eyes, I was drawn to Gov. Bill Clinton's call to "invest in people"—a principle he seems ready and well-qualified to back up with specific legislation.

However, I deeply dislike the support he gave to the Persian Gulf war, which I regard as having been a gigantic folly and diversion. On the other hand—closing my own eyes now and starting to look at Clinton through others voters' eyes—I am aware that this support recommends him to most people as president. In the smoke-filled room of my mind, I note that I may be able to get the social legislation Clinton offers if I'm ready to stomach his support for the Gulf war. It seems that I—a simple voter, not a corrupt "politician"—am tempted to compromise my principles even before I get into the voting booth. What hope, then, is there for the principles of politicians, who face all the temptations of power in their quest for votes? We have a word—"pandering"—for the politician who abandons his principles to align himself with a majority of voters. But what is the word for the voter who does likewise?

There is a word for the quality that is supposed to inspire this derivative loyalty—electability. Electability, however, is more than popularity. It is an aura of success—almost a sort of charisma—attracting to the candidate's side all of those for whom success (success in no matter what) is the dominant consideration.

In earlier times, knowledge of what and whom voters might prefer was sharply restricted, for the most part, to hunches. But with the rise of public opinion research such calculations have become a light industry. What is more, by a process that no one has yet described, an apparent rule has developed that political commentators on television must restrict themselves almost entirely to analysis of how well the candidates are doing in the race—of whether candidate X met "expectations" that were set for him in Florida, whether candidate Y did better than before with voters who want politicians to "care for someone like me," whether candidate Z succeeded in "defining himself" or let his opponent define him. (In politics today, it's taken for granted that a "self" is something that can be manufactured by the person who wants one, or even by his advisers.) Rarely is anyone heard giving his own opinion on the merits of a candidate. For example, in this election year I have yet to hear a single discussion on television among supporters of candidates—unless, of course, those supporters were the candidates themselves.

It is this stream of analysis that the campaign propagandists called spin-doctors seek to direct when they offer their self-serving interpretations of political debates and other events. The spinning arts are substance-neutral. The spinners never say that their candidate has the best program for the economy, that he will help the poor, that he will bring world peace. They always say that his campaign is succeeding in making lots of voters think those things. They always say that he is on his way to being elected, not that he deserves to be.

Probably, some compromises by voters are inherent in elections—inherent, that is, in democracy. If a mandate to govern is to emerge out of the votes of tens of millions of people, it seems unavoidable that voters, even as they consult their own judgment and consciences, will cast a sidelong glance at what they think the rest of the electorate is likely to do. The danger, though—greater in our time than ever before—is that in the process an elementary datum of political life will be lost: each individual voter's preference for president. It would be strange indeed if, in our passionate curiosity to know what the will of the people is, we meddled with that will. An election then would produce a result never anticipated by our founding fathers: the choice not of the president the people wanted but of the president that each person thought all the others wanted.

MARCH 22, 1992

WHEN THE AFFAIR OF THE BANK IN THE U. S. HOUSE OF Representatives rocketed into prominence, the outrage was seemingly universal. The invitation to anger offered on all sides was tempting. Of course, the notion that people in public office have abused their power, and are in need of a rebuke from a virtuous, indignant public, always has its appeal. A moment's thought, however, raised doubts whether this story belonged in that category. There was, to begin with, the surprising fact that the affair, routinely described as a "check-bouncing scandal" (for example, *Newsweek* called Congress "Bouncers Anonymous"), and referred to as "Rubbergate" by many, was patently misnamed. For not one check, as far as we know, had in fact bounced. No tradesman had presented a congressman's check to the bank only to discover that he was cheated and deceived, that no funds were available. On the contrary, every check was honored. Indeed, the scandal, if there was one, consisted exactly in this: Checks that, if written against an ordinary bank account, would have bounced, did not, for it was the policy of this bank to permit members to write checks against their next month's pay check. It was a check-honoring scandal, not a check-bouncing one, and the checks, far from being made of rubber, were coated with infallible adhesive.

It remains to ask whether the honoring of the checks was a scandal. At my local bank, I can sign up for a check-covering arrangement under which, for a certain fee for each uncovered check, and payment of interest, the bank will cover overdrafts. The house bank did the same without charging a fee or interest. (On the other hand, it paid no interest on deposits, either, as accounts that hold more than a certain minimum do at my bank.) In escaping such costs, it's true, the congressional check-writers were getting a small benefit that the average person does not. The benefit was extended, however, not by taxpayers, none of whose money was involved, but by some seventy congressmen who kept adequate balances—for the funds in the bank consist entirely of deposits made by the members. In other words, what we know so far is that a few dozen prudent congressmen have knowingly and cheerfully been covering the temporary imbalances of hundreds of less prudent congressmen. All in all, it sounds like a rather collegial thing to have done. That is the great "scandal," which some have said is as important as Watergate. That is all.

Why, then, is the public so deeply outraged—more so, if reports are to believed, than it is by the half-trillion dollar savings and loan scandal, which is reaching deep into the pocket of every taxpayer? (The outrage is so widespread that accused congressmen scarcely dare to defend themselves. Apparently, they judge a defense of innocence more dangerous politically than contrition for uncommitted offenses.) The flat-out misnomer of the affair, which turns the facts completely on their head, suggests a reason. The public, we're told, is "angry." An ABC poll has made it official by adding "Angry" to its list of types of voters whose inclinations it inquires into. The voters, it's said, are disgusted with the whole government. Yet herein lies a paradox. If our leaders have been taking the country in the wrong direction (and I agree that they have), they have been doing so at the invitation of the very voters who now are angry. For the plain truth is that the policies that have got the country in trouble—the expenditure without adequate taxation, the lax regulation, the gross neglect of social welfare, to name a few—have been the policies that the voters wanted, and have rewarded at the polls. In these circumstances, shame would be a more appropriate response than anger. Yet no "Ashamed" group appears in the pollsters' tables.

In the United States in recent years, the people have, at best, been slumbering. Almost half of the eligible voters have not voted at all in recent presidential elections. Now, displeased with the consequences of the choices they have listlessly made, they are angry. Yet the voters on the whole do not, it seems, want to go as far as to be angry at themselves. That, I think, is where the supposed "check-bouncing" scandal comes in. It deflects attentions from the mistaken policies that the voters wanted and that the politicians slavishly gave them and concentrates attention on supposed individual lapses for which the public obviously has no responsibility. It is a way of blaming "them" for the country's travails without recognizing that all along they were obeying "us."

APRIL 12, 1992

AN ELECTION IS THE MEANS BY WHICH A SELF-governing people is supposed to express its will, but in the presidential election of 1992, this is plainly not happening. The people are obscuring their will. They are hiding.

A few statistics make the point. Forty-seven percent of registered voters in New York State are Democrats. The turnout in the Democratic primary was twenty-seven percent. Of these, forty-one percent voted for the winner, Bill Clinton. However, Voter Research and Surveys has reported that among those voting only three in ten actually favored any candidate. The others were choosing the lesser of evils, or trying to stop some other candidate from winning. It emerges that Clinton won the primary—and, many believe, clinched the Democratic nomination—by winning the support of about one percent of the voting population. (A similar reductive mathematics can be applied to the Republican results in recent primaries.) This performance suggests something more than mere boredom or apathy; it amounts to an active rejection—a sort of boycott—of politics.

The results of the Democratic primaries suggest a similar mood. As many observers have pointed out, including Clinton himself, the moment someone emerges as a front-runner, the voters turn against him. They are not trying to put someone in the White House, it seems; they are trying to stop anyone from getting there. This contrarian spirit was expressed recently by the surprisingly large vote on Tuesday for Paul Tsongas, who had dropped out of the race. It's hard not to conclude that in the voters' minds this was his main virtue.

The most common explanation for this state of affairs—that the voters are angry—is said so often that it's hard to say whether the news media are hearing it from the voters or the voters are hearing it from the media. (The person on the street these days shows a disturbing tendency to answer questions about politics in phrases that obviously originate in poll questions—saying for example that he or she has "doubts about Clinton's character and integrity," or that "the United States is on the wrong track.") The interesting question, however, is, Angry at what? Well, at "the politicians," in "Washington." But what have they done to provoke anger? It's another commonplace to say that this year the voters want "the truth," and are angry because they haven't gotten it. However, this is far from clear. If, for example, the voters would like to hear the truth about the federal budget, then it must be that they'd like to hear either that their taxes must be raised or that services must be cut back. But no such message has been delivered by any of the major candidates, who all evidently calculate that such a message would make voters angrier still. There is good reason for the candidates' fear. For at least twelve years, the voters have been voting against politicians who preach austerity, and for ones who promise to spend more while taxing less. In the Democratic field this year, the man who came closest to telling the truth about the budget was Paul Tsongas, who, to be sure, did not propose to raise anyone's taxes, but did at least oppose the "middle-class tax cut" offered by Clinton. If these results are any indication, the voters are not so much angry at the lies of the politicians as they are angry that those lies, which the voters eagerly swallowed for more than a decade, are not true.

Such anger makes choice in the voting booth difficult. On the one hand, the public senses that the politicians who promise them both tax cuts and improved services are not telling the truth, and it holds them in justified contempt. On the other hand, the public fears the sacrifices it would have to make if some politician did tell the truth and acted on it. The easiest course is to turn one's back on the dilemma, while blaming it all on "politicians" and "Washington." The choices for the candidates, meanwhile, are equally difficult. How do you obtain a nomination for office when, after winning one primary, the voters turn against you in the next one? New Yorkers were exposed to one device for dealing with this problem. In a television ad late in the campaign, one of those tough-but-warm male voices intoned, "Looking for a different candidate for president?" This candidate "actually has a serious plan to move this country forward," among other good things. Who, I asked myself, could this mysterious "different" person be? Was there a new candidate in the race? The answer came. "His name? Bill Clinton, the real Bill Clinton," the voice said. Different, though, from whom, I wondered? Then I understood: Different, of course, from Bill Clinton, the front-runner and incipient member of the hated tribe of politicians. Talk about slick! At the last minute, Clinton had decided to run against himself, and he had won.

APRIL 26, 1992

WITH EVERY DAY THAT PASSES, POLITICS IN THE United States become more mysterious. The questions now looming up go far beyond the matter of which candidates the public prefers and why. The questions that need asking now go to the very heart of what democracy is, how it functions, and how it breaks down. Consider, for example, four paradoxes that have presented themselves in recent months.

1) The voters tell anyone who asks that they are interested in putting "outsiders" in office, but the moment one of these outsiders starts to win votes they turn against him. The latest twist in this tale is the boomlet for the Texas billionaire businessman Ross Perot, who now has taken over the "outsider" mantle from Democratic candidate Jerry Brown, in decline since his defeat in the primary in New York. Those favoring "outsiders" seem to forget what they are favoring them for—namely, political office, which is to say, "inside" status. The voters, realizing that, thanks to their votes, this unwelcome transformation might actually occur, set about looking for fresh outsiders to support.

2) The voters are angry, yet in recent elections they have returned more than ninety percent of incumbents in Congress to office. The voters, it turns out, tend to like their own individual congressmen much better than they like the institution. Recently, according to the *Times*, Rep. Tom Foley (D-Wash.), the speaker of that despised institution, which is now supposedly in particular disrepute because of the House bank scandal, returned to campaign in his district and was received on all sides with warmth and respect—even, in some places, with standing ovations. One almost suspects that his constituents think they are protecting him from the anger of the rest of the public.

3) The same voters who have been putting incumbents back in office have been showing increasing interest in term-limitation bills, which would prevent them from doing this. I said, "the voters," but "nonvoters" would be a better description. Turnout in some of the recent presidential primaries has dropped into the teens. Some of these nonvoters, it seems, want legislation to do a job that they decline to do themselves in the voting booth.

4) The voters are upset that the federal budget deficit is out of control but are unwilling to contemplate the steps, such as cutting entitlement programs or raising taxes, that could bring it back under control. A few years ago, Congress, unable to arrive at a consensus on budget cuts through the normal political give and take, passed the Gramm-Rudman bill, which imposes automatic cuts if overall limits are exceeded. This year, Foley is telling his constituents, Congress may pass a constitutional amendment to balance the budget.

In each of these paradoxical situations, the voters seem at odd with themselves, yet there is a certain consistency in their inconsistency. The balanced-budget amendment, for example, has a family resemblance to the term-limitation bills. In each, legislation is made to stand in for political will. Each is a *deus ex machina* designed to force decisions that the representatives find themselves unable to make in the legislative process. But standing behind the representatives' paralysis is the voters' paralysis, exhibited both in their widespread failure to vote and in their manifest ambivalence when they do vote.

To govern, someone said, is to choose. In this presidential election year—supposedly the nation's season for making fundamental choices—neither the public nor its representatives have shown a willingness to make choices. For democracy is more than campaign speeches, press coverage, and voting booths. Required also is the people's will, for whose expression this machinery is meant to be only a vehicle. No technical device—not even the Constitution itself—can make good its absence. At the heart of the political disorder of this election year is the absence of any clear expression of that will. The public, for reasons that are not clearly understood, has abdicated the public realm.

MAY 17, 1992

POLITICS THESE DAYS HAS A WAY OF GENERATING little phrases—celebrity phrases, if you like—that are on everyone's lips for a few days and then are forgotten. They are the lexical counterpart of the fifteen minutes of stardom that Andy Warhol famously predicted for every American. (These phrases, let it be noted, are not the same as buzz words. Buzz words—for example, "enterprise zone"—usually lend themselves to projects of one kind or another. As such, they have a certain modest durability. They cause a little tingle of excitement because around them careers may be made or unmade, political campaigns won or lost. Celebrity phrases, on the other hand, are as evanescent as the sound bites of which they are the makings. They merely serve the momentary need of people in the public eye to define—or, more likely, gloss over—some unexpected phenomenon.)

One of last week's celebrity phrases was "playing the blame game," an expression used to refer to a response to the Los Angeles riots that everyone was supposed to avoid. The first step in the chain of events leading to the phrase's popularity was White House Press Secretary Marlin Fitzwater's suggestion that the cause of the riots in Los Angeles was the Great Society social programs of the late 1960s. Shortly, the Democratic presidential candidate Bill Clinton riposted that in fact the social neglect of the Reagan-Bush years was to blame. Meanwhile, Attorney General William Barr had repeated Fitzwater's accusation, and Sen. Daniel Patrick Moynihan had thundered back that his statements were "depraved" and "a lie." These exchanges set the stage for President George Bush to say, "We all want to solve the problems. This is no time to play the blame game." Later, Clinton chimed in with a call for an "an end to the blame game." Thereafter, it seemed obligatory for anyone speaking about the riots to shun playing the blame game, otherwise known as "playing politics," with the serious issues raised by the riots.

The phrase, suggesting that any harsh feelings were unnecessary because everyone now was united in wanting to "solve the problems," had a noble ring to it. It soon became clear, however, that the promised problem-solving was not to be forthcoming. The president offered a few warmed-over plans, including a proposal for enterprise zones, which would offer certain advantages to businesses founded in poor areas, but none of these was thought likely by any disinterested observer to have a real chance of reversing the deterioration of American cities. The Democrats offered somewhat more ambitious, yet still inadequate, programs. For a moment, there even seemed to be agreement between the White House and the democratically controlled Congress on a package of these inadequate plans, but this already appears to be unraveling. What everyone wanted, evidently, was not to solve the problems but to make enough commotion to appear to be solving the problems. On this program, there was a chance that Republicans, Democrats and even maverick independents could get together.

Everyone was renouncing blame, it has turned out, in the name of bold action that none was ready even to propose. The obstacle to that action, it became clear, was not the temptation to blame but simply an unwillingness to devote the large sums (let's say, $100 billion) that would be necessary to reverse the deterioration of American cities—the very unwillingness that set the stage for the riots in the first place. And this unwillingness, in turn, is founded on the unwillingness of the public, demonstrated in election after election for more than a decade, to elect politicians who would raise and spend that money. To a stranger listening to our political debates in the last two weeks, it might have appeared that every last American was ready to pay almost any price to heal his country's grave, and now explosive, social ailments. But that appearance deceived. For this seeming consensus concealed another, unspoken one, which was not to spend government money for these purposes. The first consensus was expressed in politicians' words, the second in their actions.

As for "playing politics" with the issue, the shame was that no one was ready to try it. What, after all, are politics for, if not for identifying serious problems, debating them, and then doing something about them? And what, in particular, is a presidential campaign for, if not to muster the country's will to do these things? Casting blame, it is true, is one of the less attractive aspects of the process, but it may be a necessary by-product of discovering what went wrong. Better blame, political scrapping and then action than the high-minded bipartisan paralysis that now is parading as virtue. In this context, avoiding the blame game means abdicating responsibility.

JUNE 14, 1992

THE 1992 ELECTION IS, OR SHOULD BE, ABOUT MANY things—repairing the economy, taking care of the poor, preserving the environment, building a new world order in the aftermath of the Cold War—but before these problems can be addressed, a prior issue must be faced: whether the American public is prepared to pay for any of this.

As it happens, an exchange that the unannounced presidential candidate Ross Perot had with a caller during his recent appearance on the "Today" show defined this issue with exceptional clarity. If Perot is to stand for anything coherent in this election, he must stand for honesty in fiscal matters. At the core of his campaign is the promise to take action that others are afraid to take to close the budget deficit, as a first step towards putting the country's economic affairs in order. He has said that we in the present must sacrifice so that future Americans can enjoy "the American dream," and he has sworn that he will not "talk, talk, talk," but "deliver, deliver, deliver." But which sacrifices will they be, and what will he deliver?

One "Roberta," of Vero Beach, Fla., called in to get clarification of a detail of particular interest to her. She and her husband, who are about to retire, she said, had been "among the first" in Florida to sign the petition to put Perot on the ballot. But she had read in the current issue of *Newsweek* that a Bush administration official had claimed that Perot would eliminate Social Security and medical benefits for retired people who made more than $60,000 annually and now she and her husband were "absolutely shocked." She would like to know whether the allegation was true.

For the next several minutes, Perot ran in circles around the question. The Bush administration, he began by saying, used figures from 1988 rather than 1992. But before he could explain the meaning of this he interrupted himself to say that "the point" was that an economist had once told him that if rich people like him would surrender their benefits "we could make a tremendous dent in the budget." Making use of that comment as a sort of bridge from the specific to the general, Perot began to expound on the generosity of the American people. "Most Americans are very generous," he said. He praised the American Association of Retired People, which had successfully opposed a Congressional move to restrict the benefits of high-income retirees. But it was not this that he praised. "Every one I've talked to so far certainly has to make an acceptable standard of living," he noted, "but, God bless them, these are people who have given all their lives. They are absolutely preoccupied with the world their grandchildren are going to live in." Did this mean, as he seemed to be hinting, that people with incomes above $60,000 should be required to give up their benefits?

Not really. When Roberta observed that he hadn't answered

the question, Perot offered the idea that the surrender of benefits might be "voluntary." A computer would make a "rational analysis" showing which people could afford the sacrifice, and then they would be invited by letter "or a postcard" to do so. The response, Perot was sure, would be "heartwarming."

However, Roberta's response was not heartwarming. "You can afford to give it up," she told Perot at one point.

Although Perot's next answer remained on the level of generality he preferred, it had a sharp edge. "Now if everybody in our country who could help other people won't help other people, and just say, 'I've got mine, and to heck with you,'" he said, "we're dead as a country." Then, remembering Roberta, he assured her that he didn't think that she was saying that. The encounter—a skirmish on the front line of presidential politics today—was inconclusive. Perot had successfully evaded the question. Yet he had been led to shift from basking in the admiration of supporters to preaching to one the virtues of generosity and sacrifice. The exchange played out in miniature a drama that the whole country will enact in the five months that remain of the election season. The willingness to pay is the lethal, hidden shoal in the political waters that all the candidates must navigate. Will Perot—or Bush, or Clinton—dare to ask Roberta to reach into her wallet to pay for the welfare of her grandchildren? If one of them does, will she overcome her absolute shock and vote for him? If she does not, will her grandchildren have to pay? Will we then be dead as a country?

JULY 12, 1992

AS NEW YORK WELCOMES THE DEMOCRATIC PARTY to town this week, it seems only polite to mention some of the better qualities of our guest. This seems all the more fitting in view of the widespread evidence that political parties in general may have had their day in American political life. Any praise, in these circumstances, may turn out to be valedictory.

Political parties have filled a gap left in our political system by the Founding Fathers, who made the citizens king but gave them only one day every couple of years—Election Day—on which to issue their royal commands. There is no need to romanticize the checkered history of parties to acknowledge that they have offered citizens a crucial field for political expression and action for the period between elections. In barely a generation, this function of the parties has been all but washed away. First, the legendary smoke-filled room in which political operatives chose candidates was supplanted by the system of primary elections. Second, the public rallies and stump speaking that once made up campaigns were largely replaced by television appearances of various kinds, notably including, this year, appearances on talk shows.

Nevertheless, thousands of Democrats are descending on New York for their convention. In recent decades, the Democrats have served the United States best through their political failures. The first instance of this was the party's embrace of the civil rights movement. The nation's repudiation of racial discrimination was certainly its greatest domestic achievement in the last half-century, just as the principal leader in the struggle, Martin Luther King Jr., was the greatest American of the period. (Anyone who doubts this has not yet read Taylor Branch's inspired account of King and his movement, *Parting the Waters*.) The Democratic Party did not originate the civil rights movement, and it adopted it with reluctance, after many bitter fights—many of them taking place in full public view at conventions. And yet it was through the Democratic Party that the movement produced legislative achievement. The Democrats' embrace of civil rights was as bad for them politically as it was good for the nation morally. It cost them the South in future presidential elections.

The second great nationally beneficial political disaster for the Democrats was the opposition within the party to the Vietnam War, which forced its own President Johnson into retirement, and compelled Richard Nixon to make his long, bloody, grudging withdrawal from the war. The political price was paid in 1972, when the antiwar Democratic presidential candidate George McGovern lost to Nixon in a landslide, and in future presidential elections, in which the Democrats were invariably portrayed as weak in opposing the nation's enemies.

Today, the message of the antiwar movement is perhaps as widely accepted as that of the civil rights movement.. There are probably as few people who think that the Vietnam War was a wonderful idea as think that black people should be barred from voting. The frustrating paradox for the Democrats is that in forging the national consensus on what were perhaps the two most important issues of the time they lost ground with the voters. What could be a greater service than twice to stand for principle and twice to pay the political price? What are parties for if not to take risks such as these? Unfortunately, an ambivalent public sees things differently, and, even after the passage of many years, gives the party no credit for these stands. Accordingly, the party now seeks to return to a "mainstream" that it supposedly had wanted to abandon. It mightily strives to atone for its virtues and to make amends for its greatest services.

In spite of all that, the history of the times remains what it was, and does credit to the party that now assembles in our city.

JULY 19, 1992

LAST THURSDAY, THE DAY ROSS PEROT DROPPED OUT of the Presidential race, and Gov. Bill Clinton gave his acceptance speech at the Democratic convention, and he was revealed by a *Washington Post*-ABC poll to be leading President George Bush by twenty-nine percent, may one day be seen as a pivotal moment in American politics—the moment when our politics, immobile since the collapse of the Soviet Union and the end of the Cold War, finally began to move and change on a big scale. Though our final destination remains anything but clear, a few observations may be in order.

The Democratic Convention was a carefully crafted, hugely elaborate, technically up-to-date piece of major surgery on American public opinion. To judge by the poll results, it succeeded brilliantly. It showed that as a propaganda machine the Democratic Party now is fully the equal of the Republican Party. The phrase heard on all lips was that at the convention Clinton "did what he had to do." One of the things he apparently had to do was engineer the abandonment of certain tendencies deeply ingrained in the party but unpopular with the public. One of these was a great reluctance, born largely out of the Vietnam war, to resort to the use of force in foreign affairs. For more than a decade, this reluctance, exhibited in the vote of most Democratic senators against authorizing the use of force in the Persian Gulf war, had left the Democrats open to charges that they were weak on defense. History, it is true, went far toward solving this problem for the party by permitting the public's attention, in the post-Cold-War world, to turn almost entirely to domestic affairs. Clinton's support of the Persian Gulf war, though half-hearted, further safeguarded him against attacks of weakness.

The party's second politically dangerous tendency has been its historic dedication to helping the disadvantaged, including those on welfare—a dedication increasingly unpopular with the middle class, which has demonstrated in recent elections that it wants either to pay less in taxes or to receive more in services for itself for its tax dollars. Clinton shored up his position against attacks from this angle by, among other things, promising a tax cut for the middle class, vowing to force people on welfare to work, and distancing himself from the Rev. Jesse Jackson, who is the country's most prominent spokesman for the disadvantaged. To rein in their tendencies of the party without provoking a public fight required considerable skill.

Trimming principle for political advantage and calling the result a new faith is no easy trick to pull off, but a second part of the surgery was harder still. At the center of Clinton's platform is a promise of increased social investment—for schools, for job training, for transportation, for child care. The promise is central, because it is his prescription for addressing the chief anxiety of the voters in 1992: the decline of the American economy. The difficulty is that he has offered no plausible way of paying for investment on the scale suggested, especially in view of his promise of a tax cut or child tax credit for the middle class. His acceptance speech simply avoided the issue of how to pay. It's a question, of course, that not only candidates but presidents, too, have been avoiding since 1980. It was President Bush's promise not to raise taxes, many believe, that won him the White House in 1988. Because taxes went up, he may lose it in 1992. The question today is whether people are angrier at him for raising taxes or for breaking his pledge. If they are angrier because he raised taxes, they may prefer a candidate who, like Clinton, promises to cut taxes for most people. If they are angrier because he broke his pledge, they might prefer a candidate who, like no one running in 1992, acknowledges that life in the real world will force him to raise taxes. The candidacy of Ross Perot, too, was derailed by the fiscal issue. He began by making the issue of the federal deficit central to his campaign. He promised to deal with the problem in a businesslike way. If he was to keep his promise—if he really was going to stick his head under the hood of the car, and fix it—then he was bound to tell the owner, beforehand, what the bill was going to be. The weeks went by, and the plan was never presented, as, indeed, it could not be if he was not willing to raise taxes. He became another waffling politician. His ratings in the polls immediately began to sink, and shortly he was gone.

Now Clinton has pulled off the feat that eluded both Bush and Perot. He has promised to fix the car without presenting a bill. He has led Madison Square Garden in a chant of "We can do it!" and the public at large has yet to ask, "How much will it cost?" But it will ask. And that will be the moment of truth for Bill Clinton.

AUGUST 2, 1992

WE IN THE UNITED STATES LIKE TO THINK OF POLITICAL propaganda as an art that flourishes best in totalitarian societies. In recent years, however, American propaganda has far surpassed its totalitarian antecedents. We have attained a diagnostic dexterity, a technical sophistication, a strategic subtlety in the molding of opinion that Hitler and Stalin never approached.

The principal reason for our dubious triumph, admittedly, is one that reflects credit on us: American political life still is based on consent. Hitler and Stalin could simply dispatch to a concentration camp anyone who insisted on holding the wrong opinion. American propagandists, on the other hand, really do have to persuade. By the time the voter gets to the voting booth, his brain may be pickled in cliches carefully engineered at campaign headquarters (this year, for example, he will have had the word "change" burned into his consciousness by the 75,000 repetitions of Democratic hopefuls), yet his decision finally remains his own.

The latest notable episode in the annals of such persuasion has been the Democratic Party's brilliantly successful effort to "reposition itself" (the phrase itself is a fruit of the public relations revolution in politics) to line up with "mainstream values." Some of the elaborate techniques by which the Democrats have made their move were on display in a recent story on ABC News. First, the program showed some scenes of the Clinton campaign's recent bus tour from New York to St. Louis. Then the anchorwoman, Diane Sawyer, let us know that all was not as it seemed. "The Clinton caravan," she knowingly observed, "doesn't just happen; it requires advance planning to make it look so spontaneous, and so good on television." She then introduced the correspondent Jim Wooten, who proceeded to give us a supposedly behind-the-scenes look at the staging of a whistle stop in a farm setting. "What looks natural on television is as choreographed as a Broadway play," he noted. On camera, there appeared a staff person standing behind a table covered with boxes of strawberries. He is rehearsing the event. "And Senator Gore and Governor Clinton are there, and they are saying, 'Da-da-da,' " we hear him saying, as he points to a spot next to the strawberries. Then we see not just the whistle-stop scene, with bales of hay in front of a barn, but all of the television cameras ready to film the scene.

ABC next shows us Fred Keely, at Clinton headquarters, in Little Rock. We hear him explain that he has had his people lock the press in their bus momentarily upon arrival because "the arrival is not the shot." The staged episode near the hay bales is to be "the shot." Finally, we see Bill Clinton, his wife, Hillary, and vice-presidential candidate Al Gore and his wife, Tipper, all sitting on the bales eating a box lunch. This is the shot, but by now we are undeceived. We may even feel superior, for a moment, to all of those who saw only the staged scene, without Wooten's unmasking of it.

We may feel this, at any rate, until we remember that we are seeing it all on ABC News, and that just as the Clinton campaign has decided to refuse to let the news people see Clinton arrive at the whistlestop, so it has decided to permit them to film Fred Keely explaining this. In truth, then, "the shot"—one more calculated by far than the scene on the hay bales—is really Fred Keely, explaining to the voters (for Keely, we can be sure, has not suffered a temporary mental blackout and forgotten that ABC News reaches millions of voters) how cleverly he has set out to shape their impressions.

Wooten's unmasking seemed to invite a second unmasking. In this one, we would see Wooten's cameras filming the cameras filming the scene. We would hear the Clinton staff members rehearsing the scene in which they rehearsed the hay bale scene. And we would hear Fred Keely's explanation of why he thought explaining his techniques of press manipulation to Wooten would benefit his candidates. That unmasking, however, would of course require a further one, which would require another, and so forth.

We can still wonder why the Clinton people thought their explanations of their techniques would help his campaign. If the magician explains his tricks, isn't the effect ruined? One effect—the charm of the foursome sitting on the hay bale—was indubitably ruined, but another—the shrewdness of the manager who has contrived that scene—was created. Yes, the Clinton campaign seems to be saying, we are deceiving you, but look how skillfully we do it. In this case, at least, the "mainstream values" being embraced were not our nostalgia for the charming rural life of middle America but our seeming admiration for the immensely elaborate and refined means by which we continue to be manipulated by people in high places.

SEPTEMBER 20, 1992

IN THE 18TH CENTURY, GENERALS AT TIMES SOUGHT to win victories by maneuver alone—by marching and countermarching so cleverly that the opponent found himself beaten without a shot being fired. The Republicans attempted such a strategy last week in the campaign wars. For several days, Republican speakers attacked Gov. Bill Clinton for having managed to avoid the draft in the late 1960s, at the height of the Vietnam war. They also floated a rumor that the president himself would attack Clinton's draft record in a speech at the convention of the National Guard Association. But Bush drew back, and spoke only in sly, vague terms of "the controversy swirling around Gov. Clinton," and of the "awful authority" of the commander-in-chief, who "might have to decide if our sons or daughters should knock early on death's door" (a peculiar locution, reversing the common notion that it is death that knocks on our door).

In the meantime, though, Clinton, readying himself for a riposte, changed his schedule in order to come to Salt Lake City and speak to the Guard on the same day. It was this forced detour that the Republicans claimed as their battle-free victory. "We can't believe he walked into this," the Bush campaign's press secretary, Torie Clarke, announced. "This guy wants to be commander-in-chief," she added, stretching a point about as far as a point can be stretched, "but he can't avoid the land mines on the campaign trail."

Whatever President Bush's view of Clinton's draft record may be, his understanding of the powers of the commander-in-chief seems to be built on a false premise. Under the Constitution, it is not the commander-in-chief who decides whether America's sons and daughters will go to war. That responsibility rests with Congress, which is given sole power to declare war. Only when it has done so does the president decide how and when American soldiers should go into combat. (At that point, in fact, if he failed to go to war in one way or another, he could be impeached.) This authority to conduct war once it has been declared is awful enough, but it is not the authority to take the country to war. In the Cold War years, of course, Congress's war-making power has largely eroded. The nadir came in the Persian Gulf war, when the president, though he finally invited the Senate to express its "support" for his war policy, declared throughout that the power to go to war against Iraq was his and his alone. When Bush questions Clinton's competence to handle this particular power of the presidency, the citizens would do well to remember that it is a usurped one.

In the days when Congress's war power remained intact, it declared war only in response to a president's request to do so. In practice, therefore, the constitutional arrangement worked in the same way as much legislation did: The president proposed, the Congress disposed. Yet even in his role as proposer of war—a role which, though not mentioned in the Constitution, is constitutionally proper—the president is emphatically not acting in his role as commander-in-chief. He acts entirely as a civilian—that is, as president. A commander-in-chief acts by giving orders. But when presidents have sought to take the country to war through constitutional procedures, they have not given an order but made a request. When it comes to deciding upon war, the president does not command but is himself commanded—by Congress.

These distinctions, though ignored in recent years, are important to keep in mind in the debate about Clinton's avoidance of military service because they remind us of the difference between the decisions a commander-in-chief makes once the nation is at war and the decisions a president and Congress make together about whether the nation should go to war. It is with respect to this latter sort of decision that Clinton's record regarding the Vietnam war is especially pertinent. The question has been asked whether, not having served in the armed forces, Clinton would be qualified to send others to war. A more crucial question is whether he has the judgment to decide which wars should be fought at all. Clinton adamantly resisted the Vietnam war. He worked "every day against a war I opposed and despised with a depth of feeling I had reserved solely for racism in America," he wrote, in his famous letter to a director of the ROTC program. If he had been president then, we may assume, the thousands of American lives lost in the last half-decade of the war would have been spared, as would hundreds of thousands of Vietnamese lives. The whole hateful, misbegotten, wasteful, immoral venture—the fruit of the most calamitous presidential decisions of 20th Century American history—would have been brought to an end. This is no small point in Clinton's favor as the country considers him for the office of president.

SEPTEMBER 27, 1992

DOES GOVERNOR BILL CLINTON REPRESENT A political challenge by a "new generation" to an older one, as he has claimed? His generation—the '60s generation—was defined politically by three struggles: the struggle for civil rights, the struggle against the Vietnam war, and the struggle to drive President Richard Nixon from office when his abuses of the Constitution were made known in the Watergate scandal. (This last struggle was also fought by many people of other generations—including that of Sen. Sam Ervin, the scourge in the Senate of menacing, hard-edged, dull-eyed, double-dealing Nixon aides—but I include it in the list of '60s causes because it drew them together in a single constitutional showdown.) All three causes were crowned with success. The three outcomes—the dismantling of legally enforced segregation, the liquidation of the ruinous war, and the removal of the driven, repressive Nixon—were the fruit in the United States of a youthful political activism that boiled up all over the world. They are the vindication of the honor of that generation.

Clinton was deeply engaged in all of this. He agitated for civil rights in college; he helped organize protests against the war . . . In 1972, he organized Texas for antiwar candidate George McGovern. It soon was clear, however, that these victories of the '60s were to prove paradoxical. In each case, the activists won over a majority to their cause at the crucial moment. In the civil rights movement, the moment was Martin Luther King Jr.'s "I have a dream" speech, in 1965. In the antiwar movement, the moment was the Tet offensive, in early 1968, which drove President Lyndon Johnson from the presidential race and brought Robert Kennedy in. In Watergate, the moment was the Saturday night massacre, when Nixon fired the special prosecutor, who was asking for Nixon's famous tapes.

Yet in each case, the political consequence of successful activism was not credit but blame. This pattern first emerged in 1968, when Nixon, playing on southern whites' resentment over civil rights, made political gains. This pattern repeated itself in 1972, when the public, which had concluded that the Vietnam war was unwinnable and wrong, voted in a landslide for Nixon over McGovern. The pattern was repeated again after Watergate, which many at the time believed would make the Republicans a minority party for a generation but instead heralded victories in three out of the next four presidential elections—a turn of events that set the stage for a repetition of Watergate-like abuses in the Iran-contra scandal. Meanwhile, icy winds from some new quarter withered the activist spirit of the '60s at its roots. Young people began to worry more about their careers than about political causes. Where had all the flowers gone, indeed. Gone to investment banking, with a starting salary of $70,000, every one. The young voted in droves for Ronald Reagan. The big chill—the withdrawal of a large part of a generation from political action—was under way.

By the time Clinton, who got himself elected governor of Arkansas in 1979, at age thirty-two, arrived on the national stage, a record of '60s political activism was hardly a ticket to higher office. For the Democratic Party, which had incubated all three of the key struggles, these events were not something to be celebrated but lived down. This was the job for which Clinton volunteered. After long work, it came to fruition in the new image of the Democratic Party born in that spectacular exercise in public relations, the 1992 convention. The elements of this changed image included Clinton's support (equivocal though it was) for the Persian Gulf war (thus erasing the party's "McGovernite" reputation for dovishness); the promise of a tax cut for the middle class (overcoming the party's reputation for excessive attention to the poor); the careful distancing from Jesse Jackson (showing the party's independence from black activism); and support for the death penalty (showing toughness on crime). As Clinton said on Wednesday, "We had to change the Democratic Party, so the Democratic Party could command the confidence of a majority of the American people." In other words, the changes are a sort of mild national-political version of the big chill—compromise arrived at to succeed in the world. In that respect, Clinton is indeed a representative of a new generation.

OCTOBER 4, 1992

CNN ANNOUNCED THIS WEEK THAT IN CONJUNCTION with The Gallup Organization and *USA Today* it will conduct a "tracking" poll of the voters' preferences for president until election day and release the results daily, on its program "Inside Politics." As Tom Hannon, who is the political director of CNN, explained to me, in this case 350 voters will be interviewed each day. The daily published results will be based on the most recent three days of polling. The poll, in other words, is a sort of shifting assembly of voters in continuous session. In the last week of the campaign, the size of the batches will be increased to 1,000 a day, and the number of batches used in the sample reduced to two.

The inauguration of a daily poll in a presidential campaign is one of those ideas that seems inevitable once the thing is done. It's easy to foresee the day when, during presidential election seasons, such polling results will join the class of figures that, heard over the radio, America brushes its teeth to: temperature, forty-two degrees, (thirty-five with the windchill factor); Dow Jones down 49.71 to 3200.61; Clinton, fifty-two percent, Bush, thirty-eight percent, Perot, seven percent. However, for all the importance attached to polling—or perhaps because of it—poll results are surrounded with a certain embarrassment. My candidate for least-believable statement by a politician last week was the one by Democratic vice-presidential candidate Albert Gore to Judy Woodruff of "World News Tonight" that "We do not read the polls." Of course, the Clinton campaign, like the Bush campaign, not only reads the polls but adjusts every detail of its strategy to poll findings. The press, too, is made uncomfortable by poll results. One reason, certainly, is that an important part of its function—reporting on how the public is responding to the campaigns—has been taken over by polling. There is more to campaign coverage than polling, but that "more" has been reduced to a kind of annotation and embellishment of the shifts that the polls have revealed. In a week in which George Bush dropped ten points in the polls, reporters generally will not write stories saying how brilliant his campaign has been, no matter what their individual perceptions may have been. A candidate who delivered the Gettysburg Address in a week in which he sank in the polls would be judged bungling and incompetent. Polls introduce a monolithic quality into campaign coverage. A candidate is either going up or down. Stories that do not reflect this seem out of step, absurd.

Hence the consequence of polling is to add overwhelming force to current public opinion. The weight of the public's judgments has proved, so far, irresistible to both the candidates and the press. Polls are in fact like repeated instantaneous elections in which the campaigns latest gambits are voted up or down. If, for example, the Republicans' flogging of "family values" is discovered to be unpopular in the polls, as seems to have happened, then the press will describe the theme as a blunder and it will be dropped. The candidate who does well in the polls, on the other hand, will stick monotonously with his original message (provoking complaints, as Clinton has done, that he is "sitting on his lead").

There seems no chance, however, of escaping from the tyranny of the polls by driving them out of political life. Polling results, though sometimes mistaken, are a form of knowledge. Like other kinds of knowledge, polling information is powerful. And, like other kinds of knowledge, it is, once made obtainable, all but inescapable. The campaign organizations, as Hannon pointed out to me, will gather this information whether news organizations do or not. Should the public alone be excluded from knowledge about its own opinions?

Knowledge, in a free society, cannot be suppressed. It should not be ignored. Freedom, from poll results or anything else, cannot be based on ignorance. Such freedom, if it can be found, can begin only after the poll results are in. For candidates and newsmen alike, this means at least a provisional assertion of independence from current public opinion—an independence that would permit them to do better than just deliver back to the public the opinions it already holds and actually challenge the public, argue with it, enlighten it, lead it. For the candidates, this would mean daring to champion views that at first were unpopular but later might (or might not) gain a following. For the press it would mean entertaining the idea that a campaign had been brilliant in spite of falling in the polls—that it had succeeded in some other terms. Let the numbers pour in—weekly, daily, hourly. Then let those in public life, consulting the evidence of their own eyes and the promptings of their own minds and hearts, find the courage to tell what they see and speak what they believe.

OCTOBER 8, 1992

I WANT TO TAKE NOTE, BELATEDLY, OF A SMALL miracle. (Where miracles are concerned, it seems to me, belatedness is no objection.) It happened at, of all places, the Republican convention in August. I am speaking of the brief speech about AIDS by Mary Fisher, who is infected with the virus and has just been appointed by President George Bush to the National Commission on AIDS.

The presidential campaigns this year have been notable for their negative tone and deceptiveness. It has to be added that the Republican record has been much worse than the Democratic. (It's important to resist the temptation to fall into the brainless, nonpartisan style of castigation that automatically attributes equal blame to "both sides"—except, of course, in those rare cases when both sides really are equally to blame.)

The attacks at the Republican convention on homosexuals, on feminists, on a supposed cultural elite, among others, have been duly criticized and appear to have backfired with the voters, who, happily, are more interested in making their own lives better than in making someone else's worse. The many outright deceptions of the Bush campaign—including the famous claim that Clinton raised taxes 128 times as Governor of Arkansas—have also been noted and rebutted in detail by commentators. Democratic distortions, though less flagrant, have also been noted and criticized. For example, many observers have shown that Clinton's budget figures don't add up.

These rebuttals perform a service, and yet even if the campaigns were purged of every slur and lie, they would remain an essentially ugly sight. What goes unnoticed, because we are all so used to it, is the tireless, inhuman partisanship of everyone who speaks—the indefatigable bragging, the relentless, obligatory jeering at opponents. Even the most "serious" speeches are insults to people's intelligence. This degraded discourse—this specialized, bullying, mechanized speech—is extremely rare in daily life, and always despised when found there, yet somehow it is accepted by everybody as normal in politics. Even nice politicians feel obligated to employ it. And yet, like all systematic manipulation and aggression, whether subtle or harsh, it grates, however unconsciously, and drives ordinary people away from all things political.

How did it happen, then, that when Mary Fisher rose to speak at the convention, it all stopped—the way great machinery is sometimes stopped by a single touch, the way the column of tanks in Tiananmen Square stopped when a lone unarmed protestor stepped before them? She spoke of the "silence which has been draped over" AIDS and said, "I have come to bring our silence to an end." Yet as soon as she had spoken three sentences, a different silence fell over the hall—a silence of attention, respect and deep emotion.

She did not attack Democrats. Nor did she attack her own party—another way she might have created surprise and drama for her cause. She said, "I ask you . . . to recognize that the AIDS virus is not a political creature . . . Though I am white, and a mother, I am one with a black infant struggling with tubes in a Philadelphia hospital. Though I am female, and contracted this disease through marriage . . . I am one with the lonely gay man sheltering a flickering candle from the cold wind of his family's rejection." She said of AIDS, "We have helped it along—we have killed each other—with our ignorance, our prejudice, our silence." And, "To all within the sound of my voice, I appeal: Learn with me the lessons of history and of grace, so my children will not be afraid to say the word AIDS when I am gone."

As she spoke, the clamorous presidential campaign seemed to evaporate. It was a shock to discover that it still had to go on when she finished. Her words welled up from a source of truth we had all covered over and yet was still, as we now knew, there within us.

OCTOBER 15, 1992

AT THE END OF THE DEBATE AMONG VICE-presidential candidates, Vice President Dan Quayle, who had the last word, took the opportunity to impugn Gov. Bill Clinton's honesty. Clinton "has trouble telling the truth," Quayle said, and asked, "Do you trust Bill Clinton to be your president?" He spoke with a calculated, slow, heavy emphasis, like a prosecutor leveling charges, as if to suggest that in the presidential debate tonight, Clinton is going to be on trial and will have to defend himself.

Political campaigns these days seem to consist in great measure of repeating a single word over and over. The word the Democrats have chosen is "change." (They have said it so often I hope it's stricken from the dictionary when the campaign ends.) The Republicans have chosen the word "trust." The choice is surprising, because the record is crammed with obvious deceptions practiced by President George Bush. No investigative reporting is needed to discover them. They're in plain view, where anyone can see them.

One example is Bush's answers to the question whether he knew about the deal, made in violation of the Reagan administration's stated policy, of trading arms to Iran for the freedom of American hostages. Broadly speaking, there are two kinds of public lying. One is the lie about hidden things—the claim that you didn't do what you secretly did do. This might be called the protected lie—protected, that is, by the concealment of the truth. The other is the lie about known things—the claim, for example, that you didn't say something you publicly did say. If the first depends on concealment, the second depends on forgetfulness. It is an interesting question which sort of lie violates the public's trust more egregiously. The protected lie deprives the public of information it needs, but at least pays the public the compliment of assuming that if the facts came to light it would care. The brazen lie, on the other hand, being in public view, seems to hold the public in utter contempt.

Bush's record on the hostage deal is a tangle of both kinds of lying. The story begins with Bush denying not only his own but also President Reagan's knowledge of the deal. "I can tell you that the president is absolutely convinced that he did not swap arms for hostages," Bush said in December, 1986. And in January, 1988, he said, "I have said over and over again that the original proposal was not presented as an arms-for-hostages swap." This was false. Memos by Vice President Bush's chief of staff, Craig Fuller, and the Israeli official Amiram Nir have come to light showing that Bush was fully apprised of the arms-for-hostages deal at a meeting with the two men in Israel.

By June of 1988, however, Bush's account had begun to shift. "I didn't say I didn't know anything that was going on," he said. "I said it never became clear to me, the whole arms-for-hostages thing, until it was . . . fully debriefed by [Senator Dave] Durenberger." This statement marks the midpoint in a shift from the protected lie to the brazen lie. In saying, "I didn't say I didn't know anything that was going on," he sacrificed some of the protection of the earlier lie by ambiguously revealing a degree of knowledge, but he compensated by denying the existence of his own public statements that he had been wholly ignorant.

Just this week, the shift was completed. During a surprise visit to the "Today" show, where his wife, Barbara, was being interviewed, he was asked by NBC's Katie Couric if he "knew about the arms for hostages."

"Yes," he now answered, "I've said so all along, given speeches on it."

To summarize, Bush's positions regarding his knowledge of the deal have been: 1) I didn't know about it (full-fledged protected lie); 2) I didn't really know about it, but neither did I ever really say I didn't (half protected, half brazen lie); 3) I knew about it all along, and I've always said so (full-fledged brazen lie).

As Dan Quayle said during the debate, "The American people should demand that their president tell the truth."

OCTOBER 18, 1992

SOME PRESIDENTIAL ELECTION CAMPAIGNS REVOLVE around a single issue. The campaign of 1932, for example, revolved around the Depression, the campaign of 1968 around the Vietnam War. In a way, this year's campaign, too, has revolved around a single issue, but with the difference that, instead of facing the issue, the campaigners have devoted their efforts to avoiding it. Indeed, the arts of denial—of evading unwelcome facts, of catering to unreal wishes—have, in the hands of today's political professionals, reached an unprecedented pitch of sophistication. We have been living in a heyday of avoidance—a kind of golden age of self-deception.

Defined narrowly, the issue in question is how to close the federal budget deficit, which now is running at an annual rate of about $400 billion, or more than a billion dollars a day, and will push the national debt above $4 trillion by the end of the year.

Defined more broadly, the issue is whether the American people are prepared to make the sacrifices, budgetary and otherwise, that are plainly necessary if the United States is going to pull itself out of what a majority of the country now understands to be a threat of serious economic decline. Investment is needed both in the private sphere, to strengthen old businesses, found new ones, and thereby create jobs (the measure Republicans tend to recommend), and in the public sector, to improve infrastructure, and reform health and education (the measure Democrats tend to recommend). Most economists agree that deficit reduction, private investment and public investment are all pressing needs, and the question of which should take priority is much debated; yet before that question can even be reached, there is the prior and more fundamental question whether the public is willing to pay for the pursuit of any of these aims.

Mustering this will is a problem not for economics but for politics. That is why the central issue of this year's campaign, defined more broadly still, is whether our political system is any longer capable of presenting the people with the truth about a grave national disorder, and of summoning their political will to take effective action, or whether something has gone so badly wrong with our system that we now in effect face the world blind and paralyzed. A political system that proves unequal to the tasks history places before it is itself in trouble. Therefore, the deepest issue before us is whether, in the long run, our political system can survive.

The crisis, in other words, is many-layered, like one of those Russian nesting dolls called matryushkas. At its core, it is arithmetical: The budget numbers do not balance. The necessary calculations can be performed by any competent fifth grader: If the total government expenditure is $1,475 trillion, and the total of its revenues is $1,075 trillion, the result is minus $400 billion. As long as the science of arithmetic holds good—as long as two plus two equals four—no other answer is possible.

Corresponding to this simple arithmetic is an equally simple economic theory, which might be called household economics. It teaches that the fifth grade arithmetic on the page is as true for the federal budget as it is for the budget of any household. For long years, this attractive, commonsensical truth of household economics was the creed of the Republican Party, which, until the 1980s, preached balanced budgets and fiscal discipline almost as articles of faith.

The second layer of the crisis is economic. It brings the economy as a whole into the budgetary calculation. Economic theory muddies the simple arithmetic of household economics. Since the 1930s, the Democratic Party, tutored by the economist John Maynard Keynes, has had an escape route from the rigid math of household economics. Keynes taught that when nations, as distinct from households, are slowing down economically, the solution, far from being to cut back government spending, is to step it up, thereby adding to demand, which in turn summons forth production, and starts the economic engines turning again.

For several generations, Republicans, who used to call themselves "rock-ribbed," battled this Democratic free lunch of "deficit spending" in the name of the truths of household economics. In the 1980s, however, the Republicans' ribs became rubbery, and they discovered their own path to a free lunch: supply-side economics. The key to economic growth, they began to argue, was not government spending but private investment, which the government could foster by cutting taxes. Tax cuts, the theory suggested, might stimulate production so much that tax revenues would actually increase. If revenues increased, budget deficits, of course, would decrease. Thus, to Keynesian outrages to household common sense were now added supply-side outrages: The less money the government asked for in taxes, the more it would receive. In modern economic theory, as in Einstein's physics, two and two no longer necessarily added up to four.

Today, however, with the national debt at nearly $4 trillion and rising, high economic theory, whether of the Keynesian or the supply-side variety, offers little escape from the gloom of household arithmetic. There are still some who, like Robert L. Bartley, the editor of the *Wall Street Journal*, and one of the founders of supply-side economics, largely dismiss the worry. In his recent book, *The Seven Fat Years*, he has written that "In the advanced economic literature, the big debate is whether deficits matter at all." But the majority would probably tend more to agree with Sen. Warren Rudman (R-N.H.), who writes, in his foreword to *Bankruptcy 1995*, by Harry Figgie, that inaction on the deficit risks the "collapse of our country." (Though few, perhaps, would be ready to go as far as Figgie himself, who predicts that a deficit crisis will cause the government to "cut the armed services in half" while "the other half [are] kept on, at half pay, to quell the uprisings that have begun in cities and suburbs alike.")

The third and outermost layer of the crisis is political. Examining the numbers with their arithmetical brains, the politicians of recent years have answered, as we all must, that two and two equals four. Examining the problem with their economical brains (Keynesian or supply-side), they have reached the answer, "Probably four, but maybe five next year." However, when they have examined the numbers with their political brains, the answer, which is as strictly compelled by political logic as the arithmetical answer is by its logic, has been an unequivocal "two plus two equals five."

Starting in 1980, election after election demonstrated the

political truth of this calculation. It was Ronald Reagan who first found his way to this correct answer. If you raised defense spending and cut taxes, he said, you still can balance the budget. This analysis sent President Jimmy Carter into retirement in Plains. Four years later, after the national debt had almost doubled, the Democratic presidential candidate, Walter Mondale, rediscovered arithmetical truth and made the mistake of thinking it corresponded to political truth. He announced that he would raise taxes to reduce the deficit. "Here's the truth about the future: We are living on borrowed time," he said. "These deficits hike interest rates, clobber exports, stunt investment, kill jobs, undermine growth, cheat our kids, and shrink our future. Whoever is inaugurated in January, the American people will have to pay Mr. Reagan's bills." He lost every state but his own, Minnesota, and the District of Columbia. In 1990, Reagan's bills were indeed presented, but instead of promising to pay them, his vice president, George Bush, proclaimed, "Read my lips: No new taxes," and this time it was Gov. Michael Dukakis of Massachusetts, who had maintained a tactful ambiguity on the matter of taxes, who went down to defeat.

At the very beginning of this story, supply-side economics was in its springtime, and it was possible to hope that the economy, once it had received the bracing tonic of a tax cut, would "grow out of the deficit." This hope, however, died a swift death in the inner circles of the Reagan administration. The story has been told by Reagan's budget director, David Stockman—a hellbent supply-sider who nevertheless took seriously his chief's promise to balance the budget. In early 1981, Stockman recounts in his memoir, *The Triumph of Politics*, the administration fashioned an economic forecast that came to be known around the White House as Rosy Scenario, which would permit all of Reagan's goals to be met.

Stockman, whose job it was to draw up a budget, gradually came to realize that it was "a fake." The truth was that unless domestic spending was cut beyond anything even remotely possible politically, the deficit would soar.

Stockman occupied a singular position in the government. He presided over the clearinghouse at which the promises made in the campaigns were to be redeemed. He was forced simply by the nature of his job to do something that those who made the promises—not to speak of the millions of voters who believed the promises—were not forced to do: add up the expenditures and revenues, subtract the former from the latter, and ponder the result. For democratic politics, to speak schematically, is a three-cornered game. In one corner there are the politicians making their promises. In another corner are the voters, listening to those promises and making up their minds. But then in the third corner there stands the often overlooked third element, to which one can only give the grand title of Reality—meaning all the circumstances already in place when policy begins its action. The candidates and the voters, being sentient, can easily enter into a sort of conspiracy at the expense of the third element, which is mute, and therefore at a kind of disadvantage at election time. Reality can assert itself only by forcibly intruding into people's lives, in the form of what Alexander Solzhenitsyn once called the "pitiless crowbar of events." (The Polish dissident figure Adam Michnik was referring to this intractable element in politics when he said that the decaying Communist totalitarian regimes faced a "revolt of the plumbing.")

Customarily, we think of Washington as the land of illusion and the country at large as the place where reality appears. The politicians "inside the Beltway," we like to think, are constantly at risk of losing contact with the rest of the country. Yet when it comes to budgetary matters, just the opposite, curiously, is the case. For it is not until all the numbers are added up in Washington and a bottom line drawn underneath them that discrepancies force themselves on someone's attention. Budgetary reality is a reality that appears only in the whole, not in any of its parts, and the whole is assembled in Congress and in the White House. This reality, represented numerically by the budget deficit, is a reality with which the people are more likely to be out of touch than the politicians. Therein lies its special significance for politics. Politics in a democracy is the activity whereby the desires of the multitudinous groups in society are peacefully (if raucously) reconciled with one another and with the reality of existing conditions. The budget is a kind of numerical representation of a part of this process. And failure to balance the budget (unless this is deliberate) is an indication of political disorder, because it means that this basic political task is not being accomplished. It means that the demands of the parts are not being negotiated and reconciled but merely added up, without regard for the country's ability to pay. When the failure becomes chronic, this means that the political disorder is chronic. Hence, the soaring graph of our budget deficits delineates more than a purely economic problem. It is also a fever chart of the progress of that perilous illness by which peoples collectively lose touch with reality.

Other events of the period support the notion that however serious our economic ills are, the deeper crisis is political. Participation in politics has steadily declined in recent decades, to the point at which, in 1988, barely fifty percent of the eligible voters voted in the presidential election. A failure to pay for the amount of government we continue to demand and a failure to vote may be seen as parts of a broader rejection not just of this party or that but of politics itself. It might be argued that a refusal to pay more in taxes reflects a conservative philosophy of reducing the role of government. If that were the case, however, the public would be ready to accept reduced services, and it is not. Chronic budget imbalance is not the consequence of holding to one political principal or another, it is a sign of the breakdown of all principles—a breakdown, that is, of politics itself, which shows that it is no longer able to knit the country's parts into a workable whole.

After Stockman, the gap between political arithmetic and arithmetical arithmetic proceeded to widen largely without benefit of an economic-theoretical Band-Aid. The causes of chronic deficit spending were much deeper than infatuation with the fashion of supply-side economics. The loss of theoretical support was as little noticed in the country at large as the mounting deficits themselves.

It's important to remember the role deficit spending played in the broader picture of Reagan's political appeal. At the very heart of that appeal was the claim that most criticisms of American performance were the gratuitous complaints of embittered "naysayers" who had taken over the rival party—preachers of "defeatism, decline, doom and despair," as Reagan put it at the Republican convention of 1984. . . . Implicit in the accusation was the assumption that these bad things were all phantoms and would disappear if only "pessimists" stopped talking about them. Observers often marveled (for example, during the Iran-contra scandal) at the imperviousness of his reputation to scandal and debacle. It may be that his supporters wished to protect him from the consequences of his folly, just as he protected them from the consequences of theirs—that after two stormy decades of American politics, he and the voters had reached a sort of happy concord in which both the country and its leaders could take a vacation from political turmoil and stress. If his reputation was coated with a protective layer of Teflon, as people said, its secret ingredient was not so much his ability to hide things as the public's readiness not to see what was fully visible. Rosy Scenario would be an apt characterization not just of his White House's economic forecasts but of his administration itself. In his vision, there was no place for dangerous, mounting budget deficits which might require sacrifice and pain.

At the beginning of this election season, early last winter, the two men who would emerge as front-runners had their backs firmly turned to the deficit crisis. Gov. Bill Clinton, resembling no one in this respect so much as Ronald Reagan in 1980, was promising a "tax cut for the middle class." (The difference from Reagan was that Clinton would at the same time raise taxes on families making more than $200,000 a year.) The Democratic Party, tired of exclusion from presidential power, had schooled itself in the cornucopian politics that had proved so successful for Republicans. This adjustment was a key element in the Democratic Party's much-admired recasting of its public image. Nevertheless, Clinton faced a surprisingly strong challenge from Paul Tsongas, who ridiculed him as a "pander bear" for his promise of a tax cut. In a reprise of Reagan's victory over Mondale, Clinton defeated Tsongas by charging him with policies that were too austere. Bush, of course, was in the unenviable position of having made, and then broken (as part of the budget agreement of 1990), his famous promise of 1988, "Read my lips: No new taxes!" When the right-wing columnist Patrick Buchanan, taking Bush to task for breaking his pledge, won a surprisingly high thirty-eight percent of the vote in New Hampshire, Bush reversed his reversal, and called his tax increase of 1990 "a mistake."

The double reversal shed light on the politics of avoidance that have surrounded the budget question since 1980. Polls and interviews with voters showed that they were upset with Bush's reversal in 1990 not so much because it was a "mistake" as because it was a breach of faith: Bush won power from the people on the basis of a pledge and had broken it. It was a pledge, however, that had little basis for being made in the first place. As we now know, from the recent article by Bob Woodward in the *Washington Post*, the pledge was the brain child not of any policymaker but of the speech writer Peggy Noonan, who had the support of the media consultant Roger Ailes. Richard Darman, who would become budget director in the Bush administration, found the pledge "ridiculous and stupid." Noonan and Ailes, however, believed that, in Woodward's words, "The bold pronouncement was central to refashioning Bush's image and changing the perception of him as weak and loyal to the point of subservience." In other words, it was thought up by people interested in winning an election, not by people interested in governing. Budget arithmetic and political arithmetic were still irreconcilably opposed, and, as usual, political arithmetic, which again turned out to be correct (politically), won out.

In the spring of 1990, the "ridiculous" pledge ran into the brick wall of the Gramm-Rudman-Hollings spending limits in Congress, which required that if budget targets were not met, Draconian automatic cuts would go into effect. Suddenly, budget math wore a more menacing political aspect: an automatic twenty-five percent cut in domestic spending and a large cut in defense. For a moment, Gramm-Rudman-Hollings forced political arithmetic and budget arithmetic into alignment. The result was Bush's "mistake," the budget agreement of 1990, which his budget director thought was "the most responsible and sound economic policy decision Bush had made," as Woodward put it. It was Bush's self-made dilemma that he could act responsibly only at the cost of breaking his pledged word and proving himself a liar.

If Clinton had any advantage over Bush in the competition that emerged between them to cater to the public's wishful thinking in budget matters, it lay in the fact that the illusions offered by Bush were damaged goods, while those offered by Clinton had yet to receive their comeuppance in the real world. Yet sailing was not smooth for either candidate. The voters, everyone soon discovered, were "angry." It was far from clear, however, what the target of the anger was. People were angry, they said, at "the politicians," or at "Washington," which had got "out of touch" with the people. Listening to these voters, it seemed that a familiar story must be repeating itself. In this story, the government gets out of touch with the people's will—it forgets that it is not the master but the servant of the people; then in its ignorance and selfishness it creates a mess; then a righteous public, which lives in the real world and knows how bad things really have become, gets angry, and throws the rascals out. This, you might say, is the traditional democratic—the traditional American—way of understanding our difficulties.

But what if the politicians, far from being out of touch with the people, were in fact all too closely in touch? What if, as was the case here, they had been paying hundreds of thousands of dollars year in and year out for polls, focus groups and so forth, precisely in order to monitor every nuance of the people's will, and had fashioned most of the major policies of government with a view to satisfying that will, whether or not those policies, in the view of budget directors and the like, made sense? Is there in fact the tiniest shred of evidence that the fault of the candidates who won high office in the 1980s and in 1990 has been inattention to the opinions of the public? . . . None of which is to suggest, of course, that the politicians have been the altruistic servants of the people. The point is that their own chief self-interest—getting into power and staying there—lies precisely in staying as closely in touch with public opinion as possible.

The "angry" voters, like the craven politicians, were in a false position. Where, after all, did the politicians at whom the voters were angry come from? Did they spawn in water coolers in Capitol corridors? Did they descend from Venus? The rascals whom the voters wanted to throw out had, to a man or (rarely) woman, been sent in by those same voters. Indeed, the economic crisis represented by the budget deficit arose just because the politicians were so assiduously attentive to the public's wish to cut taxes while expanding services. . . . Soon after the angry voters were discovered, "anti-incumbent fever," which had the makings of a supposed "year of the outsider," was detected. The problem with electing "outsiders," however, was the same as the problem was feeling angry. If, like Tsongas, the outsider told some of the truth about the economy and called for sacrifices to cure it, he ran into the same wall of resistance that Mondale had butted his head against, and that now finished off Tsongas. More popular (though not popular enough to win the nomination) were those outsiders who, like Jerry Brown and Patrick Buchanan (candidates who differed from each other in almost every respect but this one), blamed America's ills on an out-of-touch establishment, and invited a virtuous people to "take back America."

The dilemma of the angry voter in 1992 raises one of the most delicate and discomforting yet deepest questions about democracy: What is the responsibility of citizens for the actions of a government they have voted into power? We speak of a right to vote. We sometimes speak of a responsibility to vote. But what is the responsibility for the consequences of the vote? The idea that the public should hold itself responsible for the country's mistakes runs counter to deeply ingrained habits. Our government was born in protest against a king who ruled from the far side of an ocean ("out of touch," indeed!). A sovereign, the colonialists believed, should be accountable to the people, and when he failed to serve them deserved to be overthrown. Yet when, under our Constitution, "we the people" became the sovereign (to the extent that anyone can rightly be called a sovereign in the American system), the question naturally arose: To whom were we accountable? The answer could only be: to ourselves.

The problem with the answer is that it violates another fundamental principle of lawful government: that no person should be a judge in his own case. The founders were aware of the problem and, specialists that they were in crafting checks and balances, built into the system institutions that, while themselves ultimately dependent on popular will, would stand at a certain distance from majority opinion of the moment. One was the Senate, whose members serve for six years, and another was the Supreme Court, whose members are nominated by the president and serve for life. More important still were powers within society—universities, the press, and the innumerable private associations so admired by Alexis de Tocqueville—which, enjoying a certain independence from the majority's momentary will, would help to prevent the public from slipping into an uninterrupted reverie of deluded self-approval. Much more than minority rights was at stake. The minority, if it could make itself heard, the founders saw, might be the salient edge of a new majority in the making. Thus could the country as a whole perceive its mistakes, and change course.

If in our system the people are the king, then politicians, the press, and all other visible characters in the public realm are like servants and counselors to that king. It's well known that a king whose counselors are all flatterers is at risk of losing touch with reality, and, perhaps, of losing his throne. It's less often remarked that when the counselors to a sovereign people are flatterers, the same loss of touch with reality can occur. Are the voters of the 1980s, then, to blame for their blindness to the clear signs of national decline, of which the figures for the budget deficit are only a kind of numerical representation? If so, it was only after relentless self-serving advice from their counselors—obsequious, false, poll-reading, pandering courtiers to the king.

Since our country threw off the tyrant on the other side of the ocean, two centuries have gone by, and in that period, under the Constitution, the people have ruled. Our democracy today is mature, even venerable. Its characteristic disorders are those of democracy, not those of an oppressed people battling aristocrats and kings. The protest we make against the sovereign must in great measure be directed against ourselves. The habit of always blaming someone else for one's problems is as unappealing and unproductive for the voting public as it is for anyone else. It is conduct unbecoming a sovereign.

When a king loses touch with reality, the next step, often enough, has been his downfall in a popular revolution. However, if the problem is not a government out of touch with the people, but a whole country out of touch with the realities of its state and circumstances, the case is different. For when the people are themselves the monarchy, against whom are they to rebel? Of course, the public may manage to enlighten itself, face the facts, and take appropriate action. If it does not, however, dark possibilities open up. Some of these have been placed on view in this year's election campaign.

While the outsiders were falling, one by one, by the wayside, and those two consummate insiders, George Bush and Bill Clinton, were clinching their parties' nominations, another deep shift in public opinion was quietly occurring. The optimism about the country's future that characterized the Reagan years was running out. Bush's approval rating was running out with it, falling from a high point of ninety percent in one poll just after the Persian Gulf war to below forty percent today. Voluminous press interviews revealed the reason: not any political ads but deterioration in the conditions of people's own lives. The immediate cause was the recession, and its refusal to end. The deeper cause was the growing conviction that the recession might not be a recession at all but the beginning of decline. Economic reality was descending from the clouds of budgetary abstraction into daily life.

The voters found themselves in a box. Poised between two eras, they had acknowledged the problem but not yet braced themselves to accept the solution. It was at this moment that Ross Perot stepped onto the scene. The diminutive billionaire came before the voters as one acquainted with the ways of money. He presented himself as someone who would cut through the thickets of false, political arithmetic with a businessman's unsparing arithmetic. And immediately he began, with many a pithy phrase ("the least we can expect of politicians is that they should be able to add"), to decry the deficit, which became his dominant theme. His approval ratings shot up in the polls. Yet his popularity stood on an ambiguous foundation. It was not clear whether his voters saw in him a magician who would finally serve the free lunch that Reagan and Bush had failed to provide, or whether they saw in him the leader who would at last tell the country that there was no free lunch and summon it to sacrifice.

For a while, it seemed that he might attempt to be the latter, and take his chances. But then he faltered. He claimed that he could cure the deficit "without breaking a sweat." And on June 3 he said on the "Today" show, "We will not raise taxes." He added, "It's like giving cocaine to an addict while you're trying to take them through detoxification." The moment he said this, he joined the very large class of recent politicians who, while paying lip service to deficit reduction, shrank from advocating the specific steps that alone could bring it about. (President Bush was calling for a constitutional balanced amendment that would not come into effect until his hoped-for second term was over.) In the meantime, however, Perot had asked a group of experts to study the budget and make recommendations, and this group had decided, as any group that seriously addresses the question has to, that an increase in taxes was indeed necessary. We do not yet know whether dismay at advocating this step played a role in convincing Perot to abruptly drop out of the presidential race on July 16, but it's a matter of record that at just the moment he was asked by his own advisers to challenge the budgetary lie that has stood at the center of American electoral politics for more than a decade, he not only broke a sweat but collapsed completely. It was the pivotal moment in the campaign so far. It was now Clinton's turn to climb in the polls, while Bush continued his steady slide. Perot's withdrawal released Clinton from pressure to be more specific about his own budget figures.

The campaign, certainly, supplied no pressure of that kind. If the figures for Clinton's plan failed to add up, the figures for Bush's plan, which he unveiled at the Republican convention, laughed aloud at mathematics. Unable believably to repeat his "no new taxes" pledge, and unable to reverse himself on the pledge a third time and advocate taxes, he chose to plunge even further into fiscal unreality and promised an across-the-board income-tax cut as well as a capital-gains tax cut. Specification of which spending cuts would pay for the hundreds of billions of dollars thus lost to the budget was left until after the election.

All of this, however, was presented almost as an afterthought.

The received wisdom of the moment was that the state of the economy was the main—almost the only—issue in the campaign. The Bush campaign, however, came up with something entirely different. Unable, apparently, to offer any plausible economic plan, it sought to change the subject. The main enterprise of the convention was a sudden, unexpected, virulent attack on a host of internal domestic enemies. The attack, which dismayed moderate Republicans such as Warren Rudman, who deplored the party's lunge to "the far right," carried the campaign into wholly new territory. All but gone from the speeches were such ills as the deficit, vanishing jobs, deteriorating education, declining economic productivity, all of which had been the stock-in-trade of the campaign so far. In their place was summoned up a pack of demons—homosexuals, the press, radical feminists, "radicals," Hollywood producers, single mothers. Patrick Buchanan set the stage the first night by declaring that "a religious war is going on in America," and stating that Clinton and his wife were on "the other side." The Democrats were "20,000 radicals and liberals . . . dressed up as moderates and centrists," while Bush was the "champion of Judeo-Christian ethics." Vice President Dan Quayle, who defied "those who look down on America," saw an apocalyptic struggle between forces that were "fighting for what is right" and forces that were "refusing to see what is wrong." The fundamentalist preacher Pat Robertson had discovered that Clinton and his wife were advancing "a radical plan to destroy the traditional family and transfer its functions to the federal government."

An alternative to a political program that grappled with economic reality had been revealed. The question of just what a people unwilling to face its own responsibility for its decline might rebel against was answered. They could rebel against reality itself. Giving up rational plans to battle real economic and social ills, they could go to battle against the sort of imaginary demons that haunt the psyches even of the best countries but normally play little political role. An old, old story was playing itself out: People who cannot manage their own affairs blame their troubles on scapegoats. Nothing is more positive than anger that faces realities and takes responsibility for them. Democracy depends upon this. But nothing is more dangerous than anger in flight from both reality and responsibility. Historically, the consequence has been fascism. The ultimate cost of ignoring reality is losing your mind.

After the first two days of the convention, polls showed that the attack was enjoying some success. Clinton's double-digit lead had been reduced to a single-digit lead. In one poll, taken by CBS and *The New York Times*, it declined to one point. In the days that followed, however, as a startled country began to digest what it had seen, Clinton climbed again in the polls, and observers judged the gambit to have backfired. The demons summoned up by the Republicans in August were sent for the time being back to the darkness from which they were called.

When Perot, faced with his advisory committee's bleak report on the deficit, dropped out of the race, the public lost its chance to hear the case for austerity made by a major candidate in the election. (Today, he has at last embraced his committee's recommendation, but in the meantime he has all but disqualified himself for the presidency by his mysterious departure and return to the race and his eccentric choice of Adm. James Stockdale as his vice-presidential running mate.) President Bush, whose principal further contribution to the campaign has been to try to blacken the character of Clinton, appears, for now, to have nothing new to offer in economic matters. Clinton, the front-runner, steers a middle course. In the debate on Thursday, he placed "growth" ahead of deficit reduction as the main goal of a Clinton administration.

It's a position that, whatever its economic merits, is politically suspicious. The word "sacrifice" has not (to my knowledge) passed his lips. Yet sacrifices, whether embraced by the public or not, seem inescapable. The size and shape of the task faced by the next president will not be determined by his promises this fall but by the pitiless crowbar of events, which is already visibly at work in the daily lives of Americans. The election gives the next president another chance to address the crisis by rational, democratic means. If he fails, the demons of August are waiting to return, and next time they may not go away.

OCTOBER 25, 1992

SINCE THE BEGINNING OF THE COLD WAR, A POISONOUS stream of anti-democratic demagoguery has flowed through the precincts of the Republican Party. The party has been the vehicle for creditable things as well—for example, a reasoned defense of free markets, a devotion (in the early years of this period) to fiscal prudence, and a principal skepticism toward social engineering by government—yet the poisonous stream has never completely dried up. Several times, it has overflowed its banks and threatened to inundate the nation. At its core has been the exploitation of the country's nearly universal anti-Communist sentiment to smear the political opposition as allies of the country's enemies. (The opportunity to cut the Democrats down to size was perhaps irresistible in the aftermath of President Franklin Roosevelt's domination of the political scene for more than a decade.) For example, in 1946, Sen.

Robert A. Taft charged that the Democrats were "divided between Americanism and Communism." This false but potent accusation, leveled by tireless innuendo as well as direct attack, threw the Democrats off balance, and they never entirely righted themselves. The sin of the Republicans was to make such attacks; the sin of the Democrats was to cave in to them.

The poisonous stream first flooded into the body politic as a whole in the time of the Republican senator Joseph McCarthy. The fact that a representative of a single state making baseless accusations could intimidate virtually the entire nation, including its president, into silence or worse, demonstrated that the virus was by no means confined to disreputable political professionals. The demented allegations were McCarthy's; the fear engendered by those allegations belonged to the rest of us.

In the 1960s, sordid opportunity beckoned again, when the Democratic Party, in a bitter internecine struggle, transformed itself into the party of civil rights, and began to legislate an end to legally sanctioned segregation. The Republicans, stooping to pick up the loose political change, crafted the southern strategy, which won over the white South through the use of coded appeals to racial resentment. Within a few years, the Solid South went from being solidly Democratic to solidly Republican.

Another opportunity to capitalize on strains of anxiety and hatred in the public was presented by the Vietnam War. Again, the Democrats, whose leaders had initiated the war, became the agency of change, and turned antiwar. Again, the Republicans inherited the backlash—Nixon's "silent majority," which, although it did not exactly support the war, felt upset and menaced by the style and tone of the rebellious young people who were leading the antiwar movement. Nixon, turning to a kind of covert warfare against not only the antiwar movement (which was spied on and disrupted by the FBI and the CIA) but also his electoral opponents (whose campaigns he sabotaged, and whose supporters he punished through abuse of the federal agencies) became the conduit through which the poisonous stream, now containing a brew that mixed red-baiting, racial resentment and cultural resentment of the rebellious young, invaded the body politic a second time. The ultimate consequence was Watergate, in which the Constitution was placed in jeopardy by a lawless executive branch and was saved by the only forced resignation of a president in our history.

Now, in Bush's campaign for re-election, the poisonous stream has again flooded the country. The campaign has been characterized by the neglect, amounting to contempt, of any real issue that faces the country. The American economy is in crisis, yet a Bush campaign aide actually said to a *New York Times* reporter that "the campaign has finally shifted off of where it was—twenty-four hours a day on the economy." Having supposedly been distracted from its real worries, the public has been offered a combination of strident moralizing (Buchanan's "religious war," Dan and Marilyn Quayle's "family values"), and character assassination (the suggestion that Clinton has something to explain because he traveled to Moscow as a student two decades ago, among other charges). To the many reasons for preferring Clinton to Bush, the character of this campaign adds another, perhaps overriding one. At stake is the tone and substance of American politics. Approval of the Bush campaign would send politicians a signal that in the United States the gutter is now the royal road to power. A repudiation—the more overwhelming the better—would close off that path, and send our future would-be leaders running to find more wholesome ways to win the people's assent.

NOVEMBER 1, 1992

AS THE UNITED STATES APPROACHES ITS HOUR OF decision on election day, post-Communist Russia has been moving toward what may be a more fateful political turning point. A confrontation looms between Russia's president, Boris Yeltsin, and the Russian Parliament. Yeltsin threatens to dissolve parliament; parliament threatens to emasculate the powers of the presidency. A prominent general has declared that the loyalty of the military belongs to Yeltsin. Each side accuses the other of usurpation of power. Meanwhile, Yeltsin has banned a group called the National Salvation Front, which consists of former Communists and nationalists, and he has decreed that a 5,000-man security force organized by the speaker of the parliament, Ruslan Khasbulatov, be placed under executive control. All of this transpires against the background of high unemployment and an inflation rate of five percent a week—classic conditions for the unraveling of lawful governments.

In the United States, the question is who will govern in a political system that, we hope and trust, will remain substantially unchanged. In Russia, the question is what the fundamental nature of the political system will be. Even for the United States, the answer the Russians give to this question may in the long run be more important than most of those raised in our presidential campaign. (Certainly, it will be more important than what Gov. Bill Clinton said to his draft board two decades ago—the issue apparently uppermost in the mind of President George Bush these days.) Yet the Russian question, like all questions of foreign policy in this campaign year, has been conspicuous by its absence. The most revolutionary changes on the international scene in half a century have occurred in the last couple of years, and it would seem logical to expect corresponding revolutionary changes in American foreign policy. Our thoughts naturally turn to two other great turning points of the 20th Century—the end of the First World War, in 1918, and the end of the Second World War, in 1945—and to the things that were said and done by Americans at those moments. Woodrow Wilson is of course much in our thoughts. We summon to mind his Fourteen Points, outlining the foundations of a just peace; his triumphal trip to the Versailles Peace Treaty conference; his successful international advocacy of the League of Nations; the tremendous debate that followed at home between the Wilsonians and the isolationists; and the rejection of American participation in the league by the Senate.

And our thoughts turn to the decisions after the Second World War that created the international structure that now has crumbled: to the Yalta Conference, among the heads of state of the victorious powers; to the anonymous article by "X," the then little-known diplomat George Kennan, warning of the Soviet threat and defining an American policy for "containing" it; to the Baruch plan for abolishing nuclear weapons, presented at the United Nations; to the Marshall Plan to aid the recovery of Europe (today it is scarcely possible to propose any plan whatever, whether foreign or domestic, without likening it to the Marshall Plan); to the Bretton Woods agreement, which set the stage for the fabulous economic growth of the industrialized nations—in short, to all the decisions of the gifted group of American statesmen who, in the words of Secretary of State Dean Acheson, were "present at the creation" of the new world.

Having looked back on these great deeds, we look for their counterparts today. We do not find them. Peace again has come, but no peace conference has been convened to create a new architecture for it. The global strife of the two most fearsome military powers the world has ever known has dissolved, but no Bernard Baruch appears before the United Nations to propose radical disarmament. Half of Europe is struggling through poverty, civil strife, and war to find its way to democracy and prosperity, but no Acting Secretary of State Eagleburger Plan (the real Secretary of State, James Baker, having resigned to help with the Bush campaign) is proposed to help. Once again, we are present at the creation, but so far it hasn't occurred to anyone in power to create anything.

The creativity of events, however, has by no means abated, and an array of new trials that would have been unimaginable to the statesmen of 1918 and 1945 has presented itself. These trials concern the relation not only of one nation to another but of humankind as a whole to the natural world, which is threatened by the persisting nuclear dilemma, global warming and ozone loss, among other perils to the ecosphere. In a parallel development, national economies have slipped from national control, and demand to be dealt with globally. Yet, even as nation states grope for supra-national political instruments to deal with global economic and environmental problems, nations are being torn apart from within by sub-national groups. These groups often appeal to international bodies for aid and protection, thereby seeking at one and the same time to break up nations and to transcend them. In other words, whether any particular nation cares to notice or not, forces have been loosed that are rearranging the basic architecture of the world—economic, environmental and political.

The United States, if our political campaign is any indication, does not care very much to notice. The Republicans do seem to recall that there is a world beyond our borders, but they are content to congratulate themselves on past triumphs. Grandiosely, they take exclusive credit for the dissolution of the Soviet Union—an event that, insofar as it was caused by the United States at all, was certainly the work of administrations of both parties. While taking credit for what it did not do, the Bush administration failed to do what it might have done—propose a substantial economic and political plan that might have helped the Russians get through the sort of constitutional crisis that is now upon them. The congressional Democrats, for their part, far from rising to the historical occasion that their rivals were ignoring, concentrated on placing obstacles in the way of the modest aid program that the Republican administration did propose. Meanwhile, the Democrats' presidential candidate, Gov. Bill Clinton, restricted himself to a miscellany of criticisms of administration policies. If there is a theme to be found at all in Clinton's foreign policy addresses, it is that "we must have a president who attends to prosperity at home if our people are to sustain their support for engagement abroad," as Clinton put it in a speech in Los Angeles recently. In short, his foreign policy at bottom restates his domestic policy.

It is tempting to suppose that we're witnessing a recrudescence of the isolationism that defeated Woodrow Wilson. It is a fact, however, that the only explicitly isolationist candidate in the presidential campaign—the extreme right-winger Patrick Buchanan—was defeated in every primary by a president whose popularity was slipping badly at the time. The successful strategy was not to mention foreign policy at all—or to do so in a perfunctory way. The public doesn't seem to want to reject engagement in the world so much as simply to ignore it.

The difference between yesterday's isolationism and today's indifference becomes clear if we recall the nature of isolationism at its supreme moment, when it served to inspire the defeat of Woodrow Wilson's dream of a League of Nations. America's economic and military power at the time was matchless and growing. The country's economic output, by 1918, exceeded that of all Europe. American might had just tipped the balance in the greatest war in history. "I knew," the British diplomat Harold Nicolson later wrote of his experience at the Versailles Peace Conference, "that the president possessed unlimited physical power to enforce his views. We were all, at that, dependent on America, not only for the sinews of war, but for the sinews of peace. Our food supplies, our finances, were entirely subservient to Washington." In the White House was a president who passionately believed that this matchless power should be used to deepen and make permanent U.S. engagement with the world, the better to "make the world safe for democracy." In these circumstances, to advocate isolationism—a clear and cogently argued political philosophy deeply rooted in American tradition—was an act of considerable will. Some of the most distinguished speeches in American history—for example, the addresses in the Senate by Henry Cabot Lodge and William Borah in opposition to American participation in the League of Nations—were made by isolationists. (Of equal or greater distinction were those, by Wilson and others, in favor of the League.) Isolationism was a concentrated and sustained attempt—successful after the First World War, unsuccessful after the Second—to oppose a deep-running tide of history that, as Nicolson and others understood, was drawing the United States into the center of world affairs.

Few of these conditions obtain today. The United States is in a period of economic stagnation—perhaps of decline. We are the world's biggest debtor—not, as at the beginning of the century, the world's biggest creditor. Our one act of military intervention in the post-Cold-War period—the Persian Gulf war—was paid for largely by our allies. But steeper by far than any economic decline is a decline in political will to use the considerable resources we still possess to confront issues of foreign policy. No one summons us to shoulder global responsibilities; hence no isolationist has to summon the arguments in opposition. No speeches, distinguished or otherwise, are made in favor of disengagement because no case for engagement has been made. The failure to offer consequential assistance to Russia and Eastern Europe is scarcely mentioned in political debate. This is not isolationism; it is exhaustion. It is an exhaustion, however, that goes deeper than foreign policy and paralyzes domestic policy as well. There is no Marshall Plan for the ex-Communist countries for the same reason that there is no Marshall Plan for charred Los Angeles. The symbol of this exhaustion is the budget deficit, which has become a numerical index of the nation's failure to come up with adequate means to back its public purposes. We speak of "U.S. foreign policy" as if the thing existed necessarily, and the only question was which one to choose. But foreign policy, like all policy, has certain prerequisites: the will to act, the means to carry out that will; the willingness to make the sacrifices necessary to procure those means. Only when these fundamental resources are replenished will the United States truly be able to create new policies, including one for dealing with the parts of the world we call foreign.

NOVEMBER 5, 1992

NOTHING, PERHAPS, IS MORE RELENTLESSLY scrutinized than an election. . . . Yet when all is said and done, an election remains a mysterious rite. A hundred million people go into hiding behind drawn curtains for a moment, and out of that something new is born. This something is never quite what anyone suspected.

For example, those on whom the voters' choice lands are immediately transformed. The elected man or woman is different from the unelected man or woman of a moment before. The bearer of the hopes of some tens of millions of people is invested with a quasi-mythical aura no amount of debunking can or should ever quite dispel.

Bill Clinton and Albert Gore appeared to react well to the electorate's transforming touch. In their acceptance speeches in the chilly air on the outdoor platform in front of the charmingly modest Arkansas State House, they looked buoyant without being giddy, happy without being delirious, sober without being afraid. It's worth noting, too, that President George Bush and Vice-President Dan Quayle were graceful in conceding defeat. All of this was auspicious.

Clinton's mandate, at first glance, looks at one and the same time powerful and ambiguous. His campaign was a triumph of adaptation. In an extraordinary feat of political engineering, he refashioned not only his own political image but the image of the Democratic Party to appeal to what he correctly perceived to be the preferences of the majority of the public. He was guided by the scent of victory—the victory Democrats now are savoring.

The preferences he adapted to, however, were those revealed by three consecutive victorious Republican presidential campaigns: for toughness in foreign policy (Clinton supported the war in the Persian Gulf); for toughness on crime (Clinton has supported, and carried out, the death penalty); for parsimoniousness in welfare policy (Clinton vowed that welfare would become "a second chance," not "a way of life"); and for tax reductions (Clinton promised a tax-cut for the middle class). In the "new" Democratic Party, what's new is borrowed from the Republicans. The irony is that Clinton has dispatched into political oblivion the very Republicans whose policies he studied. The Republican Party, though now in the minority at every political level in the United States, is likely, of course, to revive one day. What appears to have been swept from the scene irretrievably is the "optimistic" Republicanism of the Reagan-Bush years, which taught that any notion that the United States was in danger of decline was a political delusion of the opposition, which somehow had been captivated by visions of "gloom and doom"—as Bush, echoing Reagan, often said in his campaign. Since the United States was at bottom in sound condition, these Republicans maintained, the thing to do was not to adopt government programs to fix anything, but simply to withdraw government from the picture as much as possible (especially by cutting taxes) and let the market economy work its magic. A dozen years of essentially flat median incomes, of widening disparity between the rich and the poor, of social deterioration, and of multitrillion-dollar federal budget deficits finally persuaded the nation that its anxieties were not delusions after all, and its patience with those who said they were ran out.

The paradox for Clinton is that he embraced so much of this discredited philosophy in order to defeat it. His mandate—

decisive in what it has buried but uncertain in what it has embraced—is for dramatic "change" which, however, neither he nor the public that voted for him has defined. The demand to get moving is clear and strong, but the road ahead is in shadow.

NOVEMBER 8, 1992

EVEN AS THE LAST VOTES IN THE ELECTION WERE counted, judgments on the unsuccessful Bush campaign began to pour in. Some came from surprising quarters. Ronald Reagan said nothing for attribution, but "close associates" told *The New York Times* that he and his wife Nancy "were upset, even angry" at Bush for his failure. They were particularly distressed, we learn, that Reagan's pleasant, optimistic speech at the Republican convention was pushed late into the evening by Patrick Buchanan's snarling one. Vice President Dan Quayle is another who woke up after the election to the inadequacy of the Bush campaign. "Bill Clinton ran a much better campaign," Quayle said. Did he mean better, one wondered, than the speech in which Quayle, joining in the chorus of intolerance, distortion, and abuse that poured out of the convention, defined the election as a choice between those who defended what is "right" against the champions of what is "wrong," and said of the Democrats that they would "stop at nothing" to win? Richard N. Bond, the chairman of the Republican National Committee, could not agree more with Quayle about the campaign. "I think at the presidential level the Democrats ran a better campaign," he said. It was Bond, of course, who, on the eve of the convention, said, "We are America; these other people are not." Was this comment, by any chance, one of the Republicans' inferior moments? Moving on down the Republican hierarchy, we get to Quayle's chief of staff, William Kristol, who sees "the failure to advance an aggressive domestic and economic policy" as the "basic mistake." Is it possible that Kristol himself was making that mistake when, a week before the election, he read transcripts to the press of a secretly taped phone conversation between Bill Clinton and his alleged former lover Gennifer Flowers? Is there anyone left in the Republican Party who, now that his candidate has lost, is ready to stand up and defend the words and deeds, by which, for a year, the party sought to win the White House for another term?

In speaking of their choice of campaign themes as a "mistake," the Republicans, who just a few days before were seen in almost delirious fits of indignation at those who assailed their "values," seem to have jumped out of that role and into the role of detached television commentators. We have some notion why the usual television commentators attempt a neutral style: It is a way of commenting on the campaign without becoming a part of it. It is a way of avoiding a conflict of interest, in keeping with the old journalistic practice of separating news reporting from editorial opinion. Even in their case, the results are curious. The television commentator stands midway between the reporter, whose job it is to tell what happened, without bias, and the editorialist, whose job it is to weigh the merits or demerits of what the reporter has described. The commentator seeks somehow to combine the non-partisanship of the reporter with the freedom to opine of the editorialist. Barred from giving his own opinion of the substantive merits of the candidates, commentators are confined to estimating the candidates' effectiveness in winning over everyone else—that is, the electorate. They are like theater critics who, owing to some taboo, are forbidden to respond to the performances and the play and must restrict themselves to judging the reactions of the rest of the audience. This need to maintain neutrality is one of the hidden reasons for their much noticed concentration on the "horse race" aspects of the campaign. It is one matter that, with massive aid from public opinion research, can be addressed without appearing partisan.

What are we to make of it, however, when the leaders of one of the parties, who have the right and even the obligation to be advocates, suddenly jump out of their partisan clothing and take up positions in the ranks of the detached analysts? What can they mean when they say that the Democratic campaign was "better?" It's tempting to suppose that they mean such technical things as better organized, better funded, and so forth, but William Kristol rules this out when he says that the choice of themes was the "basic mistake." In other words, the message itself, not just its delivery, was an error. Was it a tactical error, then, to make the defense of "right" the centerpiece of the campaign, as Quayle said he was doing? Can those who defended "wrong" be "better" than those who defended "right?" Would it have been better to soft-pedal the defense of what Quayle called "Judeo-Christian values" in favor of economic prescriptions because that was what voters wanted? Was the battle between right and wrong rendered moot by the election? It is better not to ask. The election was lost. The question no longer arises. It was all a mistake.

NOVEMBER 15, 1992

THE PRESIDENTIAL CAMPAIGN THIS YEAR WAS SO intensely concentrated on the country's domestic plight that the rest of the world almost disappeared from view, yet the outcome nevertheless may have a significance abroad that no one quite anticipated. It's a mysterious fact of political life that people in the most disparate circumstances often arrive, without benefit of communication or coordination, at common ideas and common purposes. When these are widespread enough, they become known as the spirit of the age. So it was in the 1960s, when young people all over the world, acting as if in obedience to a secret universal command, launched their bold but amorphous rebellion against the ways of their parents.

The spirit of the age in recent years has been democratic. The new democratic spirit was active first in the late 1970s, in Europe, where Portugal, Greece and Spain shed dictatorships and adopted democratic government. It erupted soon in Asia, where Korean and Philippine dictatorships fell, and communist rule in China was challenged by the democracy movement. In South America, an entire gallery of military despots was given early retirement. Meanwhile, in Eastern Europe, beginning with the rise of the Solidarity movement in Poland, democracy began the march that culminated in the evaporation of the Soviet Union.

No sooner had the democratic forces prevailed, however, than a new opponent appeared in the field to challenge them. It was, in a word, fundamentalism—ethnic, spiritual, and national. "What is at stake," the Czech writer Jan Urban has recently written in the *East & Central Europe Program Bulletin* of the New School, is "not just the state borders" in the ex-Communist world but "democracy within these borders." The fundamentalist temptation is not restricted to Yugoslavia, where Serbia recapitulates the massacres of totalitarian regimes in earlier decades, or Urban's Czechoslovakia, where Slovakia precipitated a breach with the Czech lands, but also Hungary, where anti-Semitism has made strong inroads, and, to a lesser extent, Poland, where the Solidarity movement has collapsed completely, leaving a political vacuum that has been filled by scores of small parties, many of them animated by bitter intolerance of ethnic minorities, of ex-communists, or of one another. A glance across Poland's border to newly unified Germany, shaken by right-wing violence against foreigners, shows that the infection is not restricted to Europe's eastern part.

A perversion of the democratic movement itself has contributed to the intolerance that now undermines it in Eastern Europe. Democracy is the self-rule of a people. But to rule, a people must decide who is to have the rights of citizenship—who is to be included in the nation, who excluded. The process of definition lends itself to repression. Franjo Tudjman, the president of Croatia, quoted recently in an article in *New Perspectives Quarterly* by Robert M. Hayden, has written that nations should be based on "blood, linguistics, and cultural kinship." When such definitions are imposed by state power on mixed populations, the result is injustice, whose forms may range from legal discrimination, which Tudjman's Croatia practiced against its Serbian minority, to "ethnic cleansing," which Serbia is practicing against Croatia and Bosnia. The pursuit of self-determination—a principle honored in international law—can thus pave the way to that characteristic crime of our century, genocide.

We don't know why fundamentalism has revived to menace

fledgling democracy any better than we know why the worldwide movement toward democracy arose in the first place. Yet even without knowing why, we know that, somehow, the struggles to found or support liberty around the world possess a sort of moral unity. Quite independently of any balance of economic or military power, the success of democracy anywhere strengthens it everywhere. Events in the United States are as much a part of this unity as any others. At the Republican convention, and in the campaign that followed, fundamentalism, in its American version, unmistakably reared its head. . . . The repudiation of this vision by the voters was important for the United States's own future, but it also had meaning for the world. The election of Bill Clinton reaffirmed American democracy. It was a decision in favor of democracy in the country where modern democracy was born. Fighters for democracy everywhere can take heart.

DECEMBER 31, 1992

WHEN PRESIDENT GEORGE BUSH PARDONED FORMER Secretary of Defense Caspar Weinberger and five other men who were involved in the Iran-contra scandal, he was availing himself of one of the most ancient prerogatives of heads of state. According to the Old Testament, history's first homicide was the occasion for history's first pardon. For when Cain slew Abel, God first banished him "from the face of the Earth," but then permitted him to live in the land of Nod. For "Merciful the Lord is, and just, and full of pity." And the earliest known judicial code—that of Hammurabi, promulgated around 1800 B.C.—includes, along with its list of ghastly punishments, provisions for pardons.

The power to pardon is one of the most fundamental and least explicable powers of government. Seen in one light, it stands as a rebuke to all systems of government, for it acknowledges that even when all the wheels of justice have turned, injustice still may have been done by the state, and may need correction. What is more, it makes provision, even when crimes are proven, for the stain to be diluted or washed away by pity—the pity Jehovah showed to the undoubted murderer Cain. (Pity, it seems, cannot be built into the law, whose very nature it is to aim at justice. If pity is to have any role at all in political affairs, it must descend, like God's grace, from another realm.) By accepting this intrusion into its affairs, government makes a rare acknowledgement of its fallibility. A political system—even the most enlightened—that lacked a power to pardon would be a monstrosity.

The pardon is thus both one of the most democratic of the state's powers and one of the least democratic. It is one of the most democratic because it offers a last wild hope to the person condemned by the state. It is one of the least democratic because its exercise is arbitrary. Wielded, usually, by the chief executive, it normally escapes all public review. In medieval times, the power to pardon was usually vested in the king. In a system in which the making of laws, their interpretation, and their execution are vested in one person, it is scarcely surprising that the power to undo the consequences of all these powers was also vested in that person. In no act did a king more clearly exhibit his royal power than in the act of pardon. It was one way of showing that he was not bound by the laws he made.

Difficulties arose, however, when, in large parts of the world, including our own, monarchies gave way to democracies. The power to pardon had been a prerogative of the sovereign. But who, now, was the sovereign? At the time of the American constitutional convention, some argued that in a system of divided powers, there was no sovereign. Others argued that the sovereign was the people, whom Alexander Hamilton called "that pure fountain of all legitimate authority." In the democracy of ancient Athens, the power to pardon was, in fact, vested in the people. To be pardoned, someone had to obtain the signatures of 6,000 people. Such an arrangement was scarcely possible in the United States, a nation of millions, and the power was vested in the president.

The president, however, far from being a sovereign, was a mere hireling of the sovereign. The separation of the pardon from the sovereign cast the power into limbo. The stage was set for abuses. A president might use the pardon to escape accountability for the actions of his own administration. He might make himself a judge in his own cause.

This is what President Bush has now done by pardoning men involved in a scandal in which he played a role. In the harsh, truthful words of Lawrence Walsh, the independent prosecutor investigating the scandal, "The Iran-contra coverup, which has continued for more than six years, has now been completed with the pardon of Caspar Weinberger." That coverup had several stages. The first was the conspiracy of silence in the executive branch surrounding the crimes in the first place. The second was the failure, after the scandal broke, in November of 1986, of the congressional investigation to uncover the truth. This failure was, at bottom, political. The framers of the constitution, aware of the danger of executive self-exoneration posed by the power to pardon, exempted one class of crimes—those brought to light in impeachment proceedings. But in 1986, there was little sentiment for impeachment. And the Congress not only failed to discover the truth about the scandal but also helped spoil the subsequent investigation by independent prosecutor Walsh, several of whose indictments and convictions were dismissed because they supposedly had been tainted by immunized testimony given in the Congressional hearings. Other charges were dismissed when, in a further apparent abuse of executive power, the attorney general, who of course served at the pleasure of the president, refused to supply information in court on the ground that it was classified. Finally, in the coverup's third stage, the independent counsel's effort was undercut completely by the pardon.

Impeachment proceedings by the legislative branch are one means for holding the executive branch accountable for abuses. Prosecution in court is another. Both means, in a display of impotence that is full of danger for the future, failed utterly in the Iran-contra case. There is, however, a third means of holding the executive accountable—elections. It's a fact that the release in the Weinberger indictment, just a few days before the election, of information demonstrating Bush's involvement in the illegal exchange with Iran of American weapons for American hostages coincided precisely with the abrupt halt of a sudden rise in Bush's popularity with voters, which was being measured daily in opinion polls. The indictment quoted notes taken by Weinberger in which he recorded Bush's knowledge and approval of the exchange—knowledge and approval Bush had publicly denied giving. The day before this information was made public, it looked as if Bush might take the lead from Clinton. A day or so later, Bush's popularity was declining.

It would be absurd to claim that George Bush lost the election this year because of public outrage over his role in the Iran-contra scandal. No such outrage existed. However, the reminder, in the last days of the campaign, of Bush's deceptive account of his role in the scandal appears nevertheless to have played a pivotal role in the movement of public opinion. It is a cliché by now to observe that the main issue in the election was the state of the American economy. That was certainly the case in the Clinton campaign. What already tends to be forgotten, however, is that Bush was striving to divert the public's attention away from the economy and towards something else—Clinton's alleged dubious character. "Who do you trust to be president?" was the question that, at every campaign stop, Bush invited the voters to consider in the last days of the campaign. And it was this issue of "trust" that backfired on the president when the new information in the Weinberger indictment demonstrated Bush's own duplicity. Taken in its entirety, the coverup of the Iran-contra scandal has been a stunning success, as Walsh has said. Yet at a crucial political moment, a stray detail of the scandal escaped from secrecy and helped to decide an election. The Iran-contra malefactors were pardoned, but before that happened the pardoner was turned out of office. To that extent at least, justice, left unserved by the legislative and judicial branches of government, was done, in an exercise of sovereign power, by the people.

JANUARY 10, 1993

"THE MATH DOES NOT WORK," RICHARD G. DARMAN, President George Bush's budget director, said the other day, speaking of President-elect Bill Clinton's budget plans. Clinton's plans, he said, were a "circle that cannot be squared." He was speaking on the occasion of the Bush administration's announcement of its final budget. According to this document, the federal deficit for 1997 is going to be about $120 billion greater than the administration had predicted in its budget estimate a year ago.

For anyone who has followed the story of the deficit during the twelve years of Republican control of the executive branch which now are ending, Darman's comments must produce a sensation of profound weariness. The most dispiriting aspect of his accusations is their truth. Clinton's promise of a tax cut for the "forgotten" middle class, which was a central plank in his campaign, collided directly with his promise to reduce the federal budget deficit by half by the end of his term. It's true that there are variables in the economic equation—including possible savings from reform of the health system, possible savings from defense cuts, and possible increases in revenue from overall economic growth—which, if estimated optimistically, could repair the math. However, such optimistic predictions have notoriously been inspired more by political need than by interest in the truth, and Darman was right to mock them as "heroic assumptions." However, no one had to wait for Darman's comments last week in order to be enlightened about the discrepancies in Clinton's arithmetic. These were pointed out tirelessly last year by many people—including the Democratic presidential candidate Paul Tsongas, and, later, Ross Perot.

The truth, it's said, shall make you free. To this, one must add that it makes you free only if you act on it. Truths that go unacted on are, in a way, more corrupting than lies. A nation that fails to respond in an emergency because it is deceived may still act when it hears the truth. But a nation that has heard the truth repeatedly and still hasn't acted may be beyond all appeal. If hypocrisy is the tribute that vice pays to virtue, then a truth that is told and ignored is virtue scorned. When the subject about which the truth is being spoken is the budget and the person speaking has been budget director for four years, the case is more discouraging still.

The story of Darman's education in the math and politics of the budget deficit has, as it happens, been told in a series of articles by Bob Woodward which appeared in the *Washington Post* a few weeks before the election. The decisive moment came in August, 1988, when Bush, who had won the Republican nomination for the presidency, was trailing the Democratic candidate, Gov. Michael Dukakis, by seventeen points in the opinion polls. Bush's speech writers hit on the idea of Bush's promise "Read my lips: No new taxes." This pledge, the speech writers thought (probably correctly), would "put steel in Bush's image," as an aide said later. Darman, whose job it would be to deal not with Bush's image before the election but his budget after it, was horrified. He had watched federal budget deficits skyrocket in the Reagan years, and foresaw a repetition.

He knew that if the pledge were kept, the math wouldn't work. . . . Now the news comes—and who dares pretend surprise?—that the deficit is on its way up again. By 1998, if the estimates are correct, interest payments on the debt will have risen to more than $300 billion, which is a little more than the entire deficit for last year, which was $290 billion. The time for hearing the truth, whether from compromised tellers such as Darman or from worthier sources, has come and it has gone. From now on, only action deserves respect.

JANUARY 14, 1993

IN THE PRESIDENTIAL CAMPAIGN, BILL CLINTON offered himself to voters as the candidate of "change"—or "agent for change," as the instant cliché had it. The buzzword had all the attributes of one of those heavily market-tested "themes" that, since the late 1960s, roughly speaking, presidential campaigns have been organized around. It evoked an atmosphere or mood that, for reasons unknown, somehow resonated with voters. It seemed to promise something without specifying what. It created a vague shimmer of excitement. Lacking definite content, it invited voters to pour into it any particulars they pleased.

Of course, some people were left unsatisfied by a promise of change per se, and wanted to know what would change, and how. It wasn't enough that Clinton would be an "agent for change." History has shown that change can be for the worse. Stalin and Hitler, after all, were agents for change.

Clinton did, in fact, offer particulars. The difficulty was that these tended to be contradictory. The principal subject addressed in the campaign was the state of the economy, and Clinton's economic prescriptions pointed in two opposite directions: On the one hand, he promised to cut the growing federal budget deficit, while on the other hand, he promised to cut taxes on the middle class and to stimulate the economy with federal spending. In the Democratic primaries, a sort of debate ensued over whether cutting the deficit or cutting taxes was more important, and although no great degree of clarity was ever achieved, Clinton came down in general on the side of cutting taxes. Sen. Paul Tsongas favored deficit reduction. Ross Perot took an even more unequivocal position than Tsongas in favor of budget reduction. It was when Perot, the deficit hawk, left the race temporarily that Clinton, who was on the brink of accepting the Democratic nomination, shot up in the opinion polls and began, in his bus travels, to generate visible excitement among crowds of voters.

In retrospect, it's hard to avoid suspecting that the modest euphoria of that moment was connected with the escape from reminders of the deficit problem that the collapse of the candidacies of Tsongas and Perot provided. (George Bush, as it turned out, had nothing believable to offer in the way of deficit reduction nor, for that matter, any other measure to address economic problems.) Clinton was left free to turn away from the depressing subject of budget austerity and to present himself as the candidate of loosened federal purse strings, economic stimulus, and overall growth and prosperity—much as President Ronald Reagan and President Bush had done for the last twelve years. The national habit of ignoring the deficit got another—probably a final—lease on life.

Now, of course, candidate Clinton is President-elect Clinton, the mists of campaign propaganda have cleared, and the deficit again towers in clear view. President Clinton cannot deal with it as candidate Clinton did—with mere words. One cabinet nominee after another expresses astonishment at the size of the deficit, and suggests that the campaign promise to cut taxes for the middle class may not be the highest priority after all, may have to be postponed or may never happen. For "reality has come into focus here," as one Clinton transition official told *Newsday*'s Timothy Clifford. Campaign unreality—that is, almost a full year of promises to the voters—is on the way to the scrap heap.

What, then, of "change"? Clinton's spokesman, George Stephanopoulos, had something to say on the subject. "Circumstances do change," he told reporters in Little Rock. "They change every day." As for the public, a transition official told Clifford, it never really expected every campaign promise to be honored, and will be content if Clinton makes "sure they understand why things have to change." Clinton promised one thing. Now he gets ready to do another. He's an agent for change.

II
GOVERNING

JANUARY 21, 1993

EVERY INAUGURATION DAY IS A GOOD DAY. THE vessel is beautiful (as beautiful as the chill, sparkling morning that descended on Washington today), whatever the contents. We say that we celebrate the peaceful transfer of power, and the peacefulness certainly is a thing to be grateful for, but the phrase misses something of importance. In a transfer, one person hands something over to another. Yet something much more radical is in fact going on. The people, for a single, crucial moment, take their sovereign power back to themselves from the incumbent, and then vest it either in that person again or in someone new. Power is dissolved, and power is re-created.

For power has two faces. Power, on the one hand, is extension—the amplification of someone's will, through the obedience of others. This is the kind of power enjoyed by the Roman official of whom it is said in the New Testament that when he tells his servant to go, he goes, and when he tells him to stay, he stays. It is the power that, today, enables one man's voice to be broadcast instantaneously all over the globe, as Bill Clinton's was while taking the oath of office; that places some millions of people under his command; and that enables him, should he one day so wish (as we trust and believe he will not wish), to blast humankind back into its original molecules. (This last power is all but physically transferred when the gentleman holding the briefcase containing the fateful codes raises his hand in salute to his new commander-in-chief.) This is the sort of power that makes official Washington the sort of city it is—a pyramidal society, marked by hierarchical lines of power as clear and straight as the diagonal avenues that cut across the square grid of its streets, and presided over by the president.

This kind of power has of course been much in evidence during this inaugural week. Its most visible symbol has been the ubiquitous tickets and passes permitting the bearers to a seemingly infinitely articulated series of degrees of nearness to the president-elect, whose famed gregariousness, in this case, has reached monstrous proportions. Never has sheer physical access to a single individual been more widely, or more profitably, distributed. It was networking gone berserk.

Yet power has worn another face at the inaugural. This is the sort of power that, instead of presiding over the people, emanates from them. It lasts, somehow, beyond election day. In the atmosphere of solemnity and gaiety that is Washington today, it was almost palpable. Presidents sometimes grow in office. If they do, the reason may be not so much that they become better people as private individuals as that, standing at the meeting point of the country's hopes and dreads, they develop another self—a public self, which serves as a vehicle for the entire community. This is the self—which still belongs absolutely to the man in office and yet somehow is ours at the same time–we hope will grow.

And Clinton's inaugural address? It glided by, without disturbing anything very much. He took as his theme the ritual of the occasion itself—the "renewal," the "spring" that we "force" in winter. He denied what some have suspected—that he sought "change for change's sake," but never did quite say what change should, in fact, be for. The one line instantly marked out for note—if only for its rhetorical structure recalling the style of President John Kennedy—"There is nothing wrong with America that cannot be cured by what is right with America," scarcely added to the substance of the address. There had been speculation before the speech that he might embrace a theme of "sacrifice," signaling that his determination to reduce the federal deficit would take precedence over his more glad-handed promises to give the middle class a tax cut. The word "sacrifice" was in the speech, but Clinton did not pronounce it clearly. He only sidled up to it, saying that we would not be "choosing sacrifice for its own sake, but for our own sake"—a formula that came close to undercutting in its qualification the very meaning of the word sacrifice.

Yet if Clinton's speech did not redouble the radiance of an already lustrous day, neither did it spoil it. The speech evaporated in the bright air, leaving us to await another occasion on which the new president tells us what he plans to do.

JANUARY 24, 1993

HE IS SIX FEET, TWO AND ONE-HALF INCHES TALL, and his weight fluctuates between 190 and 226 pounds—between lean-jawed handsomeness and a certain puffiness. He moves with a little swagger, like a cool teenager or a prizefighter. He hugs half of the people he meets. He is a man of voracious, indiscriminate appetites. He wolfs down huge amounts of food at any and all times of night or day. He jogs every morning to get rid of the calories he put on the day before. He adores meeting new people, talking with them, charming them, and winning their votes. In this appetite, passion, and opportunism coincide. When, in the small hours, others are drooping, he wants the party to go on. On inauguration week, he threw a couple of hundred parties, and seemed to attend every one. There was no sign that he was present at any of them out of mere obligation. His preferred method of campaigning might be to personally persuade every person in the United States to vote for him. He is the greatest networker of all time.

He talks too much, in person and in public. One old acquaintance who met him by chance in a store during the campaign was amazed to find herself being treated to an extemporaneous speech on government policies. He devours books and articles, and retains a prodigious amount of what he has read. If the presidency were awarded to the winner of an SAT test, he would have won it that way, too. Like one of those sea creatures that feeds by keeping its mouth open as it glides through the ocean, he thrives on all that he ingests. His sexual appetite, too, may be voracious, but we don't know, and it's none of our business.

His preferred method of action is to win over his adversaries by persuasion. He convinces people he meets that he wants exactly what they want. The most recent group to be so persuaded was a plurality of the people of the United States. Later, though, some people discovered that in fact he wanted something quite different and they became embittered. He, on the other hand, is wonderfully free of bitterness. He does not dwell on his adversaries, as so many politicians do, but appears to surge past them, eager to move on to the next thing. He does not hold grudges. It's sometimes said, though, that his wife Hillary does this for him. In their division of political labor, he may be the software, she the hardware.

He is an emotional, even a sentimental, man, and tears come easily to his eyes on public occasions. When he was young, his political convictions were clear and strong. He "despised" the Vietnam war and "racism," as he put it in a famous letter. These were the most notable political passions of young people of his time, and in holding them, he was a man of his generation. In a word, he was a prime example of what the Republicans, on their way to twelve years of presidential victories, called "McGovernism." (Clinton ran George McGovern's 1972 presidential campaign in Texas.) His political career since those days, however, has been devoted to overcoming the political disabilities of those McGovernite enthusiasms, and he recast first himself and then his party in the mold of New Democrats—a breed more interested in the well-being of the middle-class than of the poor, and more inclined to use force abroad than the McGovern supporters. There are some New Democrats, however, who doubt the authenticity of the conversion, and fear a regress of the elected man to his Old Democratic ways.

The most conspicuous lack in his record is proof of courage. Some of the positions he has taken in his long journey from youthful idealism to the White House have the look of political expediency. These include his support for the death penalty and his meally-mouthed support for the Persian Gulf war—both issues of life and death which, one might hope, would be on the list of matters to be decided by conscience alone. During the campaign, he took no position that would affright even the most complacent voters. The only tax increase he called for was one on people earning more than $200,000. He defended the ballooning entitlements that, more than anything else, have created the dangerous federal deficit. Only after the election did he dare, tentatively, to use the word "sacrifice."

The capacity of this hugely sociable man to detect the mood of the voters and to attune himself to it has been demonstrated. It remains to be seen whether, drawing back from the rallies and the galas and the parties, he will be able, in solitude and in silence, to pass before his mind's eye the conflicting promises of the campaign, decide upon clear and consistent goals, and move his administration and the country toward them.

JANUARY 31, 1993

FOR THE FIRST TIME IN ITS HISTORY, THE PENTAGON is making public a count of the phone calls it has received on different sides of a political issue. The issue is whether to lift the ban on homosexuals serving in the military, and the Pentagon's count near week's end was 4,547 against lifting the ban, and 1,261 in favor—a tally that agrees with the Pentagon leadership's own position. The reason for the Pentagon's innovation is obvious. Just a week before, President Bill Clinton's nominee to serve as attorney general, Zoe Baird, was routed by a similar telephonic expression of opinion. Chairman Mao famously said that political power grows out of the barrel of a gun. Evidently, the joint chiefs of staff, who are in charge of more guns than anyone in the world these days, have discovered that power can also flow from the receiver of a telephone, and have decided to deploy some of this firepower against their own commander-in-chief.

Nomination battles are of course an old story in Washington, but Baird's downfall was unique in several respects. First, her rejection came with unprecedented speed. On the weekend before the hearings, everyone in Washington willing to offer an opinion was saying that she would be confirmed. By Thursday afternoon, not a supporter was in sight. Second, this galloping reversal of opinion occurred without the disclosure of any major new damaging facts during the hearings. In other nomination battles, there typically has been a steady flow of revelations, ending either with a "smoking gun," which kills the nomination, or with confirmation. Baird, however, was rejected on grounds that were known from the start—that she had hired two illegal aliens from Peru to take care of her children. On Monday of last week, her deed was said to be a negligible detail, a mere "technical violation," to which Clinton had been wise to pay small attention. By Thursday, this same deed had grown into a fatal offense, whose high significance only political blunderers and fools could possibly have failed to understand.

What changed was not the factual picture but public reaction to the picture on view already. "The public made the decision," a congressional staff aide intimately involved with the judiciary committee's hearings on the nomination told me. "The nomination was a firestorm waiting to happen," Sen. Richard C. Shelby (D-Ala.), who was one of the first to withdraw support for the nomination, said, "and the hearings provided the oxygen. However, the firestorm did not start in Washington, as has happened in the past; it started among the people."

The reactions started to pour in on Tuesday, the first day of the hearings. The calls were overwhelmingly opposed to Baird. Many callers had watched the hearings on C-Span. This channel, which broadcasts an amazing range of Washington doings—for example, State Department briefings—across the country, has given every American who cares to tune in a ringside seat at the deliberations of his representatives. It has become a power in the land. "All America is now wired," Shelby remarked to me. (Surprisingly, he finds that the new visibility of Washington in the home districts has increased rather than decreased voters' desire to see their representatives in person. Having tasted televised access, they want personal access.)

On Wednesday, Clinton was inaugurated. On Thursday, the decisive day, the flood of calls was greater still. Many people had been inspired to call by radio talk shows. For example, in Omaha, the talk-show host Jerry Hudson spent three hours discussing the nomination on Thursday. "I hadn't planned to stay with the thing so long," he said later, "but the phone stayed hot. The last time we stayed on for three hours was Mike Tyson's conviction. This time, people just thought, almost unanimously, that the chief law enforcement officer of the country should not be someone who has broken the law." At noon, Sen. Jim Exon (D-Neb.) told reporters that Baird's nomination should be "pulled by the president." At lunchtime, the Senate Democrats held a caucus, and it became clear that the flames of the firestorm kindled in the provinces were licking the walls of the Capitol. By day's end, five Democratic senators had urged Baird's withdrawal, and it was clear that her fall was only a matter of time. Clinton, offering no resistance, accepted the withdrawal.

A few days later, I asked a Senate aide whether I might see some of the letters her senator had received on the nomination, and she said that because all must first be checked by metal detectors, they had not yet been opened. Letters, it appears, are to our budding age of electronic democracy what sailing ships were to the steam age. Even public opinion polls, those sovereign arbiters of public opinion, were bypassed in the rush to judgment. The Gallup poll, racing to add its findings to the discussion, did an overnight poll between 6:30 and 9:00 on Thursday evening, but by the time the results (sixty-three percent against confirmation, twenty-three percent for, twelve percent no opinion, two percent it depends) could be released, the die was cast.

On November 4, Bill Clinton was elected president of the United States. On January 20, he took office. The next day, he was forced to abandon the person he chose to be chief law enforcement officer of the nation. Who wielded, we may well ask, this extraordinary power? Who overruled the elected representative of all the people, fresh from his election victory, on his first day in office? A certain number of self-selected ordinary citizens, acting through the newly available channels of our wired nation, did: The phones got hot, and the nomination of Zoe Baird went up in smoke. For decades, images and words have been streaming out from the centers of power across radio and television channels to a largely passive public. Now that public, or a part of it, has learned the art of sending messages back with equal speed. Techniques of instantaneous communication, both from the politicians to the voters, and, what is more important, from the voters back to the politicians, are on the verge of an undoubted revolution. This will include, for example, the Clinton administration's promised "electronic highway," which will link, among other things, most of the computers in the country. Last week, a few thousand people, availing themselves of their newfound power, made their wishes known, and all Washington, like a field of wheat in a high wind, bowed down in obedience.

FEBRUARY 4, 1993

THE FEDERAL BUDGET DEFICIT CRISIS, WHICH MANY believe to be the single most important domestic problem facing the wobbling new presidency of Bill Clinton, has given rise to an impressive refinement in the arts of evasion. When the problem being evaded was new—in 1980, for example, when Ronald Reagan was first elected president—crude methods such as the bald assertion of contradictory propositions or plain misstatements of fact would serve, but now that the problem is a dozen years old and these primitive subterfuges have been seen through, subtler methods have been developed. The art of cutting the deficit has not yet been discovered, but the arts of avoiding the problem have blossomed in marvelous profusion, and were on full display in Washington this week.

The week began with a story in *The New York Times* that the Clinton administration was considering a reduction in cost-of-living adjustments on Social Security benefits. The news, politically speaking, had the look of a bomb with a lit fuse, for proposals to cut Social Security have traditionally aroused immediate explosions of protest. The likelihood of an explosion seemed especially probable in view of the fact that two issues of much smaller concern to the voters—the nomination of Zoe Baird to be attorney general and the proposal to lift the ban on gays in the military—had just provoked blitzes of phone calls from around the country. The stage seemed set for a detonation that would rip the roof off the Capitol.

I hastened, therefore, to the likely epicenter of the coming explosion—a meeting, at the Willard Hotel, of representatives of the American Association of Retired Persons, which is 34,000,000 strong. Yet at the plush Willard all was calm. John Rother, the legislative director of the AARP, coolly disdained the idea of making the "switchboards blaze" on Capitol Hill. He had sent out no "alert" to the 34,000,000, as the organization sometimes does. Public opposition to any suspension of cost-of-living increases is "so potent," he explained, it was unnecessary to make a dramatic display. In other words, if no blaze was lighting up the Capitol Hill switchboards, the reason was not that retired people were indifferent but that the Congress was so conditioned to obey them that no action was necessary. Like the possessor of a nuclear arsenal, the AARP scorned the use of its weapon, and relied for victory on deterrence alone.

Meanwhile, at the White House, George Stephanopoulos was justifying the AARP's self-confidence. On previous occasions, the Clinton spokesman had said that all federal programs were "on the table" in the administration's deficit deliberations. Now, however, when asked whether this was true of Social Security cost-of-living allowances, he answered that he wasn't "going to get into on-the-table and off-the-table"—briefingese that effectively took the issue, for the time being, off the table. Still another proposal by the administration threatened a similar result with respect to the deficit. The White House, plainly eager to regain control of the public agenda after losing it for a week to the opponents of Zoe Baird and of gays in the military, drew back the curtains on its welfare plan. To an innocent eye, the plan looks less expensive than current arrangements, inasmuch as it requires welfare recipients to go to work after two years. A moment's examination, however, reveals that many of these jobs would have to be created and paid for by the government and thus would increase rather than decrease the federal welfare bill. The program, the *Washington Post* editorialized, was "attractive." The only problem was "how to raise the funds." It's a "problem" that will make a mirage of every attractive program offered by the Clinton administration until, putting an end to sophisticated evasion, the president tells how some of these programs (for it cannot be all) will be paid for.

FEBRUARY 11, 1993

THERE IS IN EVERY TIME A CERTAIN CLASS OF LAWS that, by virtue of a sort of tacit social consensus, go unobserved. Citizens commonly do not obey these laws, and law enforcement agencies rarely enforce them. Today, a list of such laws would include jaywalking in New York City (enforcement would put the whole city behind bars), sodomy laws (on the books in many places, including the capital city, but almost never enforced), and laws against possession of small amounts of marijuana (widely neglected by the police in favor of enforcement of laws against hard drugs).

Some of these laws are obsolete and on their way to removal from the books, and others are new and have yet to be enforced—if, in fact, they ever will be. In this latter class are the laws regarding the registration and taxation of aliens who work as domestic servants—laws broken, according to Internal Revenue Service estimates, by some seventy-five percent of the families who hire such people. Until recently, Americans were quite content to live with this widespread legal lapse. Reform of the law rather than its strict enforcement was the outlook. Through a process of rampant inflation, this "issue" has ballooned in the public eye until it has all but eclipsed every other matter, and knocked the newborn Clinton administration so far off course that, in the opinion of many, it might be unable to recover.

After the withdrawals of nominations of Zoe Baird and Kimba Wood as attorney general, Secretary of Commerce Ron Brown rushed forward to volunteer a confession that he, too, had violated the babysitter regulations. Shortly, the Clinton administration, turning itself into a zealous prosecutor of the previously ignored law, demanded that all the members of the cabinet confess their child-care crimes. Next, *The New York Times*, extending the inquisition to a new branch of government, phoned every member of the Congress with a similar demand.

By midweek, the atmosphere in the capital was one of mild, semicompulsory dementia, characterized by obsession with an issue that almost no one here, if asked for a considered opinion, would place in the first, or even the second or third, rank of issues facing the United States. In vain did the president, armed with charts and figures, announce and explicate new policies and decisions, including the administration's program for reforming welfare and its decision to cut the White House staff. In vain did aides urge that "the story of the day" should be the White House cuts, rather than Judge Wood's husband's leaks to the press.

The development reveals the emergence of a sort of parallel government that promises to exercise an instant veto over the actions of the Congress and the White House. Its components are, first, that portion of the public which, either because it is unemployed or bedridden, spends its time watching Senate hearings on cable television or listening to talk radio, and then instantly vents its opinions in phone calls to Washington; second, a press that hugely and often thoughtlessly amplifies those voices; third, a Congress that registers every change in public opinion like a pennant in a breeze, and, fourth, a White House as pliant to the pressures of Congress and public opinion as Congress is to public opinion alone.

It all sounds like democracy until one remembers who it was that, demanding in the first place that government concentrate its attention on the nation's economy, voted the president and the Congress into office. The will that the people are vetoing through the channels of the parallel government is, in the last analysis, their own.

FEBRUARY 18, 1993

THE FASTEST THING IN THE UNIVERSE, ACCORDING to Einstein's theory of relativity, is the speed of light. Now, however—if recent events in Washington are any indication—there is something that moves even faster: American politics.

The amazing foreshortening of time in American political decision-making was put on vivid display, of course, by the rise of the ridiculous issue of the tax rules for hiring babysitters. . . . The lesson of Zoe Baird's nomination is that in American politics a week, a day, even an hour is now an eternity, and that if you leave a moment empty, almost any absurd matter can rush in to fill the vacuum. The newly inaugurated Clinton administration, as the world now can plainly see, was busy framing the most ambitious program for national economic reform in a generation. It left a few weeks open to mischief, and the babysitter crisis was one result.

Then the president unveiled his economic program, and the pace became, if anything, even faster. Tutored, no doubt, by the overwhelming public pressure brought almost instantaneously to bear against the Baird nomination, the administration adopted a frantic expedient in support of its plan. The president, instead of unveiling his program in last night's speech to the joint session of Congress and then awaiting the public reaction, gave a ten-minute, nationally televised pre-speech, designed, clearly, to shape that reaction in advance. In general terms, he unveiled his proposal to raise taxes. Probably, he was not a moment too soon. Certainly the Republicans, to name just one group, were already in the field with rebuttals of the as-yet-ungiven speech to Congress. On the evening of the president's pre-speech, Senate Minority Leader Bob Dole was ready with a pre-response, in which he warned of "economic ruin." Immediately, ABC News conducted a telephone poll which showed that fifty-nine percent of the public approved of the president's hurried remarks while twenty-seven percent disapproved. No doubt ABC News thought it thereby would win the race to test the public's reaction. Too late! CBS was there first. For just as Clinton had decided to give a pre-speech, CBS had decided to measure pre-reaction to the pre-speech, and had tested public opinion hours before the president opened his mouth. (The poll showed that fifty-four percent thought taxes on people like themselves were necessary to close the federal budget deficit, while forty-three percent thought they were not.)

The next day—still a full day before the president's speech to Congress—Washington, not to speak of the nation at large, had become a tremendous battleground in a propaganda war that, before it is over, may prove the greatest in our history. (In

Washington, for example, I was one of some sixty-five reporters who assembled to hear a pitifully cold-ridden "senior White House official," equipped with newly made charts and graphs, try empirically to prove that the size of the deficit, in whose name the middle-class tax cut promised in the campaign had been jettisoned, had come as a great shock and surprise to the new administration.) For the physics of the new politics dispenses with the formality of waiting for something to occur before you react to it. Waiting for things to happen takes too long. Now, the light beam hits the wall before the flashlight is turned on. The audience gasps, and then the magician pulls the rabbit from the hat.

By Wednesday afternoon, there wasn't a person in Washington who hadn't made up his mind about the president's speech. Around the country, citizens with microphones thrust in their faces were giving their opinions. Even the president, in his pre-speech, gave his reaction to his speech. Last night, finally, the president gave his speech.

FEBRUARY 21, 1993

THE CLINTON ADMINISTRATION HAS EMBARKED ON A great and good and necessary enterprise: putting the finances of the American household in order. If Clinton is successful, as I believe there is an excellent chance he will be, the benefit will extend far beyond the economy, on which all eyes are now focused. The greatest good would be the beginning of a restoration of the body politic, which in recent years has been dangerously crippled by a collective disorder at whose root lies a virtually systematized fight from unwelcome realities, including, above all, the country's swiftly deteriorating fiscal condition. Democracy, if it is to inspire confidence—not only here in the United States but around the world—must be seen in action, and the Clinton administration has begun to act.

The decisive moment came on Monday when, in his brief, televised pre-speech, the president said, "I had hoped to invest in your future . . . without asking more of you. But I can't, because the budget deficit has increased so much . . ." The words "I can't" sounded in the land with a sort of click. It was the click of the gears of government meshing with the wheels of the economy and society, after more than a decade of spinning idly. The government had achieved traction. Or, to vary the old ship-of-state metaphor, the aircraft of state, having taken off into the wild blue yonder of fiscal fantasy with the election of Ronald Reagan in 1980, was touching down on solid ground again.

The pre-speech's heavy emphasis on new taxes was criticized for having alarmed the public—not to mention the stock market. But precisely this emphasis was its great virtue. It announced the difficulty and sacrifice that are inseparable from authentic action. By placing this aspect first, Clinton signaled the honesty—the reality—of his undertaking. Only after he had done that could anything else be believed. The statement, it is true, also contained an element of dishonesty. He pretended that he had not known all along that his promised tax cut for the middle class was incompatible with deficit reduction—that new estimates of the deficit had changed his mind. Yet whatever the truth about the figures may be, it was obvious not only during the campaign but for years before that tax cuts in a time of rocketing deficits were senseless. . . . Now Clinton and his aides obnoxiously claim that because he did not say, "Read my lips," his promise to cut the taxes of the middle class was not to be taken seriously—as if all promises are now to be considered void if not accompanied by the phrase "Read my lips."

To the extent that Clinton's program gives the lie to his campaign promise, his honesty makes him a liar. The lie, however, is one that the public apparently wanted to hear. Inasmuch as Clinton and the public embraced the lie together, now, perhaps, in a spirit of mutual repentance and forgiveness, they can embrace the truth together.

Appropriately, ex-President Ronald Reagan, the prime author of the economic tangle the country now is in, was heard from, in an article in *The New York Times*. The piece read well. The familiar cadences of the ex-president were audible even in print. Yet in the new atmosphere the old refrain sounded off-key. It is one thing to hear the arguments for a plan that may lead to fiscal disaster before that disaster has occurred, and another thing to hear them after it has occurred and the hard work of cleaning up the mess has begun. There were the "facts" that are not facts: "Most of the economic gains of the 1980s were made by low- and middle-income citizens, not the wealthiest" (in fact the income of average low- and middle-income citizens stagnated or fell). There were the sensible-sounding formulas that left out obvious truths: "Let us remember that deficits are caused by spending" (as if cutting taxes could not also lead to deficits).

As a candidate, Clinton adopted Reagan's illusion that taxes can be cut and the deficit reduced at the same time. As president, he has abandoned the illusion, and proposes to raise taxes. The press and others bestowed the title The Great Communicator on Reagan during his time in office. In a day when politicians have learned to live or die by their images, it seems the ultimate accolade. But if Clinton, challenging the appealing but deceiving images established so successfully in the public mind by The Great Communicator, is able to undo the ill effects they produced in the real world, a title more honorable and more fitting to the leader of a democratic country—that of a great doer—can be his.

FEBRUARY 28, 1993

A NEW POLITICAL LANDSCAPE HAS ABRUPTLY TAKEN shape in the United States. The exact moment it occurred was not Clinton's speech to the joint session of Congress—crucial as that was in consolidating the change—but two days before, when Clinton gave his brief televised pre-speech announcing large tax increases, and the public, revealing to pollsters that very evening a response that has not altered since, signaled its acceptance. The Clinton administration has learned what every politician who wants to survive in the incredibly accelerated political processes of the 1990s must learn: The response to scheduled events before they occur—the "preaction," if you like—is as important as the response after they occur (the traditional reaction). The pre-speech was like a great preemptive karate kick in this speeded-up political combat, and the opposition has been on its back ever since.

Not the least surprising feature of the new atmosphere, in fact, is the helplessness of the Republican Party, which just a few years ago appeared to many to be the master of the political scene for the indefinite future. The Republicans so far have not merely failed to find an adequate response to the president's proposal; they have not found any response at all. There were hints of this helplessness before the election. The first hint, perhaps, was the decision of the party at its convention not to offer an economic plan but instead to sermonize on "family values" and the evils of homosexuality. The Republicans gratefully turned again to these themes when Clinton, in his first weeks in office, embroiled himself in the debate about gays in the military; but when the president turned his attention back to the economy, the Republicans fell all but speechless.

The incapacity to respond was unforgettably caricatured by Sen. Trent Lott (R-Miss.) during testimony at the Senate by Office of Management and Budget Director Leon Panetta. Over the years, the Republicans have shown a penchant for brandishing lists and plans whose contents they will not reveal to the public. The prototype was Sen. Joe McCarthy's secret list of supposed Communists in the State Department. (In fact, there were none.) Another was Richard Nixon's secret plan to end the war in Vietnam—a war that continued throughout his first term in office. Lott's contribution to the tradition was a secret list of spending cuts that allegedly would accomplish as much deficit reductions as the president's plan but without raising taxes. He displayed the list before the TV cameras; yet when Panetta asked to see it, Lott declined, and returned it to his jacket pocket. Whether the list contained any more budget cuts than McCarthy's list contained the names of Communists in the State Department is still unknown.

Later, at a news conference, Senate Minority Leader Bob Dole likewise refused to offer any alternative plan, urging instead that everyone concentrate on discovering what was wrong with the president's plan. However, Dole and his colleagues did provoke a glimmer of public response with one accurate observation: that the plan depends more on tax increases than on spending cuts. But since the Republicans insisted on hiding in their jacket pockets any further proposals of their own for cuts, they set the stage for the president's demand that they "put up or shut up."

Their ploy and its failure so far may point to the deepest reason for the sudden reversal of their fortunes. Boiled down to its essence, the Republicans' objection to the president's plan is that it increases taxes. This fact alone, they seemed to believe, would, once duly pointed out, discredit the plan. And experience, of course, was on their side. For twelve years, the party had been trading on the public's resistance to taxes, which appeared impervious to argument and oblivious to consequences, including the gargantuan federal budget deficit.

When, in a historic shift, the public changed its mind about taxes, the foundation of Republican political success was destroyed. To be sure, Clinton did nothing in the campaign to bring about the change, but he fell heir to it as president, and had the good sense to build a policy on the new foundation. The Republicans, remembering past triumphs, had no better idea than to refresh themselves one last time at the well of public indignation at high taxes, but the well was dry.

MARCH 11, 1993

ON TUESDAY, SEN. STROM THURMOND, A MAN WHO ran for president in 1948 on the segregationist "Dixiecrat" ticket ("I want to tell you," he said then, "that there's not enough troops in the Army to force the Southern people to break down segregation and admit the Negro race into our theaters, into our swimming pools, into our homes, and into our churches"); a man who championed the Vietnam war from start to finish; a man who defended Richard Nixon in the Watergate scandal up to the moment the president resigned (at one point he blamed the scandal on Ralph Nader and the American Civil Liberties Union, among others); a man notable, in short, for supporting a host of causes the country at large eventually came to regard as mistaken if not sinful, turned 90.

The event was amazingly free of specific content. None of the events listed above was mentioned. They had all vanished, it seemed, from collective memory. Yet not only had the man survived but—and this is the key point—he remains in office. He is that rarity among American politicians; a man whose life in office has been almost coextensive with his life on Earth. And so all of Washington came to pay tribute. President Bill Clinton came. Ex-President Nixon came. Senate Majority Leader George Mitchell, Senate Minority Leader Bob Dole, Sen. Joe Biden—everyone came. The celebration turned out to be a kind of memorial service turned upside down. At memorial services, speakers are likely to say that although the person has died, the causes he supported live on. But here it was the causes that had died and the person who lived on. Nor was it the case that, as sometimes happens, the causes had been trampled by evil forces but they lived on in people's hearts, for these causes—segregation, for example—had died out in people's hearts, including, as it happens, Thurmond's. Once the civil rights legislation of the 1960s had passed, the South Carolina Republican hastened to integrate his staff. He became a monument to integration in the way an enemy fortress that falls in war becomes a monument to victory.

What, in these circumstances, were the speakers to say? Were they to sing the praises of integration? Praise Thurmond for changing his mind? Defend Nixon's innocence in Watergate? They opted to speak of virtues that a person can display in pursuit of any goal whatever: vigor, steadfastness, fidelity. Bob Dole, the Senate's most sardonic member, who seems to survive the hypocrisy of political life by permitting himself an incessant *sotto voce* mockery of it, indulged himself, as the program's emcee, in black comedy. His most daring jibe, in response to many speakers' tributes to Thurmond's longevity (one giddily wished him "another 90 years"), was to ask if Dr. Kevorkian was in the house. Mitchell's list of encomiums was a masterpiece of omission. As in Japanese painting, the artistry lay in what had been left out. He said of Thurmond, "By his sheer longevity, his energy, his force of will, his overwhelming persuasiveness, he has shaped the history of our time."

The most elaborate moment came when Nixon rose to speak. The former president was, as usual, in the midst of a comeback. He was championing the cause of Russia and had met recently with Clinton. But it was the comeback of a ghost. The fallen Nixon is a spectral figure, and his peregrinations through the lecture halls and op-ed pages of America are a kind of life after death. Yet the ghost is a far pleasanter personage than the man-in-power ever was. It fell to Nixon to add poetry to the occasion. He quoted Sophocles: "One must wait until the evening to see how splendid the day has been." Coming from Nixon, it was a surprising affirmation. It seemed to forgive Thurmond for whatever mistakes he might have made, to forgive himself for his own mistakes, and to forgive the rest of us for having had to condemn them. In an evening of merciful omissions, he gave voice to a sentiment of absolution that somehow was real.

MARCH 18, 1993

AS CONGRESS POSTURED AND MANEUVERED IN preparation for its vote on the Democratic resolution in support of President Bill Clinton's budget proposal, a minor episode illustrated the remarkable changes that have taken place in recent months in the very terms of the debate on economic issues in this country.

Rep. Gerald Solomon from Glens Falls and other Republicans held a news conference announcing the introduction of an amendment to the Democratic resolution. For several weeks after Clinton's speech setting forth his economic plan, the Republicans seemed to have lost their voice. The president challenged them to offer a specific alternative, but they remained silent. It was a curious hiatus: The forms of partisan debate were preserved, but its substance was missing. Senate Minority Leader Bob Dole carried the Republican standard, and there was a paradoxical heroism in his effort. It's harder, after all, in speech after speech, and interview after interview, to defend a party that has no position than to defend one that has a position. Dole, in these dispiriting moments for the Republicans, seemed not so much to be carrying on a partisan debate as holding open the possibility of debate for such time as his party decided what it wanted to say.

A slow evolution began in Republican ranks. Its first fruit was a proposal by the hitherto little-known congressman, John R. Kasich (R-Ohio), of an alternate budget. The principal difficulty faced by the Republicans was their resistance to any tax increases—which, for more than a decade, had won them the enthusiastic support of a like-minded public. Clinton, however, had proposed tax increases, along with spending cuts, as the means to cut the deficit, and opinion polls now showed the public accepting his plan. Kasich proposed to achieve budget reductions comparable to Clinton's with spending cuts alone. Those cuts, however, were so severe that the Republican leadership kept its distance.

The stage was set for the amendment Solomon offered on Tuesday. This plan, according to Rep. Olympia Snowe (R-Maine), "took the Kasich plan as a foundation" and then went "beyond that" to add something else—tax increases, including several of the taxes on the wealthy that Clinton had proposed. This "going beyond," of course, marked a sharp reversal for a party that had adamantly opposed tax increases in the last election. Deliberately missing from the list of taxes, however, were all those that, like Clinton's energy tax, fell on the middle class, whose overtaxed condition received much sympathy at the news conference. In the name of "fairness," the representatives said, only the rich would be taxed.

As the congressmen and congresswomen sounded the call for deficit reduction and fairness, lamented the plight of the middle class and congratulated themselves on their courage in calling for tax increases on the wealthy, a certain feeling of *déjà vu* crept into the proceedings. It fell to Jim McLeary (R-La.) to identify the reason. "If you want to characterize this plan," he said, "it's the Clinton campaign plan." It had "no new taxes on the middle class," he pointed out, and it "got the deficit down"—the two principal things that Clinton had promised. The Republicans, of all people, had stepped forward as belated supporters of candidate Clinton. The Solomon amendment, offered scarcely two days before its virtually certain defeat in the vote scheduled for today, is unlikely to figure large in the history books. But to anyone who one day takes an interest in the rapid and deep political shifts in our period, the emergence in the winter of 1993 of Jim McLeary and his Republican colleagues as champions of the Democratic economic policies they fought in the fall of 1992 deserves at least passing note.

MARCH 21, 1993

WHEN THE HISTORY BOOKS ARE WRITTEN, THE MOST important tale of the early 1990s may well prove to be the story of something that didn't happen: the creation of a serious, well-funded, comprehensive program for supporting the democratic governments that suddenly and miraculously arose in the ex-communist countries. No one can be sure that such a program, if it were instituted, would succeed; all we know is that it has not been, and that today aggression and atrocity are triumphant in former Yugoslavia, while democracy fights for its life in Russia. In 1991—to give just one instance of squandered opportunity—Russian President Boris Yeltsin offered to join NATO. The response was an embarrassed silence, and the bid was allowed to lapse. Had the invitation met with a favorable response, there might now exist a level of cooperation among the former adversaries in the Cold War that would give them significant influence both in Yugoslavia and in the republics that have succeeded the Soviet Union.

The question posed by this record can be framed in the following way: In 1980, President Ronald Reagan began a defense buildup that, before it was finished, cost a trillion dollars. Just this week, President Bill Clinton, alarmed by events in Russia, proposed increasing aid to that country from $300 million to $700 million. These figures, in view of the dimension of the peril that has now arisen, are not merely low; they are low by several orders of magnitude. How has this happened? Why is the United States, having spent a trillion dollars at the tail end of the Cold War, unable to find one or two percent of that amount to secure the peace?

The answer must begin with the Reagan buildup itself. Some observers say that it was important in bringing communism to its knees; others disagree. However, the consequences for the United States are not in doubt. The trillion, we now know, was a trillion that the United States did not have, for during the buildup the national debt increased by $3 trillion. Hence, the mistake was not so much the buildup itself as the failure to pay for it. When the Soviet Union unexpectedly disappeared, the American government's coffers were empty. Every dollar in them was already spoken for by several other parties. In these circumstances, proposals to substantially aid the ex-communist world did not even have to be defeated; they were never brought to a vote in the first place. The political parties, you might say, vied with one another in ignoring the growing danger. The abdication, whose price now is becoming clear, occurred in silence.

As it happened, at the crucial moment, a distraction arose: the Persian Gulf war. The purpose of that war, according to President George Bush, was to lay the foundations for a new world order, to be based on the principle that the international community was resolved to drive back aggression wherever it might occur. In fact, the war turned out to prove a nearly opposite point: that the world (with the United States providing most of the armed forces) was ready to halt aggression whenever the effort promised to be brief and comparatively easy. Today, the very soldiers who, like Colin

Powell, commanded the Gulf war have successfully argued that the United States should remain on the sidelines in former Yugoslavia, on the ground that engagement there would be protracted, messy, and costly. In retrospect, it's clear that the Gulf war was not the first in a series of long and difficult battles to secure a new world order but the last of a series (the first two were the invasions of Grenada and Panama) of comparatively short and painless battles whereby the United States sought to persuade itself that it had recovered from the humiliation and injury of the defeat in Vietnam.

That, perhaps, is why public enthusiasm for the gulf war, which most people had thought would carry Bush to a second term, faded so quickly. It was the last hurrah of an age that was passing, not the welcome given to the new age. As the martial music of the gulf war died away, the public, much to Bush's surprise, turned, with a vengeance, to domestic woes. Instead of concluding that, thanks in great measure to the fiscal imprudence of the 1980s, domestic tasks and international tasks were now threatened by a common neglect, the public decided that unwarranted concentration on the foreign sphere (supposedly Bush's failing) was distracting government from concentrating on domestic problems (something Clinton promised to do). Pushed aside first by Bush's gulf war, then by Clinton's virtually exclusive concentration on domestic ills, the crisis in the ex-communist countries fell into a double obscurity—an obscurity from which Clinton, who must deal with the world as it is, not as he presented it in his campaign, now seeks to rescue it.

APRIL 8, 1993

ONE OF THE MOST INTERESTING SUBPLOTS IN President Bill Clinton's Washington is the tale of the Republican Party's trek through the wilderness. They face not only a Democratic presidency but a Democratic majority almost everywhere else—in most state legislatures, in governorships, in the House of Representatives and, of course, in the Senate, where a Republican filibuster against Clinton's economic stimulus package has been launched.

In recent years, the two most important pillars of Republican ideology have toppled. One—anti-communism—was removed by events. The collapse of the Soviet Union left the GOP at a loss for a coherent foreign policy. The extent of the disarray is suggested by an editorial in the current *National Review*. Finding liberals "soft on communism" has long been a stock in trade of the right. Now the conservative *Review*, still apparently eager, even in the absence of communism, to find the Democrats soft on something, accuses the administration of failing to announce its support for Boris Yeltsin in the event that Yeltsin should decide to "prevail and preserve sound policy, even by authoritarian means." "Sound policy" here means support for free market reforms. This failure to support an authoritarian capitalism in advance of anyone's having proposed it, the *Review* finds, amounts to "liberalism as an infantile disorder." The second pillar of Republican ideology was fiscal conservation—the principle of keeping the government out of debt—and it was laid low by the Republicans' own action. It was in the name of fiscal conservatism that a generation of Republicans battled Democratic social spending, from Franklin Roosevelt on. In the '80s, however, the Republicans, lured on by a public that wanted to receive government services without paying for them, abandoned fiscal conservatism and ran up more than three trillion dollars of federal debt. The loss of these two pillars preceded the party's defeat in 1992. George Will is right when, in the same issue of the *National Review*, he writes, "There was no sense of an honorable banner borne in an honorable defeat"—as there had been, he adds, when Barry Goldwater lost in 1964. This time, the banners were lost first; then came the defeat. Now the party is casting about for new banners. It toyed for a while with opposition to gays in the military, but that issue looked unpromising as an organizing principle—especially since, in the view of many, the party's antigay militancy at its convention contributed to Bush's defeat. The party next sought some budget plan to offer in place of Clinton's but failed, finally, to settle on one.

It is into this vacuum that the party has thrust its filibuster. The Democrats, for their part, complain that the Republicans are bringing our system of government to a halt. Clinton, for example, said that the filibuster blocked "majority rule." However, these complaints are exaggerated. The filibuster began only after the Congress had swiftly passed the resolution that left Clinton's budget proposals virtually intact. The stimulus package, at a cost of $16 billion, is in truth not much more than the ghost of a campaign promise. During the campaign, voters may recall, Clinton placed the goal of economic stimulus above the goal of deficit reduction, promising a large stimulus plan and a tax cut for the middle class. As president he has reversed these priorities, and the main act of his first 100 days has been the passage of tax increases and spending reductions that will cut the deficit. The great pitched battle in the Senate has come after the war has ended.

In these circumstances, it's hard to escape the feeling that the filibuster is a triumph of pure form over substance—that the

Republicans are reminding everyone of their existence pending such time as they discover an important message to deliver. Worse things have happened. The forms in question—even the filibuster—are forms of democracy, and democracy is a bit of substance to which both parties can agree to give support.

APRIL 11, 1993

THE CLINTON ADMINISTRATION, IN ITS EIGHTY-FIRST day, appears to have entered a second stage. The first stage opened when, in his first television address to the nation, the president announced his tax increases and spending cuts, and polls instantly made known the public's acceptance. (The silly season between inauguration and the television speech—Clinton's babysitter period—doesn't count.) The tonic effect of facing basic truths made itself felt. Clinton, riding the wave of opinion he had created, seemed to carry all before him.

Now, however, this initial burst of energy appears to have spent itself, and a new mood is crystallizing. This is most obvious in foreign affairs, which, disrespectful of the Clinton administration's wish to concentrate on domestic affairs, has intruded itself in the form of the constitutional crisis in Russia and the worsening aggression in former Yugoslavia. In a speech at Annapolis, Clinton made a case for assistance to Russia that seemed unarguable. He said that the struggle of the states that once made up the Soviet Union was "the greatest security challenge for our generation." He recalled the "trillions of dollars" the United States had spent on the

Cold War. For these reasons, he said, the United States must "put Russia and its neighbors first on our agenda abroad."

That weekend, he unveiled his plan: $1.6 billion dollars in aid. To anyone who took the speech seriously, it seemed that Clinton must have left a few zeros off the figure. For how could help to Russia be "the greatest security challenge of our generation" and yet deserve only $1.6 billion? Any number of individual weapons systems in the budget will cost more. (We will spend more—$1.7 billion—on the Trident II ballistic missile submarine, designed to blow up a Soviet Union that is no more, than we'll spend to rescue a Russia that still exists.)

The pattern is repeated in the administration's policy toward Serbian aggression in Bosnia. In the administration's first major speech on the subject, Secretary of State Warren Christopher defined that crisis, too, in the most drastic terms. Serbian ethnic cleansing had been "pursued through mass murders, systematic beatings and . . . rapes . . . prolonged shellings of innocents in Sarajevo and elsewhere," he said. Beyond that, the very shape of the international order was at stake, he said, for "the world's response to the violence in the former Yugoslavia is an early and crucial test of how it will address the concerns of the ethnic and religious minorities in the post-Cold-War period." He pointed out that "bold tyrants and fearful minorities are watching to see whether ethnic cleansing is a policy the world will tolerate."

So far, the answer is that the world, including the United States, will tolerate it. Suggestions by Clinton in the campaign that bombing Serbian positions might be necessary were abandoned in favor of food drops. (It must be added, though, that in spite of signs that the administration's reluctance to intervene is actually growing, policy remains deeply ambivalent, and might well reverse again. The recent decision to enforce the no-fly zone points in this direction.)

These policies resemble nothing so much as Washington's response to the budget deficit before Clinton became president. Eloquent speeches replace action instead of announcing it. Big talk is accompanied by small deeds. There is no mystery why: The public, having accepted certain sacrifices, isn't yet ready to make further ones. There is a danger, too, that the gap will reopen in domestic affairs, as it becomes clear that further austerities are necessary to put the economy in order. For the most important issue that the administration and the country face is not the budget deficit, or assistance to Russia, or intervention in Bosnia, or any other specific goal of policy, but whether the nation has the reserves of political will to meet these and the other trials that the real world, which does not follow the results of opinion polls, is creating. Clinton, to his great credit, broke the impasse in the crucial area of fiscal affairs in the early days of his presidency. Now the permission to act he won then is maybe reaching its limits. If so, he'll have to return to the public once again, and make the harder case for facing the further challenges that events are forcing upon us.

APRIL 29, 1993

THE 100TH DAY OF THE CLINTON ADMINISTRATION IS upon us, and the numerically triggered avalanche of journalistic assessments is well down the mountainside. The impression is widespread that the administration is floundering. One explanation for Bill Clinton's troubles, offered by, among many others, his budget director Leon Panetta, is that he has lost control of the public debate by concentrating on too many issues at once. Another explanation, offered by Republicans, is the self-fulfilling argument that by failing to persuade any of them to abandon their unanimous support of their filibuster in the Senate against his economic stimulus plan, he has displayed a lack of leadership. But behind all this, it seems to me, is the force of a broader influence. It is the pressure of coverage itself—of "communications," or whatever it is we now call the digitized procedures of public speech and writing in our day.

It's no secret that the technology of communications has burgeoned hugely. . . . This communications machine is the electronic equivalent of a standing army. Just by existing, it calls for use. Though available for any partisan purpose, its uses are not necessarily partisan. Its bias, like that of most immense man-made machinery, is in favor of its own needs. First and foremost, twenty-four hours a day, it wants a story. It is unthinkable that any arm of it should ever lie still for even a minute—that the screens would go blank, that the transmitters would fall silent, that the sheets of newsprint would stay rolled in the plant. Once, people tended to speak in public because they had something they wanted, for better or worse, to say. Now they are likely to speak because the machine requires feeding, and the price of silence, politically speaking, may be death. The machine's influence is best understood, perhaps, as a kind of omnipresent suction, demanding a constant flow of words and deeds from all in its vicinity. Needing, as it does, a perpetual diet of new stories each day, it is by implication an enemy of yesterday's story: It is an adversary of memory, and so of continuity. Because it must operate at full stream all the time, and must stuff all events into a frame of unvarying size, it tends to raise the trivial to the level of the awesome and degrade the awesome to the level of the trivial: It is the enemy of proportion. In short, it is a consumer, and, like all consumers, it tends to destroy what it swallows.

No one is more at risk of being swallowed than a president, for he is expected at all times to dominate not only his political opposition but the machine itself. In the political parlance of our day, keeping ahead of the communications machine is called "defining the agenda"—that obsession of modern candidates and office-holders alike. It means feeding the machine first, and with the most. The next step is "spin control": another attempt to seize the initiative in the communications wars. (No one ever accused, say, Abraham Lincoln of inadequate spin control.) It would be absurd to suggest that Clinton has not made policy mistakes in his first hundred days. Yet, when Panetta advises Clinton to pick his issues more sparingly, and the Republicans accuse him of failing to lead, they are taking him to task not so much for his failure to frame good policies (although the Republicans certainly dislike Clinton's) as for poor superintendency of the communications machine. For if he fails to get a grip on it, then the machine, they know, being self-propelled, will roar ahead without him, drowning him out with sheer static (for example, the horrors of illegal babysitting). If the Republicans don't beat him, he can still lose to this impersonal rival.

MAY 6, 1993

ACCORDING TO THE CONVENTIONAL WISDOM OF THE moment, the Clinton administration has temporarily lost its way and the reason is that it has attempted to do too many things at once. Clinton, after hearing this reproach on all sides for some weeks, has ratified the consensus by confessing the error. "One of the things that you risk when you try to get a lot of things going," he said, "is . . . maybe getting a little out of focus. And I think we can . . . tighten the focus a little bit . . ."

The key phrase, certainly, is "out of focus." It not only sums up the current conventional wisdom, it resonates strongly with other recent stock phrases. One of these was the famous sign on the wall of the Clinton Campaign headquarters: "The economy, stupid." This advice demonstrated "focusing" in action. It divided the world into two realms: 1) The economy (implicitly, smart); and 2) everything else (the preoccupation of the stupid). Russia? Stupid. Bosnia? The same. Thinning ozone, warming global climate, decaying cities, declining schools: all stupid. The same division of the world was implied in another famous stock phrase: Clinton's promise to concentrate "like a laser" on the economy. Laser light is focused light. It is blinkered light. Every photon is sent like a bullet toward the same target. In the vision suggested by this phrase, the president, now himself a sort of high-tech gadget (the better, presumably, to compete with his Japanese counterparts), remains dutifully "on message," and shuts out the rest of the world. Monomania becomes policy.

As a method of campaigning, the technique proved its worth. Today, Clinton sits in the White House. Deliberate monomania showed itself a superior method for surmounting one of the greatest challenges faced by a political candidate: getting his message through to the voters in a world of virtually infinite distraction by the proliferating media of our day. For these media are not only instruments for conveying the "message"; they are an ocean in which a message can drown. Once Clinton had been elected, the question naturally arose whether other techniques might now be appropriate. Administration officials, however, soon noted that the techniques of the candidate had their uses for the president. Instead of pressuring legislators directly, he would use the new media to bring his message to the public, which, in turn, would indirectly pressure the legislators. The technique of monomania was deployed anew. The passage of Clinton's initial budget plan was testimony to the technique's success.

Then things began to go wrong. For one thing, the Republicans defeated Clinton's economic stimulus plan with their filibuster—but that's another story. (In effect they discovered an issue on which they could inflict a defeat on him without suffering too seriously in public esteem.) What is more important, the world continued to turn. That is, history continued producing a fantastic profusion of events, including the constitutional crisis in Russia and a worsening of the crisis in Bosnia. It is a profusion that since the end of the Cold War has, if anything, increased. Clinton responded, as any president worthy of the office had to. He gave strong support to the Russian president, Boris Yeltsin, shortly before the referendum on Yeltsin's presidency and policies. Clinton's support unquestionably helped Yeltsin win on all questions on the referendum. Yet in the battle for "focus" Clinton's highly successful initiative must be considered a defeat. The same will be true for whatever Clinton does in Bosnia, although to neglect that crisis would be an unthinkable dereliction of a president's duties.

The political needs of the presidency, everyone now seems to agree, require him to focus like a laser beam on one thing only. But if that is so, then American politics is heading toward a dangerous collision with history, which has a way of producing many things to deal with at once, and does not countenance delay. Monomania may be a way of winning elections. It cannot be the way to run a country. It is a formula for misrule.

MAY 20, 1993

IN A SHARP REVERSAL OF POLICY, PRESIDENT BILL Clinton, who in last year's campaign excoriated President George Bush for failing to address the crisis in Bosnia, is pulling back from intervention there. The retreat comes in the aftermath of a misguided initiative, in which the administration urged arming the Bosnian Muslims and bombing Bosnian Serbian positions while prohibiting the use of American ground troops. European nations, some of whom do have ground troops in Bosnia, carrying out a humanitarian mission under the United Nations flag, rejected the initiative, for fear that it would jeopardize their troops without reaching the desired objective—a political settlement.

The American proposal was shaped by a domestic political requirement that normally would be considered crippling to military activities: the need at all costs to avoid American casualties. The United States wanted to settle everything from the air—to untie Bosnia's Gordian knot from 10,000 feet. The origins of this singular strategy of winning wars without risking lives go clear back to Vietnam. At the time, many in the military and elsewhere, baffled by the American defeat, concluded that victory had been snatched from their hands by the American press and the war's opponents at home. The military, after all, had won almost every battle in Vietnam, and yet the war was lost. How could that have been, they wondered, if their efforts had not been undercut on the home front?

Then reflection set in. Thoughtful military men began to understand that their fundamental problem had been in Vietnam itself—that their fighting there had not been directed toward any clear political goal. If anything, their victories, by destroying civilian society in the South, undercut the precondition of any lasting success: the creation of a stable government in the South, thus permitting American troops to leave. To amount to much, the military men gradually concluded, victories in battle must be won in support of defined political objectives.

This lesson has now been applied to Bosnia. Top American military officials—including, above all, Chairman of the Joint Chiefs of Staff Colin Powell—now insist on having a full roadmap to political success before they introduce a single soldier on the ground. Anything short of that looks to them like a pursuit of mirages. Above all, they want to know how and when they are going to get out of the war, and this has publicly been made a condition of involvement by Secretary of State Warren Christopher in testimony to Congress.

The military men, however, have been misled by their conclusion. Military policy, it is true, should be connected to clear goals, yet the goals in different situations may differ greatly. In Vietnam, no goal worth achieving could have been obtained without the creation of a popular, self-sufficient government in the South. In the absence of that, all other policy was senseless. But in

Bosnia, there is a goal worth achieving that falls short of creating a durable government there. Radovan Karadizic, speaking with an audacity unusual in even the most brazen political criminals, said recently, "Bosnia never existed, and it will never exist." Is this clear enough for everyone to understand? He frankly announces to the world his intention to obliterate a nation. Stopping this should be the primary goal of international policy, and it can be done—it must be done—before reaching a full political settlement in the former Yugoslavia, an admittedly hellish task whose burdens the international community should frankly accept. There is to be no end, it seems, to the confusion brought by the Vietnam war. Even our hard-won wisdom regarding this war betrays us. Once it was the war itself that did the damage—to Vietnam, to the United States, to the world. Now, the lessons of Vietnam, learned too late to help us in Vietnam itself, have sunk in just in time to darken our understanding of a new crisis in a new age.

MAY 23, 1993

NEWS STORIES ARE MADE UP OF COUNTLESS EVENTS, in much the way newspaper photographs are made up of countless dots, and each story, in turn, is one among innumerable events making up a larger story. The largest story is the story of one's time. It's hard, though, while living through contemporary events, to make out what the larger stories are. I suspect that when the history of American politics of recent years is written, it will turn out to have revolved around a lasting tension between certain powerful and attractive fantasies and certain disagreeable realities, the principal fantasy being that the power and prosperity the United States enjoyed since the end of the Second World War was secure, and the principal reality being the steady economic and social deterioration of the country.

Seen in this light, Ronald Reagan emerges as a master of illusion. The illusions he propagated, however, were not lies put over on a gullible public; they were dreams the public wanted to dream. In his new memoir, Secretary of State George Shultz remarks that when Reagan got a piece of misinformation fixed in his mind, nothing could dislodge it. This quality served him well with the public, which also was clinging doggedly to comforting misconceptions. Often it was said that after a period of national self-doubt, he made America "feel good about itself again," and no doubt he did. Looking back on this period of feeling good from a period in which people no longer feel very good, it's at least some small comfort to reflect that, if people had to fool themselves, they got some comfort from it.

In domestic policy, the illusion has a convenient numerical measure—the $4.4 trillion national debt, which represents the gap between the wealth the country thought it had and the wealth it actually had. One day, some graduate student will get a Ph.D. analyzing the fabulous array of techniques—the crackpot economic theories, the fiscal sleight-of-hand, the legislative posturing, the gorgeous political advertising, not to mention the outright lying—whereby the country managed to avoid the truth for so long. Suffice it to say that around 1992, the bubble of self-deception burst, contributing heavily to the defeat of President George Bush.

In the foreign sphere, the illusions were of like kind. By carefully choosing military campaigns—in Grenada, in Panama, in the Persian Gulf—in which the United States could achieve swift, spectacular-seeming results while suffering minuscule casualties, Reagan and Bush sustained the country's image as a superpower. These wars without casualties were the equivalent in the foreign sphere of the free lunch that a fiscally irresponsible government was serving at home. As soon as a real, costly engagement, such as the one in Bosnia, threatened, this illusion, too, stood revealed. By the time Bill Clinton arrived in office, the public had lost its illusions but not yet recovered its belief that government could deal with the mountain of difficulties it now saw on all sides. Clinton, largely turning his back on foreign affairs, had campaigned on a platform that combined cries of alarm about the economy with a Reaganesque fiscal proposal—the improbable, irresponsible promise of a tax cut for the middle class. Nevertheless, when he arrived in office, he sharply changed course, scrapped the tax cut, and called instead for a large tax increase, together with spending cuts. It was the greatest victory for realism in almost a generation.

This realism has not endured. Clinton's half-hearted initiatives regarding Bosnia have stalled or been dropped. In the Senate and the House alike, rebellions are afoot against the taxes that are at the heart of Clinton's proposals. Senate Minority Leader Bob Dole, for instance, says he opposes any new taxes whatsoever. How he will address the budget deficit without them he does not say. Clinton's popularity has sunk in the polls. A host of voices, none of whom has any coherent or politically acceptable plan of his own to offer, is raised in complaint against one aspect or another of the president's plan.

Are we, then, in for a return of Reaganism—of rosy illusion? We might well hope so. The illusions he offered had at least the virtue of commanding wide belief. The same cannot be said of any of Clinton's detractors' plans. They not only fail to address reality; they fail even as illusions. In the Reagan years, people thought all was well, while in fact the country deteriorated. Now, people know things are deteriorating but lack faith that anything can be done about it. If Clinton fails, the outlook is for neither reality nor illusion, but only incurable fragmentation, bitter and futile. Illusion, we may be about to learn, is preferable to realism without the capacity to act.

MAY 30, 1993

WE HAVE JUST WITNESSED WHAT APPEARS TO HAVE been a quiet but deep shift in the foreign policy of the United States and in the country's role in the world. The most tangible sign of this shift was, of course, the Clinton administration's abandonment of its plan for intervention in Bosnia and its acceptance of the European and Russian plan in its place. The Clinton plan called for bombing Serbian targets and lifting the embargo of arms to Bosnian government forces, and the Russian-European plan called instead for creation of safe havens for refugees in Bosnia. It was a shift that signaled the world's acceptance—for the time being, at least—of the results of the ethnic murders and expulsions in former Yugoslavia. Whether that acceptance is final now appears to be largely up to the Europeans and Russians. The United States, it is clear, will be playing a subsidiary role.

The war in former Yugoslavia has carried—probably inescapably—a burden of significance far larger than itself. It was doomed from the outset to be a symbolic, a "defining" war. Geography alone—its location in the "heart of Europe," in the very territory where the First World War was set in motion—guaranteed that. Its timing—the first years of the post-Cold-War period—was even more important. It was inevitable that, at the outset of a new era whose nature was unknown, the war would be looked to as an early indication of what might be in store for everybody. Certainly, the great powers (if any such remain in the world) saw it that way, and said so. The first possible clue of things to come was the brazen, extreme brutality of the war itself, including such apparent innovations as mass, organized rape as an instrument of policy. The second clue was the response of the other powers of the world. Would they do anything? Which ones? How much? If the international community intervened, what principles would thereby be established? If it kept out, what precedents for future crimes would be set? The war could not have shed more light on these questions if it had been expressly devised by some demon for the purpose.

Naturally, the response of the United States—called by some "the world's only superpower"—was of particular interest. Bill Clinton, both as candidate and as president, made many statements suggesting that the outcome of the war was of the highest importance and that he would take a strong stand against Serbian aggression. For instance, soon after arriving in the White House, he fell in with the tendency to generalize and suggested that if nothing was done, "the terrible principle of ethnic cleansing will be validated—that one ethnic group can butcher another if they're strong enough." And Secretary of State Warren Christopher said, "Our conscience revolts at the idea of such brutality . . . Our answer to ethnic cleansing," he said, "must be a resounding 'No!' " None of these words was taken back last week. Only American actions contradicted them. In an event unusual for Washington, however, an anonymous "high State Department official" saw fit to discuss with reporters at a lunch the reasons underlying the manifest American disengagement from Bosnia. "Friends" of the United States, he said, could not understand "how much has changed in the U.S. after the Cold War." And he went on, "We simply don't have the leverage, we don't have the influence, the inclination to use military force. We don't have the money to bring positive results any time soon." Our economic interests were "paramount," he said. Reading his words, one had the impression of hearing what people in the Clinton administration think as opposed to what they say. His sentiments accorded with other long-expressed views of the administration . . . The official's sentiments accorded, too, with poll results which, on a regular basis, have shown strong resistance to American involvement in Bosnia. At a time when observers were saying in a chorus that Clinton's political strength was on the wane, the poll results were, perhaps, of particular importance. If Clinton was ducking international responsibilities, he was doing it in the company of the voters.

Almost instantly, the remarks of the candid official, since identified as Peter Tarnoff, the undersecretary for political affairs, were repudiated. Christopher said, "There is no derogation of our powers and our responsibility to lead." And a senior White House official said of the remarks, "That is not our foreign policy." But it was.

JUNE 3, 1993

BEHOLD DAVID GERGEN! HE IS ALL THINGS TO ALL men. If our age, like the ancient Greeks, believed in gods, he would have to be one. He is a Republican. He has worked for three of the last four Republican presidents: Nixon, Ford, and Reagan. Yet he is a Democrat. Now he will work for President Bill Clinton. Yet, at the same time, he is an independent. ("I've always been a registered independent," he says.) He is a newsman (he covers the news and comments upon it). Yet he *is* the news (he is that which is covered). At one moment, he points the camera at those in power—he's outside looking in—but the next moment, the camera is pointed at him—he's inside looking out. Even in his outside capacity, he has two roles. He's a print man—an editor for *U.S. News and World Report*—yet he appears on the "MacNeil/Lehrer NewsHour" as a commentator, together with Mark Shields. In some vague way, Gergen is the "Republican," Shields the "Democrat." (The remarks one heard most often from these genial controversialists were "Mark is completely right . . ." and "David is completely right. . . .")

As adviser to Clinton, Gergen will have multiple roles, too. As he told *The New York Times*, the people in the Clinton administration "said they were looking for someone who will be at the intersection of policy and politics and communication." Has Gergen, in the government or outside it, ever been anywhere else? Will he, then, be confined to some particular area of policy, such as domestic affairs? No need to worry. In the Reagan administration, he had no role in foreign affairs, but in the Clinton administration, "They have assured me that I will be in the loop across the board on policy." No wonder, then, that, at the ceremony announcing the appointment, the president seemed to take a back seat. In the Reuters photograph of the occasion, Clinton, facing the camera, smiles at Gergen and shakes his hand, while Gergen, unsmiling, and not looking at Clinton, seems to ponder the responsibilities of office. (The famously wooden presence of Vice President Al Gore adds further solemnity to the occasion.) In another photo, Gergen grasps the podium while Clinton, his face wrinkled with an appreciative smile, applauds, courtier-like, in the background.

If Gergen seems all things to all men, perhaps that is because he, above all others, is versed in the art of making politicians appeal to the greatest number of people. In the Nixon administration, it was he who presided over the scripted Republican convention of 1972, in which even the applause and "spontaneous" demonstrations were timed to the second. In the Reagan administration, he was the author of a famous memo outlining that administrator's first hundred days.

What, then, does Gergen stand for, and what does he bring to the Clinton administration? "I have been very concerned," Clinton (favorable poll rating, thirty-six percent) said at the announcement ceremony, "that the cumulative effect of some of the things which are now very much in the news has given to the administration a tinge which is too partisan, and not connected to the mainstream, pro-change, future-oriented politics." On all sides, it is agreed that Gergen's job will indeed be to bring the Clinton administration back into "the mainstream."

But the mainstream is not, in fact, a "position." It is a piece of demographics—or, what is more to the point, a hunk of votes. It is good poll numbers, victory in elections. Like Gergen himself, the "mainstream" cannot be pinned down over the long run to any particular view. Gergen represents the principle of entropy in politics—the overwhelming tendency of American politicians—including, it's now clear, Clinton—to tell the public whatever it wants, at a given moment, to hear.

JUNE 6, 1993

IF THERE IS ANYTHING THAT PROFESSIONAL POLITICAL observers agree on these days, it's that the presidency of Bill Clinton is in sharp decline. *Time* refers on its cover to the "Incredible Shrinking Presidency." Jeff Greenfield, of ABC News, wonders aloud whether Clinton's ills are not "almost terminal." Albert Hunt, of the *Wall Street Journal*, opines that if Clinton doesn't improve his performance, "he's going to be a figure of such ridicule that it'll be too late . . ." Thomas L. Friedman, of *The New York Times*, finds that Clinton has lost his footing on the "Washington high wire."

The judgment that Clinton is in decline is so widespread (dissent is mostly limited to reminders that he is a resilient politician, and may recover) that it may seem perverse to ask what we really mean these days when we say that a president is in decline. How can we tell? What are the signs? If one were to decide solely on the basis of concrete accomplishments, the record, I suspect, would appear merely mixed: He failed to win passage of his economic stimulus program but now has won passage in the House of his more important tax package; one initiative in foreign affairs—his support in Vancouver for Russian President Boris Yeltsin—

succeeded, when Yeltsin won the support of his own people in a referendum, while another—his attempt to win European approval for his plan for Bosnia—failed.

Yet other elements enter into the judgment. One is the press itself. The most conspicuous sign of the decline, of course, is the sort of pronouncement by news commentators quoted above: Clinton is in decline because the press says so. Friedman writes that "what many Clinton supporters . . . say is troubling them is that they see a president who is coming perilously close this early in his term to being typecast in a way that will only reinforce his troubles." In other words, they are afraid that Friedman and others will write articles like the one in which this sentence appears. For who is it but the news media that can "typecast" a politician? To a certain extent, therefore, press opinion on a president's performance is self-fulfilling. One day, the *Gotham Bugle* in its wisdom declares that the president is in decline. This makes it a political fact, for what the *Bugle* says influences the thinking of many, and what many think is, of course, a datum of prime importance, which the *Bugle* can then report, and so forth.

It would be a foolish exaggeration, however (and a megalomanic one on the part of a columnist), to suppose it is the news media that decide whether the president is in decline. It is certainly true that the media can lead the public to think about one thing rather than another (Clinton's $200 haircut rather than his budget plan, his tax increases rather than his spending cuts), but its capacity to tell the people what to think about those things is sharply limited. In the last analysis, news commentators do not establish whether the president is in decline; public opinion polls do. If every news organization in the country said that the president was succeeding brilliantly, but polls showed that sixty-five percent of the public thought he was failing, the latter judgment would be the one with political weight. The polls almost certainly influence coverage more than coverage does the polls. It would be simply impossible to write a story titled "The Incredible Shrinking Presidency" if Clinton's popularity were high. There is no possibility, as things stand today, of a sentence which ran along the lines, "Although the president performed brilliantly this week, his ratings dropped still further in the polls." What is more, the president's standing in the polls is instantly reflected in the fortunes of his legislation, as Clinton, whose levels of approval in the polls are low, is learning. Thus does the mere opinion of the public that the president is in decline become identical with the fact of decline. For in our day, polls, not the media, are true political bedrock. Unlike news commentary, the opinions they give voice to are truly self-fulfilling. If the polls say the president is in decline, then he is well and truly in decline.

Perhaps, then, all is well, for public opinion is prevailing, just as it should in a democracy—and not just on the occasional election day, but year in and year out. Perhaps we have quietly moved from a system of quadrennial judgment of presidents to one in which judgment is passed every few weeks. If so, a serious obstacle remains: the formal, constitutional system which provides that a president, having been elected, shall remain in office for four years. We may have found the way to render judgment on our presidents—to declare them beyond "cure," even "terminal." If so, our reward will be that we are governed for the next three-and-a-half years by a dead man.

JUNE 10, 1993

WITH THE APPOINTMENT OF DAVID GERGEN, insiderism in Washington has reached a new extreme. Anyone who doubts this has not been watching "The MacNeil/Lehrer News-Hour," on which Gergen regularly discussed politics with the columnist Mark Shields. The "NewsHour's" first response to the appointment of one of its own to the highest councils of power was to assemble four former staff members of the White House. Their praise for "David" was unanimous. Ken Duberstein, Ronald Reagan's last chief of staff, thought the appointment "a very bold move and a good move." Jimmy Carter's press secretary, Jody Powell, also thought it "a good move." Martin Andersen, Reagan's first domestic policy adviser, couldn't have agreed more. Why? Gergen had "a streak of decency," Andersen said. Not only that, but "David" has "a healthy respect for the truth and realizes . . . you've got to be extremely careful to be accurate, to not misrepresent and never, never lie." (Never, never lie, at any rate, unless, like Richard Nixon or Ronald Reagan, your administration gets caught in such wholesale violations of the law as the Watergate or Iran-contra scandal.) Duberstein added that "David" was going to be a "reality therapist" in the White House. (Yet the last time Gergen was a reality therapist—that is, when he served as communications adviser to the Reagan White House while the budget policies were set that led to the $4-trillion deficit Clinton now has to reduce—the cure was to throw reality out the window.) George Christian, Lyndon Johnson's press secretary (and the only one not to use the chummy, audience-excluding "David"), thought Gergen an "outstanding public servant."

The "NewsHour's" next response was its regular Friday discussion with Gergen and Shields, this time with Gergen in his new role. Gergen, who said he "didn't apply for the job" at the White House, described himself as "moderate, centrist." He needed to assure himself, in a private conversation with the president, of something that the public record apparently had not divulged—that Clinton, too, was "centrist" and not too far "left," as he sometimes had appeared to be. Gergen left the distinct impression that in this highly privileged conversation it was Clinton, not Gergen, who was on trial. A viewer tuning in at this moment might easily have thought that President Gergen had been interviewing a job applicant named Bill Clinton to see whether his views were "moderate" enough for White House employment. And indeed such an interpretation would not have been far from the conventional wisdom, which holds that if Clinton fails to return to the "center," supposedly personified by Gergen, he will wind up a one-term president. In that sense, Clinton's conversation with Gergen was his first job interview for his second term. The rest of the program was spent on the sort of encomiums regarding Gergen that the "NewsHour's" viewers were already familiar with. It's true that one guest—Linda Chavez, the director of Reagan's Civil Rights Commission—did say she wished that Gergen ("a friend of mine") had not taken the job, but that was because she feared that he might be disappointed with Clinton.

Once in the White House, Gergen made a decision that was of a piece with all that had transpired so far. He announced that the door between the White House press room and the communications director's office (which, to the annoyance of the press, had been closed early in the administration) would be opened. In one light, the move might seem a victory for the freedom of the press. However, in light of the circumstances surrounding the appointment of Gergen—the White House adviser turned reporter turned White House adviser again—it looks more like the final disappearance of any barrier between those who cover the news and those who are the news.

JUNE 13, 1993

LATELY, I'VE BEEN A LITTLE PREOCCUPIED WITH David Gergen. . . . Could professional jealousy play a role? Gergen is a columnist who, in a single bound, has leaped from the sidelines, from which he merely commented on the action, to the center of power, where, if his own account is correct, he'll have a hand in virtually everything that goes on. He'll "go to all the major policy meetings . . . and have a voice in them." His position in the White House scheme of things will be at "the intersection of policy and politics and communication." It sounds almost as if Gergen's commentaries are about to be implemented as policy by the Clinton administration—a columnist's dream or nightmare, depending on one's point of view. (To be fair, though, it should be said that Gergen also characterized his likely contribution to the administration as "modest.") But my interest in Gergen cannot be solely a matter of professional rivalry. After all, most commentators believe that Gergen personifies the "center"—the very bull's eye of American political life, at which every candidate for office apparently aims when he draws a bead on today's voters. This is why Clinton chose Gergen as the repairman for a presidency that commentators were starting, in a massed chorus, to describe as botched. But first Gergen had to satisfy himself about Clinton. . . . It turned out, Gergen said, Clinton wanted to be more "the new Democrat that he campaigned as"—in other words, closer to the center.

Since the center apparently has become the holy grail of American politics, I think the concept warrants a little analysis. Gergen said his own view of life was "moderate, centrist." Then he added, "I'm moderately right of center"—a seeming contradiction. But in fact there is no real contradiction, because in the last decade or so the center itself has been on the right. (For example, the word "liberal"—a title with a noble and proud heritage—came to be called the "l-word," as if it were an obscenity.) The center, you might say, has been a little bit off-center. There is nothing to be surprised at in this. Formally, the word "center" refers to a point wholly conditioned by other givens—for instance, the circumference of a circle. In politics, the center is the mere midpoint of whatever spectrum of opinion happens to exist. In Confucian China, mourning your parents for three years was the center. In Hitler's Germany, wiping out "inferior" races was the center. In Ronald Reagan's America, cutting taxes, raising military spending and cutting the budget deficit (preferably by constitutional amendment) was the center. That didn't make any sense, but it was the center, anyway—a center established, in part, by Gergen, who served Reagan at the time as a communications adviser. For there is no rule that says that the beliefs of the center will make sense. There is only a rule that says that whatever wisdom or nonsense thrives at the center will be respected by a majority, for it is this very respect that places those views there.

The center came up in Gergen's recent remarks two more times. Asked by MacNeil what his approach to service in the White House was, Gergen answered that when one is young, "a certain arrogance creeps in" because you "confuse who you are with what you are." With experience, though, "you've got a bit of a center of your own," and you can say to the president, "Let's not do that." Then, shortly after his remarks about his own "centrist" views, the word came up again, this time with a crucial twist in meaning. He noted that Clinton had claimed that his withdrawal of the nomination of Lani Guinier as assistant attorney general for civil rights had not been about "the political center" but about "his center," which "had more to do with his political philosophy." Gergen said that the broader change in direction of the administration was of the same kind. We were left to ponder the happy coincidence of three centers—the center of the American electorate, Clinton's philosophical center, and Gergen's own center. It is Gergen's ability to devise such explanations, one feels, not the contents of his center, that has brought him to the White House.

JULY 18, 1993

AT 4:30 IN THE AFTERNOON ON TUESDAY, MAY 18, President Bill Clinton boarded Air Force One, at Los Angeles International Airport, after playing a game of basketball with children in the city. Waiting for him there was Cristophe, a renowned hairdresser of Belgian extraction who catered to Hollywood stars and had on occasion cut Hillary Clinton's hair. At 4:52 P.M., the Secret Service and airport officials closed two of the airport's four runways, as is customary when Air Force One takes off or lands. A few minutes later, they requested a delay of twenty minutes. Meanwhile, Cristophe cut Clinton's hair. Air Force One took off at 5:48. Air traffic came and went on time, with the exception of an unscheduled air taxi, which took off seventeen minutes after leaving the gate—two minutes late by Federal Aviation Agency standards. The bare fact that the president had had a haircut on Air Force One was reported the next day by Reuters. On that day also, Valery Kuklinsky, a reporter in the L.A. bureau of UPI, called Elly Brekke, a spokeswoman for the FAA in L.A., to ask whether the president's haircut had delayed air traffic. Brekke stated that the air control tower had told her that the arrival of two incoming flights—one from Yuma, Arizona, the other from Palmdale, California—had been delayed. On the twentieth, Kuklinsky's findings were released, and Lois Romano, of the *Washington Post*, revealed that the hairdresser had been Cristophe, and that his fees were in the $200 range. The two crucial elements of the story, the airport delays and the high price of the haircut—the two wings, so to speak, on which the story would fly—were now in place.

The day after that, Glenn Kessler of *Newsday* filed a Freedom of Information request for information about delays. Some five weeks later, he got his answer, which revealed that in fact there had been none. In the meantime, however, the story of the haircut, including the misinformation regarding delays, had been winging its way around the world. It created a lasting sensation. The headlines of the news stories, which eventually numbered in the thousands, give the tenor of the coverage: "AIR TRAFFIC WAITS FOR BEVERLY HILLS HAIRCUT" (*Boston Globe*). "PRESIDENTIAL TRIM LEFT TRAVELERS IN THE AIR" (*Dallas Morning News*). "CLINTON: MAN OF THE PEOPLE OR JUST ANOTHER ELITIST?" (Gannett News Service). "HAIRCUT GROUNDED CLINTON WHILE THE PRICE TOOK OFF" (*The New York Times*). As in some updated version of the classic caricature of aristocrats galloping down the street in a luxurious carriage and splashing the common people in the street with mud, Clinton was suddenly revealed lolling in plutocratic luxury on his airplane while ordinary people circled in helpless frustration overhead. The president, the news stories suggested, had lost touch with the lives of ordinary Americans. He had abdicated as "president of the common man," in the phrase of one reporter at a White House briefing.

As it happened, just as the story of the haircut was being made known, "Travelgate"—the tale of the abrupt, unfair, inadequately explained firing of seven employees of the White House travel office—broke, and the two stories were immediately linked, under the general heading of White House incompetence. At the time, the president's approval ratings in the polls were in steep decline. That week they were sinking through the forty percent range, on their way down to the high thirties—a record low for a president at that point in his term. The haircut story, which quickly assumed gargantuan proportions, unquestionably played an important role in this decline. By midweek, Eleanor Clift was observing on "The McLaughlin Show," on CNN, that the administration had permitted the haircut story to "overwhelm the news." And by week's end, Jeff Greenfield was asking on ABC's "World News Tonight," "How does a presidential haircut come to dominate the news?"

Commentary on the performance of the administration—most of it mentioning the haircut—began to border on the lugubrious. On May 28, Albert Hunt, of the *Wall Street Journal*, told viewers of CNN, "This is the most inept White House operation I have ever seen," and he apocalyptically warned the White House to reform before it was "too late." And Margaret Garrard Warner, of *Newsweek*, added on the same program that if Clinton didn't improve his performance, "I think he's finished." The next week the *Washington Post* ran an article whose headline asked simply, "ANOTHER FAILED PRESIDENCY?"

In this period, too, Clinton's budget package—the centerpiece of his presidency—was moving toward a vote in the House of Representatives. However, the *Boston Globe* noted on May 21 that among the White House press corps, at least, "the case of the runway coiffure eclipsed the president's battle with Congress over his economic plan . . ." Stories that "dominate" the news, eclipsing the most important business of state, observers generally agree, have a strong influence on the president's standing in the polls; his standing in the polls, in turn, has a strong influence on the passage of important legislation; and the passage or rejection of legislation, finally, has everything to do with whether the country indeed winds up with Another Failed Presidency. The haircut story was by no means a marginal political phenomenon; it lay at the heart of the process by which presidential power is won or lost today in the United States.

From the foregoing it might appear that owing to a few innocent factual mistakes, an impression of the president formed that happened to do him great political harm. The truth of the matter, however, is much stranger. May 20 was the pivotal day in the story's development. The UPI story assured that the White House press secretary, Dee Dee Myers, would be asked at that day's press briefing whether there had been delays. She categorically denied it. "Absolutely not; absolutely not," she said. What now was on the record were two flatly contradictory accounts: the wire service claim that there had been two delays and the White House claim that there had been none. Which version was correct? The press stories had identified the point of origin of the flights. Had they been delayed or not? The situation seemed to cry out for investigation—calls to airlines, interviews with passengers on the flights in question and so on. At just this critical moment, however, the two institutions that might have resolved the issue—the White House and the news media—backed away from further inquiries.

Later on the 20th, the White House communications director, George Stephanopoulos, held a second briefing. "There were no delays at all," he said. Then, however, he was asked specifically about the wire service report that two flights had been held up. This time he answered, "All I know is that no hold" was placed on any flights—a slightly evasive-sounding wording that might seem to leave room for the discovery later that, somehow or other, a flight or two had been delayed, after all. Nevertheless, the categorical White House denials remained on the record. It was at Stephanopoulos's briefing that the first sign appeared of a shift in emphasis that was to prove decisive for the whole future of the haircut story. At one point, a reporter asked, "What does it do for [Clinton's] image?" The reporter went on, "Forget about whether it cost any extra money. Is that perceptually . . . the kind of image he wants to convey to people?" If we think of the haircut story as a kind of helium-filled balloon straining to lift into the stratosphere but still tethered to the ground by doubts regarding the factual truth of one of its critical elements, then this reporter's question would be the moment when the tethers snap, and the balloon lifts clear of mere factuality. Into what stratosphere was it lifting? Into the stratosphere of image. The question being asked was changing from "Did this actually happen as reported?" to "What effect will the story, true or false, have on the president's image?" The president's image could be battered—as it was—even if the story were untrue.

The same shift from fact to image was broadly apparent in the avalanche of news stories that followed the next day. For example, Richard Benedetto, of *USA Today*, led his story by telling his readers, "While Bill Clinton's image-makers have worked carefully to craft a persona that suggests the president is in touch with real people, every once in a while he does something silly that tarnishes that." And a story for Reuters began, "The White House insisted Thursday that President Clinton did not betray his image as a common man by having his hair cut aboard Air Force One as it sat on the tarmac in Los Angeles, delaying air travel." The president, it seemed, had not betrayed the common man with elitist ways; he had betrayed his "image as a common man." There once was a time when the lead to a newspaper story was supposed to convey something tangible and precise, on the order of "Killer bees have invaded the city." Now the lead is as likely to read, "An invasion by killer bees has tarnished the city's image." Mere images have acquired the solidity of facts.

Of particular interest was the coverage by the *Los Angeles Times*, whose reporters Paul Richter and Greg Krikorian did more than almost anyone else to resolve the factual impasse. Most reporters either took the wire service reports at face value, ignoring the White House denials, or simply recorded the allegations and the denials side by side. Richter and Krikorian took further steps. First, they got in touch with a spokesman for the L.A. airport, Diane Reesman. She, unfortunately, "could shed no light" on the delays, and merely remarked, "I've heard both stories." Second, they contacted Earl Vonbuck, of Skywest, a commuter airline, but instead of confirming or denying a delay, he only commented, "But if somebody told me I was going to be late so the president could get a haircut, I would frown." With Vonbuck's hypothetical frown at a hypothetical presidential obstruction of his travel plans, the factual trail grew cold. Richter and Krikorian noted that it remained "unclear" whether there had been delays.

That conclusion, however, came in the second half of the

story. The lead of the story, like so many other leads, concerned the president's image. "A presidential haircut by a high-placed celebrity stylist," it read, "left the White House Thursday sweeping up questions on whether President Clinton is living up to his carefully groomed image as a regular kind of guy." And before the unclarity of the facts was discussed, the political analyst Kevin Phillips was quoted as saying that Clinton's deed had been "a political mistake and cultural myopia." Commentary on the story's deeper significance had not been slowed by the factual doubts scrupulously recorded later in the text.

The *L.A. Times*'s editorial commentary was of a piece with its reporting. It is hard to imagine that any of the news people writing about the haircut themselves had looked on Clinton as a "regular kind of guy" but then had had to discard that pleasant illusion upon learning that Clinton had had an expensive haircut. Anyone who has observed presidential politics even briefly knows that the president's image is his most valued political possession; that its creation and management are the object of huge expenditure and nonstop counseling by platoons of public relations experts, pollsters and "handlers" of various kinds; that the policies of the government, not excluding its military policies, are shaped by the requirements of the president's image; that if the president, whose life is necessarily utterly unlike that of any other person in the United States, manages to appear as if he lives like "a regular kind of guy," this appearance is itself nothing but the product of hugely elaborate public-relations efforts; and that in the midst of all these expenditures and labors the payment of $200 is a negligible event. (For all we know, Clinton told Cristophe to give him a regular-guy kind of haircut.) The *L.A. Times* editorial reflects this knowledge. "The Clinton haircut story is the stuff of political image-polishers's worst nightmare," the editorial noted, adding, "Here is a populist taking full advantage of the trappings of the imperial presidency." Was the populist president wrong, then, to have an expensive haircut? Should he return to the simple ways of the common man? That was not the *Times*'s conclusion. It only wanted his expensive haircuts kept out of sight. "A good hair day," it concluded, "but it didn't produce a pretty picture. Next time, Mr. President, try getting it cut in a less public place." The newspaper demanded more efficient concealment of the president's imperial ways from the public.

And the White House? Its spokesmen abandoned the investigative field after their original denials were ignored, evidently calculating that further efforts at rebuttal would only give added life to a story that they wished would disappear entirely. The FAA was silent. When *Newsday*'s Kesler asked why, Fred O'Donnel, a spokesman for the FAA, explained, "Once the story has run, it has a life of its own . . . and . . . to get the story corrected is virtually impossible."

Indeed, by week's end, the White House went a step further. Despairing of rebuttal, Clinton tried repentance. He apologized. Asked on "CBS This Morning" about the haircut and "delays," he described his performance as a "boner" and a "mistake." Explaining why the president had changed his mind, Dee Dee Myers said, "We read numerous accounts that flights indeed were delayed." Such was the imperative to serve the needs of the president's image—an entity which, though created to serve him, now forced him, like the victim of a Stalinist trial, to confess to misdeeds he had never committed.

AUGUST 5, 1993

IT'S A DISCOURAGING FACT ABOUT AMERICAN political life that politicians who lead the country to do what it knows in its bones is the right thing often are rewarded by defeat at the polls. The politics of recent decades offers several examples. One is the civil rights legislation of the 1960s—probably the most splendid achievement of the American political system in the domestic sphere since World War II. However, that achievement, together with certain other factors, very likely cost the Democratic Party, which led the way, the presidency for the better part of the next twenty-five years. The impulse for civil rights legislation came from outside the government—from the civil rights movement, led by Martin Luther King Jr. Fundamental political change in this country almost always originates among the public at large, rarely in the halls of power. Yet if the call to change born outside the government is not heard within it, it may be stillborn. It was the presence of President Lyndon Johnson in the White House, responding to King's call, that brought the energy of the civil rights movement to fruition in the form of the Voting Rights Act of 1965 and other legislation.

Although the change was accepted by the country as just, no serious attempt was made to reverse it and the Democrats paid a heavy price, for the Republicans, capitalizing on white resentment, helped bring most southern states into the Republican column in subsequent presidential elections.

A second example is the movement to end the war in Vietnam. Like the civil rights movement, it eventually won public acceptance. Just how profound that acceptance ultimately became is revealed by the extreme reluctance of the American military today to intervene in Bosnia. The soldiers, who once resisted the antiwar movement's arguments against military intervention, now turn out to have absorbed them so deeply that they will not contemplate intervening in any conflict in which a clear, quick, and comparatively painless victory is not in view. Once again, the country's change of heart began outside the government. Once again, the popular movement struck an answering chord among people in power—in particular, among three Democratic presidential candidates, Eugene McCarthy, Robert Kennedy, and George McGovern. Once again, the change occurred within the Democratic Party, which first led the country into the war, and then, in protracted tumult, turned against the war. And once again, while the change in opinion eventually forced an end to the war, the party that had brought the change about paid a political price. The charge of "McGovernism," standing for military weakness, became a potent weapon in the hands of Republican candidates, who won four of the five presidential elections between 1972 and 1988.

Now another fundamental national issue, that of the budget deficit, threatens to fall into the same pattern. Once again, the Democratic Party is leading the way, and the Republicans are resisting. (This is somewhat surprising since, historically, balanced budgets have been a Republican cause.) Once again—as with the decisions to end both segregation and the Vietnam war—the country is being asked to do something it reluctantly recognizes to be right. And, once again, there is a clear danger that the Democrats, if they win the vote to reduce the deficit by raising taxes and cutting spending, will succeed in doing the right thing and yet will suffer for it at the polls. It's hard to know, looking at this record, whether to be more surprised that the public ever accepts the need for painful but necessary action, or that, afterwards, it rejects those who have carried out its will. There is something in us, it seems, that wants to do what is right, but also something else that wants to take revenge on those who have asked us to do it.

AUGUST 15, 1993

ON THE DAY OF THE SENATE VOTE ON THE Democratic budget bill, Rep. Tim Penny (D-Minn.), a conservative Democrat, who had voted for the bill in the House of Representatives, announced in a one-minute speech that, when he had finished his term—his sixth—he would not seek re-election. The first reason he mentioned for his decision was that Congress had just "failed" to "dramatically reduce the deficit in a bipartisan fashion." "I have always said that nothing would make me more proud," he explained, "than to cast a vote for a tough budget-balancing package—one full of deep and controversial program and entitlement cuts as well as tax increases—and then retire knowing I had done the right thing for the country. The deficit-reduction program just adopted by the House—though certainly controversial—is far short of the plan I envisioned." The failure to go far enough in cutting the deficit wasn't Penny's only reason for retiring from Congress—he also wanted to spend more time with his family, he said—but his explanation placed him in the company of a growing band of American politicians who might be called the deficit dropouts. They are a breed that leaves politics with a parting blast at its failure to deal with the deficit. One, for example, was Sen. Warren Rudman (R-N.H.), who decided last September not to seek re-election, in large measure because of his "frustration" at the Senate's refusal to deal forthrightly with the deficit crisis. "In history," he warned at a news conference at the time, "when there is enormous debt and hyperinflation, then the political system looks for easy answers and produces demagogues on the far right . . . It looks for scapegoats and people to blame." The Senate, he said, had proved "unwilling to make the hard choices or to explain to the American people that there is no such thing as a free lunch."

A more prominent deficit dropout was Ross Perot, who made deficit reduction the centerpiece of his presidential campaign, but then abruptly quit the field—only to return to it in the campaign's final weeks. . . . In recent television appearances, he has persistently declined to reveal the details of a deficit-reduction program that he supports, becoming a kind of parody version of the politicians whose evasions he mocked at the start of his presidential campaign.

The lesson of the deficit dropouts seems to be that those who are in power are prevented from dealing honestly with the budget issue, while those who are out of power can at least speak freely about it. . . . This is the lesson now being driven home by the sour public reaction to Congress's passage of the Democratic budget plan. Most observers agree that a vote for the plan was "courageous"—a "heavy lift," in the words of Rep. David Bonior (D-Mich.). . . . For modest as the tax increases are, they apparently still are too much for most people. (A recent ABC News/*Washington Post* poll, for example, found that fifty-four percent of the public opposed the 4.3-cent gas tax while forty-six percent approved.) Since many of these same observers agree that the package's fault is that it doesn't do enough to reduce the deficit, it's hard to escape the conclusion that the representatives, far from lagging behind the voters, as the conventional wisdom would have it, are actually "ahead" of them—maybe only a millimeter ahead, but indubitably ahead.

Is it possible? Can it be that a noble, self-sacrificing political establishment is risking its political neck for the sake of a greedy, self-deluding public? Are the people unworthy of the despised "politicians?" Public opinion polls cannot give us the answer. The final verdict—not on the politicians but on the people who put them in office—will come in the next elections, when the public must decide whether to reward or to punish the representatives who permitted themselves this modest act of courage.

OCTOBER 3, 1993

SOME OF THE BEST POLITICAL NEWS OF THE ELECTION season comes from the states of New Jersey and Connecticut, where, against all prediction, two deserving governors, New Jersey's Jim Florio, a Democrat, and Lowell Weicker, formerly a Republican and now an independent, have risen high in public esteem in their respective states. The two men have some things in common. Both won passage of bans on assault weapons. Both promised not to raise taxes but then, once in office, championed and won passage for tax increases at a time when this was at one and the same time absolutely necessary for the fiscal integrity of their states and deeply unpopular. And both were thought by one and all to have thereby forfeited their chances for re-election.

For at the time—the waning years of Republican control of the presidency—tax-cutting was the tried and true path to public esteem.

Weicker, unpredictable as ever, announced on Thursday that he would not seek a second term anyway. That leaves Florio, who is running hard against the Republican Christine Todd Whitman. He has risen to a commanding lead in some polls, including one taken this week by CBS and *The New York Times*, which places him ahead, fifty-one percent to thirty percent. When, six months after his election, Florio reversed his campaign promise and championed a $2.8 billion increase in state taxes, public anger—stoked by radio call-in show hosts, as public anger usually is these days—was so great that it spilled over into the Senate race of 1992, in which Whitman almost defeated Bill Bradley, who, as a federal official, of course had no hand in the tax rise. On the same election day, control of both houses of the New Jersey Legislature passed into Republican control.

Now Whitman directly faces Florio—the man she has really been running against all along. Last week, she unveiled her economic plan for New Jersey. It proved to be a terse condensation—a sort of executive summary—of all the tax-cutting proposals that the Republican Party used to such telling effect in the 1980s and early '90s. Four pages in length, it promised to cut the New Jersey income tax by thirty percent but did not specify where the offsetting spending cuts would come from. (The document offered only "examples" of cuts, and these did not add up to the needed sum.) For all its brevity, the plan was stuffed with misleading statements. For example, the plan stated that after Florio's tax increase, "overnight we went from a low-tax state to the second-highest-taxed state in America." In actuality, as the *Philadelphia Inquirer* quickly discovered, that was true, according to certain measurements, only of New Jersey's federal taxes, over which the governor has no control. In a ranking of states according to local- and state-tax burdens, New Jersey stands at number twenty-five. In the not-so-distant past, such proposals worked magic with voters. Now, however, several things have changed. For one thing, the Republicans who won control of the New Jersey legislature had to translate their anti-tax philosophy into action. They failed even to seriously propose cancelling the Florio increases, which had been used to fund education and reduce property taxes. The Republicans's only tax-cutting success was to repeal a one percent rise in the New Jersey sales tax (a step accomplished, however, only by cutting back on certain rebates of property taxes). Their failure to translate their promises into action cast more than a little doubt on Whitman's ability to carry out her plan.

More recently, of course, President Bill Clinton, in the name of deficit reduction, succeeded in winning adoption of some $500 billion worth of tax increases and spending cuts. In doing so, he became one more politician who had promised the voters tax relief in the campaign but gave them tax increases once in office. The question that hung fire, however, was what the political consequences would be for the politicians, including Clinton, who supported this program. The defeat in the Texas Senate race of Democrat Bob Krueger (who opposed the Clinton plan) by Kay Bailey Hutchison, who took a vociferous anti-tax stand, suggested that there was a high price to pay. Now, Florio's apparent reversal of fortune casts this conclusion in doubt. Of particular interest is the finding of the CBS-*Times* poll that forty-nine percent of the voters now think Florio did "the right thing" in raising taxes. If so, it may prove that it is possible for a politician who falsely promised the public a free lunch, and then changed his mind later and presented the bill, to win re-election. Whether it's possible for a politician honestly to present the bill before the election and get himself elected anyway is as yet unknown. This is a pinnacle of boldness and courage that has yet to be scaled.

OCTOBER 28, 1993

JONATHAN EYAL OF THE BRITISH NEWSPAPER, *THE Independent*, spoke for a good portion of international opinion recently when he wrote of the United States that "the country that claims special privileges as the world's only remaining superpower has neither the stomach nor the vision to lead efforts for international stability." How has this happened? How has the country that was about to establish George Bush's "new world order" been reduced to an international nonentity that, in every crisis from Bosnia to Haiti, seems only to search for the quickest way out—the best "exit strategy," in the currently fashionable phrase?

Offhand, one might guess that the reason is that the fighter pilot of World War II, George Bush, has been replaced by the Vietnam war evader, Bill Clinton. However, a glance at Congress reveals that isolationism is, if anything, stronger on the Republican right (its traditional stronghold) than on the Democratic left. Moreover, Bush's last remark on the subject was a word of encouragement for Senate Republicans seeking to place congressional restraints on Clinton's freedom of action in Haiti—a radical reversal for a man who until then had stood for presidential supremacy in foreign affairs. As Bush's remarks suggest, the explanation for the shift in policy lies elsewhere than in the change of administration.

The beginnings of understanding, it seems to me, are to be found in the Persian Gulf war, when American belligerence seemed at a peak. In a *tour de force* of executive manipulation, Bush maneuvered the nation and the world into the war. He presented Congress with a virtual *fait accompli*, while denying its constitutional right to decide whether to take the country to war. (Eventually, he relented to the extent of inviting their approval of his action.) The imperial presidency seemed to reach its zenith. What was more, the public, succumbing to a kind of orchestrated delirium, responded with joy to the victory. Its attitude to war itself seemed transformed. . . . In one poll, Bush's popularity rocketed to an unreal ninety percent. His re-election, most observers agreed, was now a formality. Yet, in the two years that followed, this picture of the United States and its future was swiftly shattered. In retrospect, we can see that the cracks were appearing even in the flush of victory. The first sign was Bush's reluctance to proceed to Baghdad to remove the Iraqi leader, Saddam Hussein, from power. His reasons were most Vietnam-like: He did not want to spoil the painless victory with protracted embroilment in Iraq's domestic affairs. The Gulf victory did not so much cure the "Vietnam syndrome" as overlay it.

The recrudescence of the syndrome was even more marked in Bush's policy toward Bosnia. The United States would not send troops to Bosnia, he said, because we wouldn't know how "to get them out." Acting Secretary of State Lawrence Eagleburger pronounced himself "horrified" by "those armchair strategists" who "aren't the ones who have to worry about the Americans getting killed if we get into a situation . . . from which we cannot extricate ourselves." Thus it was not Clinton, but Bush, who first trained American eyes on the exits from crises. But most important, perhaps, were the astonishingly few casualties America suffered in the war. Looking back, we can see that the celebrations of the war combined elation at our victory with relief that our soldiers had come through almost unscathed. As soon as, in crises that followed, casualties occurred or even threatened—in Bosnia, in Somalia, Haiti—the American resolve that seemed to have been born in the Gulf war was revealed for what it was: an illusion based on the profoundly misleading expectation that great things can be done in the world without paying a great price.

NOVEMBER 4, 1993

ALL OF THE EXIT POLLS ON THE NEW JERSEY SIDE OF the Hudson (now a kind of Republican river on both its banks) agree: Gov. Jim Florio was defeated by the Republican Christine Todd Whitman because of the $2.8-billion tax increase he imposed in 1990 after promising not to raise taxes in the campaign of 1989. Notwithstanding the efforts of the White House to interpret this outcome, along with Tuesday's other major Republican victories around the country, as a "local" matter, its significance is obviously national.

Just a few weeks ago, when Florio was ahead in the polls, Democrats saw the meaning of the race in a clearer light. Back then, they rightly placed Florio's campaign in the context of an unfolding tale that not only was national but also extended back to the beginning of the Reagan years. James Carville, the principal strategist for Florio's campaign, was telling reporters Florio's resurgence marked the end of the public appeal of the tax-cutting proposals that had been winning elections for Republicans since 1980. "The electorate just doesn't believe that you get something for nothing," he said. The "something" Florio's opponent was offering "for nothing" was an assortment of tax cuts, including a thirty percent decrease in the income tax, to be phased in over three years. In tried and true Republican fashion, Whitman did not enumerate the cuts in services that would accompany these cuts in revenue. Only "examples" were given. She would cut the waste that "I know and you know is there." "Everything is on the table," Whitman said grandly—a way, of course, of saying that nothing was yet on the table.

The continuity of the Whitman plan with Ronald Reagan's tax-cutting policies was clear from its parentage: Its chief architect was Lawrence Kudlow, an enthusiast of supply-side economics who served as deputy budget director under David Stockman in the Reagan administration. (The Whitman campaign was run by Ed Rollins, a former Reagan tactician.) Carville himself, of course, had been the strategist for the Clinton campaign and had continued to give Clinton advice when, in a move strongly reminiscent of Florio's, the new president raised federal taxes and reduced spending in an attempt to bring under control the budget deficit created by the Reagan tax cuts. In these circumstances, it is impossible not to interpret the New Jersey results as a forerunner of national political events. "This is not a message to run and hide from the tough issues—that is not what it is," Clinton said yesterday, pulling a Florio-like mantle over his shoulders. If it wasn't that, however, it was certainly a message that if you face the tough issues, you'd better steel yourself for defeat in the next election. . . . Clinton's success in winning congressional approval, in two cliff-hanging votes, for a modest budget-reduction package, created the appearance that the issue was being dealt with. The truth is, however, that virtually every politician—from Jimmy Carter, in his race against Ronald Reagan onward—who has dared either to promise or practice fiscal sanity has been punished for it in the voting booth. (Clinton's election, it's important to remember, is no exception. In his campaign, he promised that famous tax cut for the "forgotten" middle class. Like Florio, he practiced fiscal sense only after preaching fiscal nonsense.)

In short, the issue of the federal deficit, from which the country has been taking a little-deserved vacation recently, is entirely unresolved. The Florio defeat is the rumble of a sleeping volcano.

NOVEMBER 11, 1993

THERE IS A GREAT TEMPTATION TO LOOK DOWN ON the debate the other night between Ross Perot and Vice President Al Gore as a degradation, if any were needed, of political decision-making in the United States. And certainly this temptation should be indulged to the hilt. From the moment the antagonists appeared, each tensely displaying the clasped hands on the table that apparently now is the required demeanor for political debaters on television, they seemed bent chiefly on knocking each other into the mud. Perot's specialty was posing as the victim of Gore's interruptions. This reached an absurd extreme in one exchange in which Perot, having silenced Gore and won his full attention, kept reproaching him for not listening:

Perot: Give me your whole mind.
Gore: Yeah, I'm listening. I haven't heard the answer yet, but go ahead.
Perot: That's because you haven't quit talking.
Gore: Well, I'm listening (Stagily listens—the earnest student.) . . .
Perot: Are you going to listen? (Weakly) Work on it.

Gore, for his part, brought along a large bucket of tar, and applied it liberally to Perot. First, he accused Perot of having a business interest in the defeat of NAFTA—but then said that Perot had cleverly arranged to profit whichever way the vote on NAFTA went (a qualification that would seem completely to undercut the original charge of a conflict of interest). Then he accused Perot of hypocritically denouncing lobbyists when he in fact had lobbied Congress in support of his business. The essential childishness of the confrontation was probably best revealed, however, when Gore presented Perot with an insulting gift—a picture of Sens. Reed Smoot and John Hawley, authors of the protectionist Smoot-Hawley act in the 1930s. The idea was to paint Perot a protectionist. Perot, not quite ready to take the jarring step of simply refusing to accept the unwanted photo, accepted it but then, to show his displeasure, quickly placed Smoot and Hawley face down in front of him—an indignity these gentlemen scarcely deserved, however mistaken their bill may have been.

While acknowledging the emptiness of the debate, however, it is also important to recognize that it marks one more step in a broad transformation of our political system. Today, legislative battles are being decided not by deliberation in Congress but by direct appeal to what is assumed to be public opinion. Once, it was considered disreputable for politicians to abandon their convictions to win popularity with their constituents. The thing was done often enough, but rarely admitted. Now, discovering and obeying the constituents' wishes in each matter that comes before Congress has come to be seen as something like the very business of a congressman. "I'm in favor of NAFTA," Rep. David Levy (R-Baldwin) told reporter Jill Dutt, "but if there's no support in my district, I'm not going to vote for it. I didn't come here to shove stuff down people's throats."

Gore's decision to "debate" Perot (or at any rate to try to besmirch his reputation) was of course aimed at increasing the support for NAFTA that Levy and other congressmen find in their districts. If Congress will not shove stuff down people's throats, the proponents of legislation have realized, then perhaps the people can be got to shove stuff down Congress's throat. The tendency is for legislative fights to be conducted as if they were elections. Political advertising geared directly to congressional votes is already commonplace. The innovation this week was a debate obviously modeled on election debates. Naturally, as in a campaign, polls were taken immediately afterward. (They showed that Gore's performance had given NAFTA a boost.) All that's missing now is an actual popular vote.

NOVEMBER 18, 1993

THE NAFTA DEBATE, WHICH CAME TO ITS CLIMAX with the vote in the House of Representatives, made scrambled eggs of American party politics. It thoroughly divided both the

Democrats and the Republicans. Nor did the distinction between "conservative" and "liberal," which to some extent cuts across party lines, offer any key to the debate. Party leaders are looking forward to a restoration of party harmony now that the issue apparently has been settled, but those hopes may be disappointed. For the debate has confirmed the existence of a dangerous fault-line in the political landscape.

On one side is the vast preponderance of expert opinion. On the other side is inexpert opinion. A college education, the polls show, is one of the best predictors of support (among the general public) for the treaty. The fact, much-touted by the White House, that every American economist who has won a Nobel Prize supports the agreement, while more than half the American public opposes it, deserves reflection. It looks as if, in the "information age" that is now upon us, a gap of an unexpected kind has opened between the information-rich and the information-poor.

The NAFTA debate is in fact the second occasion on which this gap has opened wide. It appeared earlier in the hugely protracted debate over the federal deficit, in which most expert observers understood that increased taxes and reduced spending were necessary but the general public fiercely resisted both. The result was rampant hypocrisy among politicians, many of whom knew as well as most economists that common sense called for sacrifice, but who knew even better that asking for it spelled political suicide.

This is not to say, of course, that expert opinion has necessarily been correct on either issue. Expert opinion has been monumentally wrong often enough. (The first years of the Vietnam war are an obvious example—although I should add that, regarding the deficit and NAFTA, I happen to agree with the experts.) What is more disturbing, the opinions of the experts on NAFTA, however justified, happen to coincide, broadly speaking, with their own interests.

In 1990, Robert Reich, now secretary of labor, observed in his far-seeing book, *The Wealth of Nations*, that the globalization of the economy, which NAFTA powerfully symbolizes, tended to favor the management class (which he opaquely called "symbolic analysts") over the working class.

The key fact of the global economy, he noted, was the mobility of capital, products and, above all, knowledge ("information"), which permitted factories, together with the jobs they offer, to be moved from one part of the world to another. The one thing that could not move was labor. When a multinational corporation moves an auto-parts factory from a town in the United States to Mexico, the town cannot follow. The line that divides the information-rich from the information-poor also tends to divide the rich from the poor, pure and simple. It's not surprising, then, that when a worker whose livelihood is threatened by the liberation of global capital hears the "symbolic analyst" who runs his company advocating NAFTA, he is likely to conclude he is listening not to an economic sage but to a self-interested plutocrat of the new information age. If enough people join him in that conclusion, programs that make economic sense can lead to political disaster.

NOVEMBER 21, 1993

SHORTLY AFTER THE HOUSE VOTE IN FAVOR OF THE North American Free Trade Agreement—and just in time for the 11 P.M. news programs—President Bill Clinton appeared before reporters at the White House and made some surprising claims about the significance of the treaty. He claimed that it was a turning point in the history of the United States. Borrowing the phrase President George Bush used to describe the Persian Gulf war, he called the vote for the treaty a "defining moment" for the country. "After World War I," he said, "the United States turned inward and built walls of protection around our economy. The result was a depression and ultimately another world war. After the Second World War, we made a very different choice; we turned outward. We built a system of expanded trade and collective security." Now the country faced the same choice again, and he was "proud to say we have not flinched."

Did the United States, adrift since the end of the Cold War, reach a turning point with the NAFTA vote? Have we headed off a new depression, turned back another world war? Even when the usual temptations to boast in the hour of victory are taken into account, these remain big claims. The phrase "defining moment," of course, is bound to provoke a certain skepticism, inasmuch as the original defining moment never did manage to define much of anything. Very possibly, this expression is destined to be thrown for a second time on history's piled-high ashheap of grandiose and empty phraseology. Still, the claim deserves to be considered seriously, if only because it is the Clinton administration's first substantial effort to define the United States's role in the post-Cold War world. The claim seems especially significant in view of the fact that the NAFTA debate rearranged the domestic political landscape, splitting the Democratic and the Republican parties. If the moment does prove "defining," then we may have had a glimpse of the country's domestic future as well as its future abroad.

The most striking feature of Clinton's claim, perhaps, is that it bases foreign policy on economic programs. The shock troops of a Clintonian new world order, it appears, will not be Green Berets and Rangers but computers, fiber-optic highways, and so forth. In place of the League of Nations offered by President Woodrow Wilson after World War I, Clinton offers NAFTA—a free-trade association. In place of the United Nations and NATO, designed by President Harry Truman after World War II, Clinton offers the General Agreement on Tariffs and Trade—more free trade. The "fear" Clinton wants the United States to shake off is fear of foreign goods, and the courage he wants us to muster is the readiness to compete in the global marketplace. The basis of this position, of course, is the persuasive notion that a regeneration of the United States has to begin at home. Missing still, however, are the links between economics and the other dimensions of life, including the social, the political, and the ecological. Free trade today is something different from what it was even twenty-five years ago. In the truly global economy of our day, "free" increasingly means free not just from tariffs and other barriers to trade but from any legislation whatsoever. For economic life, born within nations, has now transcended them. While the economy is global, law—environmental law, human rights law, social law—remains largely national. "Merchants," Thomas Jefferson observed, "have no country. The mere spot they stand on does not constitute so strong an attachment as that from which they draw their gain." But it was not until 1989 that a Gilbert Williamson, then president of NCR Corporation, could say, "I was asked the other day about United States competitiveness and I replied that I don't think about it at all. We at NCR think of ourselves as a globally competitive company that happens to be headquartered in the United States."

In other words, in the global economy in which the United States and every other country is enmeshed, the framework of commerce threatens to break free from the entire framework of law. Businessmen who don't care for the legislation of one country can move their operations to another, where the "business climate" is better. This is the dilemma that the opponents of NAFTA—worried about the erosion of wages, environmental standards, and human rights supported by American law—were seeking to face. They lost this battle, and probably it is well they did, for a defeat of this particular treaty would have done little to serve their cause. But the broader dangers they drew attention to are real and immense, and remain unaddressed. Until they are, the Clinton administration cannot truly call its economic program a foreign policy.

DECEMBER 2, 1993

ON JULY 30, 1992, THE COMMERCE DEPARTMENT reported that the Gross Domestic Product had increased by 1.4 percent in the second quarter of the year—a sadly disappointing figure at a time when the country had already been waiting for some time for signs of a recovery from recession. For President George Bush, the news was politically ruinous. It arrived at the pivotal moment of the presidential campaign. Bush's victory in the Persian Gulf war was forgotten, and an economic malaise was widely reported to be gripping the country. Bush, people were saying, was preoccupied with foreign policy and out of touch with the problems of ordinary people at home. The GDP figure drove the final nail into Bush's political coffin. . . . It seemed to confirm all that Clinton had been saying about the state of the economy. . . . What was equally important, it prevented Bush from mounting a serious defense of his economic record. Once the dismal statistic was made known, any attempt to paint a rosier picture of the economy was bound to be taken as further evidence that he was out of touch with reality.

His response was twofold. First, he tried to renew his defense of his record in foreign policy. (He accused Clinton of having spoken about foreign policy for only "one minute—141 words" at the Democratic convention.) Second, he permitted the Republican far right to declare a "cultural war" (in the words of Patrick Buchanan) against feminists, gay people, and others that gave the Republican convention its extreme tone. This offensive was abandoned when it met with public disapproval. Clinton, meanwhile, was confirmed in his decision to dwell on the economy almost to the exclusion of all else, including foreign policy. In other words, a popularity contest pitting foreign affairs against domestic affairs—a contest that domestic affairs won hands down—took political shape and became entrenched in post-Cold-War American life.

Recently, the Commerce Department released revised figures for the same period, and it turns out that actual growth during the second quarter of 1992 was 2.8 percent—precisely double the earlier estimate. (There was nothing scandalous in the revelation. The Commerce Department always advises that its first reports are based on incomplete, early figures, and the "revised" figures often differ from these. If anything, the low initial figure demonstrates the independence of the department from any pressure from the White House, whose interest, of course, is in overestimating growth.)

Now the record has been corrected (for the few newspaper readers who happened to notice this statistic in the back pages of their papers). But what of history itself, including the Republicans' desperate resort to extremism at their convention, the election of Clinton, and the fateful neglect of foreign policy that has proceeded from these political events? None of that can or will be undone. It is probably impossible to undo even mentally all of the myriad conclusions we drew from the incorrect statistic, including the picture of George Bush as out of touch with economic reality. Information, even when false, is mighty only when it's current. The truth that arrives late, like a style out of fashion, or a politician out of office, is neglected, invisible, and powerless to undo the effects of the error—which, by that time, has become the inexpungible stuff of history.

DECEMBER 19, 1993

THERE SEEMS TO BE A NEW PROCEDURE FOR GETTING a job from the White House. Once, the president interviewed candidates for jobs. But now it is the candidate who interviews the president—preferably several times. He looks the president over carefully. Are the president's ideas acceptable, his policies sound? Is he up to the standards of the candidate? Is he up to the job? If the president passes his interview-test, the candidate consents to take the position. There is even a phrase for the happy feeling the president must inspire in the candidate—adequate "comfort," or "comfort level." Perhaps the first high official to get his job through this procedure was Clinton's communications director, David Gergen. . . . Last week, it was the turn of retired Navy Adm. Bobby Ray Inman—Clinton's nominee as secretary of defense—to interview the president. Inman stated at the ceremony announcing his nomination that he had not voted for Clinton. In other words, the president had not won his confidence during the campaign, or, apparently, by his conduct in office, either. The interviews were necessary to achieve that. Fortunately, the president performed adequately. "I was persuaded from our lengthy conversations of the president's absolute commitment to build a strong bipartisan support for where this country needs to go in the years ahead," Inman revealed. "Mr. President, as you know," Inman went on, "I had to reach a level of comfort that we could work together, that I would be very comfortable in your role as the commander-in-chief . . . And I have found that level of comfort." Therefore, obeying the call of "duty and country," Inman was willing to wrench himself away from "a very happy and prosperous life."

Comfort-levels were high in another quarter, too. Sen. Sam Nunn, the chairman of the Senate Armed Services Committee, revealed that he also had had several "candid" conversations with the president about the change of secretaries of defense—a revelation that, given the importance of examinations of the president for obtaining high office, could only fuel the rumors in Washington that Nunn might be in line to replace Warren Christopher as secretary of state. However that might be, it was clear that placating Nunn and other congressional critics of Clinton's military policies was one reason for choosing Inman. Ever since it was revealed that Clinton had eluded the draft, his popularity in military circles has been low, and the choice of a military man such as Inman to serve as secretary of defense was obviously designed to improve this relationship.

Strikingly absent from the discussion surrounding the appointment was any mention of the substance of military policy.

Inman described himself as "an operator" (apparently, his ear was deaf to the pejorative meaning of this word), adding, "hopefully with a strategic view." The country, too, can be hopeful on this point, inasmuch as the Clinton administration so far has notably lacked strategic views. However, neither at the announcement ceremony nor in the discussion in the press that followed have strategic views been much mentioned—nor, it seems, are any expected. Inman, surprisingly, announced that he would not discuss his views until "the confirmation process is through"—as if he were a nominee not for secretary of defense but for the U.S. Supreme Court. He did say, however, that he would "surprise" us by introducing "the best business practices" into the Pentagon.

The press on the whole seemed well-satisfied with the lack of any mention of substance. In the *Washington Post*, for example, an editorial deplored discussion of national security "in ideological terms," while Barton Gellman and Bob Woodward remarked in an analytic piece that Inman's "job" will be to preside over a decline in defense spending and to "stop senior uniformed leaders from rebelling against it."

The president, in making Inman and his military colleagues comfortable, has framed a policy toward the military. As for military policy itself, there is none yet in sight.

JANUARY 30, 1994

THE PRESIDENT'S STATE OF THE UNION ADDRESS WAS notable for, among other things, giving short shrift to two subjects: foreign policy (as I have mentioned), to which he devoted scarcely ten minutes of his sixty-five-minute address, and the budget deficit, to which he devoted two or three minutes. The first omission was unfortunate, and to the president's discredit; the second was welcome. Usually, news stories are reserved for things that happen. In this case, something that has not happened—the continued rise of the deficit—deserves note. Just a year ago, the deficit was the dominant issue in American political life. Today, not even the critics of the speech bother to mention the subject's absence. The budget deficit was deservedly given little notice, for the president, taking a great political risk, whose price may yet have to be paid, had done something about it: put through his budget plan, which plausibly schedules $500 billion in budget reductions over five years.

Is the problem solved, then? By no means. Clinton's contribution to the debt will in all likelihood be even greater than George Bush's. After that, the problem gets worse. Both adversaries and champions of the Clinton plan are agreed that in three years the deficit will start to rise again, owing chiefly to rises in entitlement payments. In his carefully reasoned recent book *Facing Up*, Peter G. Peterson offers a sensible list of the sorts of taxes and cuts that will be required to prevent this. They include "affluence" tests for all federal benefits, including Social Security, caps on mortgage-interest deductions, "cost-containment goals" for health care, and a fifty-cent per gallon gas tax—in other words, virtually every spending or taxation proposal that has proved to be the kiss of death for any politician who was bold enough to mention one of them in the last forty years or so. (The very word entitlement suggests the attachment people feel for these programs.)

Is Clinton's program responsible, at least, for the economic recovery now finally underway? Even that is true only in a negative sense. He has not been in office long enough to take credit for the conditions that have led to the recovery. There is a consensus among economists, in fact, that no politician is really responsible. Most say that the business cycle is. The negative credit that Clinton does deserve, however, points to the true nature of his accomplishment. While he cannot be given credit for creating the recovery, he can take credit for heading off a deadly threat to it. Passage of his program took every ounce of political capital that he had. So bitter was even this mild medicine that it passed the Senate only with the tie-breaking vote of Vice President Al Gore. In that climate, there was no chance whatever that, if the Clinton plan had been defeated, another, more effective one would have passed, and the lack of any plan might well have destroyed the confidence in economic conditions, including the stability of interest rates, that was essential for a recovery.

That passing this program, modest and inadequate as it was, was an act of political courage has been demonstrated by subsequent elections, including, especially, the victory in the Senate race in Texas of the Republican Kay Bailey Hutchison, who promised more tax cuts, over Bob Krueger, who himself thought it expedient to repudiate Clinton's plan, and, in New Jersey, of Christine Todd Whitman over Gov. Jim Florio. To this day, a vote for the steps necessary for deficit reduction is a *salto mortale* without benefit of a political safety net. The politicians who cast such a vote, including Clinton, can only pray that by the time of the next election one will have been woven and put in place.

In the meantime—in the precious interval before that test comes—the nation as a whole has been liberated to discuss the huge substantive reforms—of health care, of welfare—that were the centerpiece of Clinton's address. These, indeed, may be the only realistic paths to the further budget deficit reductions that are needed. In other words, with his budget plan, Clinton punctured the bubble of fantasy that in the previous decade had grown up around the budget and all issues related to it. In doing so, he restored rationality to the discussion of domestic issues. Whether there is a health care "crisis," whether the health care system should be reformed all at once or in stages, whether the new plan should be single-payer or multipayer, whether health reform should go hand in hand with welfare reform or come first are all questions on which reasonable people can disagree. But that these questions, which are the ones the United States needs to ask, are on the agenda at all is due to the president who, because of his resolute action earlier in the year, was at liberty, for the moment, to put the issue of the federal budget deficit to one side.

FEBRUARY 17, 1994

A LITTLE DEBATE HAS BEEN BUBBLING ON *THE NEW York Times* op-ed page, and I would like to join it. It concerns the announcement by Sheldon Hackney, the new chairman of the National Endowment for the Humanities, of a series of televised "town meetings" to explore the "American identity," the better to ease tensions among ethnic groups. In a piece headlined "The Identity Myth," the writer Richard Sennett asserted that efforts to discover "a national identity or an American character" were displays of "the gentlemanly face of nationalism," whose very nature it is to "define who 'we' are in contrast to a threatening 'other.'" In conclusion, he charged that "Mr. Hackney . . . seems to offer a Serbian solution to the challenge of living with one another." If the logical leap from town meetings aimed at ethnic conciliation to the ethnic massacres now taking place in Bosnia seemed broad, a response to Sennett's piece by the philosopher Richard Rorty went a good part of the way toward justifying it. Rorty was bothered by unnamed "academic leftists" who were "unpatriotic," and charged that, although they championed many noble causes, including the defense of women and African Americans, they suffered from an inability to "rejoice" in the country they lived in. Without quite identifying Sennett as one of these unpatriotic leftists, Rorty took issue with him regarding national identity. "A nation," he said, "cannot reform itself unless it takes pride in itself—unless it has an identity . . ." As if to illustrate Sennett's fears, Rorty seemed to have identified a "we"—those who share the American identity and rejoice in it—and excluded from it an "other"—the unpatriotic, left-wing professors. "A left that refuses to take pride in its country," he angrily concluded, "will have no impact on that country's politics, and will eventually become an object of contempt."

At the heart of the two men's disagreement is the concept of "identity." The word contains a built-in ambiguity. Its original meaning is sameness, from the Latin *idem*: same. But in the hands of psychologists it has come to mean something very nearly the opposite of that: the unique features that define an individual ("my identity"). How could one word express both sameness and uniqueness? The answer may lie in the verb-form of the word, "to identify with"—that is, to see yourself as the same as someone. Finding your identity, it appears, is a process whereby you define yourself according to your similarity to others.

What does it mean, then, to place an essentially psychological process, whereby an individual adjusts to a collectivity, at the center of politics? For one thing, it replaces an active process with a passive one. Consider a few older words that people use when seeking to define themselves and their beliefs: temperament, character, conviction, ideal. Temperament, unambiguously, is a given, be it by nature or nurture. All of the others must be actively and energetically sought. Character is built. By contrast, you merely find your identity. Convictions are held, ideals pursued. However, the person who "rejoices" in his "identity" is well-satisfied with what he already is. His next step may well be to insist that others become like him.

Or consider the word citizenship. Rorty writes, "A sense of shared identity is not an evil. It is an absolutely essential component of citizenship." Citizenship, however, is no vague or empty concept in need of provision from the rich storehouse of "identity." Citizenship is already a full and exacting program of shared responsibilities, which are clearly set forth in the Constitution and related law. If there must be television programs, let them inspect, with a cool and critical eye, what America is, or let them, with a warmer glance, describe the ideals embodied in our social contract, together with a vision of what we can and should become. But spare us celebrations of that half-way house, neither quite reality nor ideal, the American "identity."

MARCH 17, 1994

BY NOW, ANY NUMBER OF OBSERVERS HAVE demonstrated that the Whitewater affair is not "another Watergate"—much less "worse than Watergate," in the daft phrase of New York's Sen. Alfonse D'Amato. To summarize, there is no proof, or even evidence, that: The president orchestrated the payment of bribes to silence witnesses in court; the president ordered law-enforcement officers not to enforce but to obstruct the law; the president tried to use the CIA to obstruct the FBI; the president used other agencies of the government to punish his "enemies," including those who were investigating his many other crimes; the president presided over a campaign of illegal "dirty tricks" to win re-election; the president ordered the secret wiretapping of journalists and his own aides; White House staff organized a team to carry out numerous burglaries and other crimes. These acts and many more of like character were the basis for the charge, leveled against President Richard Nixon in articles of impeachment, that he had "acted in a manner contrary to his trust as president and subversive of constitutional government, to the great prejudice of the cause of law and justice, and to the manifest injury of the people of the United States." Finally, there is no protracted record of abuses of the sort that made Watergate only the final act in a drive for presidential power that, if it had been left unchecked, threatened to subvert democracy itself. Clinton has not, in other words, waged a secret military campaign (such as Nixon's secret bombing of Cambodia) or a campaign of spying on and disrupting domestic political dissent; nor has he usurped Congress's power of the purse by executive impoundment of funds. (If any constitution was subverted in the Whitewater "affair," it must have been the constitution of Arkansas, since the alleged wrongdoing occurred in that state, before Clinton arrived in the White House.)

The question remains why so much attention is being paid to Whitewater, even by people who have no political ax to grind. Two clichés of the hour suggest an answer. The first is the assertion, made repeatedly on news programs, that on such and such a day Clinton was "hounded" or "dogged" or "pursued" by questions about Whitewater. Characteristically, the story suggests that Clinton wished to draw attention to something else—his health plan, aid to Russia, job creation—but was prevented by the "questions." To give but one of any number of possible examples, Bob Schieffer remarked on "Face the Nation" that during Clinton's recent trip to Moscow he was "dogged by questions about this old real estate deal that he was involved in." But who, we may ask, was doing this dogging? It was, of course, chiefly the press itself. To the self-fulfilling prophecy, the press has added the self-created news story: It asks someone questions, then reports that the person was dogged by questions. (To this, one might add that the person in question was also dogged by reporters reporting that they had dogged him with questions.)

The second cliché is the advice that whatever the truth may be, Clinton now is bound to deal with the "perception" that he did something wrong. For example, Rep. Lee Hamilton (D-Ind.) recently stated that although he knew "of no evidence that the president or the first lady has done anything wrong," nevertheless congressional hearings on their possible wrongdoings should be held so that the Clintons can "overcome this inaccurate perception." But if hearings must be held to inquire into "perceptions" unsupported by any evidence, who, we need to ask, is safe from investigation? In a world in which the press creates "perceptions" by reporting its own questions as news, and Congress then feels an obligation to hold hearings to test those perceptions, the path appears to open to infinite investigation of anyone and anything whatsoever. No resemblance to Watergate, or to any other misbehavior, for that matter, is required.

MARCH 24, 1994

ONE DAY, WE MAY KNOW WHETHER THE PRESIDENT and his wife did anything wrong in the Whitewater affair. At the very least, we'll know everything that is discoverable with the fallible investigative instruments at hand. (As the Iran-contra scandal shows, the investigative trail sometimes runs cold before all the answers are found.) When that day comes, we may know whether all the investigations into Whitewater—in the media, in the courts, in Congress—were justified, or whether we all could have spent our time better looking into something else.

Of course, it is in the very nature of investigations that their value is unknowable until they are completed: If the results could be known in advance, there wouldn't be any need for investigation. The only way to decide whether and how to pursue an investigative effort is to keep it in proportion to the seriousness of the alleged wrongdoing and the weight of the evidence. Judging by this standard, what is now striking about the Whitewater affair is the gigantic discrepancy between the awesome apparatus of multiple investigations and both the triviality of the alleged misdeeds and the weakness of the evidence that they actually occurred. The most serious charge is that, as Governor of Arkansas more than a decade ago, President Bill Clinton pressured a businessman to make a loan to a partner of Clinton's in the Whitewater land deal. How Clinton might have profited from such a loan has yet to be made clear. To get to the bottom of this charge and others of no greater weight, a special prosecutor has been appointed. And now, it appears, one or perhaps two congressional hearings will be held.

How has it happened? Four collective actors can be distinguished: the Republican opposition in Congress, the White House, the media, and the congressional Democrats. The motives of the first three have been much discussed and by now are fairly clear. The Republicans have a partisan interest in holding as many investigations as possible. The White House has an obvious self-interest in limiting investigations, but is forced to agree to them for fear of seeming to engage in a cover-up. The media, which love a dramatic story, give it exaggerated attention and then, in a self-fueling process, cover their own coverage.

The most interesting, though least discussed, actors are the congressional Democrats. Just a few weeks ago they opposed almost as one person any congressional hearings. They bitterly accused the Republicans of using the affair to distract the nation's attention from President Clinton's legislative agenda. But then, in one of the most sudden and thorough-going political collapses in recent memory, almost all of them changed their minds. The collapse became evident last Thursday, when Rep. Dan Rostenkowski (D-Ill.) called hearings "inevitable." The very next day, the Senate voted by 98–0 to hold hearings. This week, the House followed suit, in a vote of 408–15.

Why did they change their minds? Was compelling new evidence of presidential wrongdoing presented? If any of them thought so, none let us know about it. Did they re-evaluate the evidence already available? Once again, none of them has suggested this. This sweeping reversal proceeded without any explanation whatever. However, it is not mysterious. When public attention to the alleged scandal reached a certain point, the congressional Democrats were overwhelmed by the fear that they would seem to be part of a cover-up. The "inevitability" felt by Rostenkowski was purely political. Thus did the presumption of innocence shift, as President Clinton has rightly complained, to a presumption of guilt. The congressional Democrats have accused the Republicans of sacrificing justice for partisan gain, and they are right, but the Democrats' own actions are more dubious still, for they have sacrificed both justice and party to stay in office. The price for their dereliction will now be paid by the country at large.

JUNE 12, 1994

THE NOMINATION OF OLIVER NORTH AS THE Republican candidate for a Senate seat from Virginia brings the Republicans to a critical turning point in the history of their party. For more than twenty years, it has been an open question whether this party is willing to live within the boundaries for political activity fixed by the Constitution. A Republican president, Richard Nixon, engaged in the multiple abuses of power known as Watergate and was driven from office under threat of impeachment. A few independent Republicans—notably, Sens. Barry Goldwater (Ariz.) and Lowell Weicker (Conn.)—joined in insisting upon a thorough investigation. When Nixon's secret tapes were revealed and the vote in favor of the first article of impeachment was cast, it was joined by most Republicans. Nixon fell, but the party's reputation as a defender of the constitutional rule was rescued.

The historically unprecedented outcome of that crisis seemed to ensure that presidents would refrain from abuses of power for a long time to come. Almost incredibly, however, in the second term of the Republican president Ronald Reagan, a new complex of abuses—the Iran-contra scandal—was uncovered. The president, it turned out, had delegated decisions on foreign policy to a secret cabal that promptly set about breaking at least two laws, one against arming the contra forces in Nicaragua, the other against bargaining with terrorist groups. Not the least surprising aspect of the abuses was the fact that the people in the Reagan White House seemed to have learned nothing from the Watergate crisis—unless it was how to escape punishment for their misdeeds, for, in a protracted, multi-stage mockery of justice, most of the defendants in the case either escaped conviction on technicalities or were pardoned by Reagan's vice president and successor, George Bush, a man who had himself played a role in the illegal activities.

At the heart of the Iran-contra scandal was, of course, North. It would be imprecise to call North a fascist. He makes no open call for democracy's overthrow, as both Hitler and Mussolini, for example, did. But in his actions he has shown himself a wrecker of constitutional government. He is a lawbreaker. He conducted foreign policy in several parts of the world in violation of the law. He is a liar: He perjured himself before Congress, and later boasted about it. He is a thief: He diverted public money to private purposes. Nearly every step of his career—the original abuses of power, the failure of Congress fully to uncover his misdeeds, the failure of the justice system to bring him to account, and now his political success—illustrates democracy's fatal tendency to undermine itself.

The question before the Republican Party now is whether it is ready to embrace North and all that he stands for. History suggests that conservative support is crucial to the success of anti-democratic, right-wing revolutions. In the words of Robert O. Paxton, of Columbia University, in the current *New York Review of Books*, "No fascist movement has so far acquired political power alone, without conservative allies." The best-known example is Hitler, who was defeated when, in 1923, he attempted a putsch against the conservative government in Munich, but later succeeded in winning power when he adopted a strategy of "legal revolution," which combined electoral strength and deal-making with conservative forces. Mussolini, too, Paxton points out, was a failure, until he hired out his infamous "blackshirts" as goon squads to businessmen who wanted to break the power of trade unions.

At the beginning of the week, there were encouraging signs that Republican conservatives were ready to draw the line against North. Virginia's Republican senator, John Warner, had long taken a strong stand against him, calling his potential election a "disgrace." Now he suggested that if North won the nomination he would support an independent candidate against him. Former President Gerald R. Ford balked at supporting North. Then the tide seemed to turn. Senate Minority Leader Bob Dole of Kansas, who earlier in the week had seemed to back away from North, embraced him, and promised to campaign for him in the fall, the better to win a Republican majority in the Senate. The National Republican Senate Committee gave North its support. At week's end the party's future still seemed undecided. Are the Republicans, the public waits to hear, ready in 1994 to trust the man who lied to them in 1988? Are they ready to make the lawbreaker a lawmaker? Are they a conservative party or a radical one? Will they let their party become a Trojan horse lodged in the heart of American democracy? Do they stand for the law or its overthrow?

JUNE 23, 1994

THE APPARENT SURRENDER OF THE WHOLE COUNTRY, led by its gigantic, multiform, all-pervading journalistic apparatus, to the morbid pleasures of the O.J. Simpson story brings to full flower a peculiarly American sickness. The obsession has been characterized by, on the one hand, irresistible compulsion, and, on the other, an obscure but pervasive feeling of shame—even of sinfulness—as when an addict, after a long but futile struggle, finally capitulates once and for all to his addiction.

The remarkable power of the story was put on display immediately, when, even in sports-crazed New York, coverage of the car-chase leading to Simpson's arrest was permitted to knock almost three quarters of an hour of the Knicks' championship game off the air. Another dimension of the response—which itself quickly became a key part of the story—was the appearance on the Los Angeles freeways of Simpson's fans—people who came out, certainly, as much to be seen by the half-a-dozen television news helicopters overhead as to see Simpson. The television audience, famously passive and faceless, had got up out of its chairs and couches and thrust itself in front of the camera. The loop of electronic coverage was closed: The audience was watching itself.

But what was the source of the undercurrent of moral nausea? Was it disgust at oneself for finding enjoyment in murder? Such enjoyment was certainly present (many people confessed their disappointment that the chase yielded no suicide or shoot-out at the end), but this is an ancient story—as ancient, at least, as the audiences that watched gladiators at Roman circuses. Was the cause of shame the near-total eclipse of serious news—for example, the nuclear crisis in North Korea? But the eclipse of substance by sensation was scarcely new, either.

The radically new element, it seems to me, was the astonishing resemblance of these extraordinary events to millions of extremely ordinary television programs. Words like "bizarre," and "unreal" were on everyone's lips, but it would have been equally fitting to call the events trite, banal. What could be more commonplace than a car-chase on television? Every element in the tale—the handsome sports star, the beautiful blonde wife, the gruesome murders themselves, the flight from justice, the evidentiary puzzle, even the presence of a Serious Issue (male abuse of women) as a sop to conscience—was familiar and over-familiar to the television audience. Only the fact that the people were real was new.

In recent years, we've become acquainted with the concept of virtual reality. In the Simpson story we see the birth of virtual fiction. Virtual reality is a full substitute for reality (its sights, its sounds, its smells, its feel), composed of artificial elements. Virtual fiction is a full substitute for fiction (its plot, its characters, its spectacles), composed of real people and events. The United States has been perfecting the craft of virtual fiction for some time. The so-called New Journalists, starting with Tom Wolfe and Truman Capote, made their contribution when they decided to render as fact what no journalists could ever really know—the thoughts inside a person's brain. Television followed with docudramas, which add "realistic" (that is to say, false) detail to factual stories. In film, Oliver Stone, who wedded fact and fiction in his rendering of the Kennedy assassination, is the pioneer. The presidency of Ronald Reagan was a giant step forward in virtual fiction: His crew mastered the art of glossing over the political life of the country with pleasing images that had little correspondence with reality ("It's morning in America," and so forth). But the Simpson story is the first full, unconstrained work of virtual fiction. Box office has been tremendous. Indulgence in virtual reality is a kind of betrayal of the real world, inasmuch as it seems to offer the weird possibility of doing without that world. Indulgence in virtual fiction is a worse betrayal, for it surrenders all the machinery of journalism, on which we rely to keep us in touch with reality, to the service of entertainment. The sin is abandoning the attention and care we owe the world beyond our personal horizons. A country that turns to its newsmen for the stuff of fantasy is a country lost in a world of dream.

III

RE-ELECTION

JANUARY 21, 1996

THE AGE OF DISTRACTION

IN THE ELECTION YEAR NOW BEGINNING, IT IS NOT only the offices of government that are at stake but the basic shapes and forms of electoral politics through which those offices are won. The changes occurring in politics are only one consequence of a much broader revolution, however. For alongside the world of our senses, given at birth, there has, in recent decades, grown up another, secondary world, made up of the images and sounds purveyed to us by the luxuriously proliferating instruments of communication of our time. Radio and, above all, television were, of course, the advance guard of this new world. Cable made possible the effective unlimited multiplication of channels. With the rise of the satellite, television soon became a global, interlocking network. The internet has duplicated that feat for computers, which add to passive viewership the possibility of interactive participation with what is on the screen. The internet is the largest *tabula rasa* ever created. It is now being covered with a stream of "information" whose volume beggars the imagination. Now that the photo-optic cable has been invented, television, the computer, and heaven knows what else may be conjoined into a single device. And, of course, "virtual reality"—the three dimensional simulation of experience—has already made its debut. There is nothing to compare this new environment to except, perhaps, the natural environment itself. Already, computers have "viruses," and there is talk of the "natural evolution" of software, which, like Darwin's organisms, will fend for themselves in the new environment—virtual organisms evolving in virtual seas. There is even "information war," in which one army sends its hostile "information" (viruses, etc.) to attack the enemy country's information. This is no light matter. A modern nation whose military information is corrupted or disarmed—its satellites flying out of their orbits, its computer screens foaming with nonsense, its missiles curving back to strike its own cities—could be as thoroughly humbled as one smashed by physical bombs. Iraq has already learned something of this through experience, in the Gulf war. The American strategy was to go for the information-jugular of the Iraqi war-machine—to snap "their spinal cord," in the words of Col. David Deptula, a target planner in the war. "Imagine Iraq like a human body," he said. "What happens if you take away somebody's ability to communicate with the rest of the body?"

The television set of the average household is on for seven hours a day, and the average person watches for more than six hours a day. If we add to that the 3.2 hours the average person spends listening to radio, and the three hours spent with other media, such as records, tapes, and movies, we arrive at a total of more than twelve hours a day spent attending to a reality other than the primary given one, which, if we suppose that people sleep about eight hours a night, receives our undivided attention for only about four hours a day. Who would have guessed, before the communications revolution, that human beings, if given unlimited opportunity, would all but discard the sensual world around them, and spend *most* of their time in a state of distraction? Formerly, when you awoke in the morning in your dwelling place, and saw the sun rise, and prepared to face your life, you were pretty much stuck with that. Today, a hundred other sun-rises, other dwellings, other lives are on call at the touch of a few buttons. Do you not like the person who stands before you? Do you not like his face? Then summon up, on some screen or other, another person, with a nicer face—say, the movie star Candice Bergen. Is your apartment drab and cramped? Then live, vicariously, in other, more glamorous and commodious apartments. Are you lonely? Cheerful people will come and keep you company. Do you not like your life? Other lives are available in abundance, twenty-four hours a day. On channel thirty-eight, congressmen and senators are orating. On channel thirty-five, if you tire of the legislators, couples, straight and gay, are coupling, courtesy of Time-Warner, or some other multi-billion dollar conglomerate that aspires to satisfy *all* of your "virtual" needs. (It's striking to reflect that whereas for the first several thousand years of history few people probably ever saw, close-up and at length, *other* people making love, now just about anyone in America can watch this twenty-four hours a day.)

For children, there are, of course, video-games—finger sports, which exercise neither the body nor the mind but merely the nervous system. Watch a child at play on the electronic playing fields: gone are the balls, the nets and goals, limbs flashing in the sunshine. Only the eyes move, the thumbs and two fingers, to the accompaniment of an inane tune endlessly repeating.

Yet of all the realms that have been invaded by the secondary reality of the communications revolution, none is more wide open to transformation than politics. Politics has always been a realm of appearances, in which men and (less often) women present themselves, their opinions, and their proposed projects and policies to their fellows for decision and judgment. In a realm governed by appearances, the ability to create imaginary worlds necessarily is revolutionary. In the early decades of the communications revolution, the totalitarian regimes of the twentieth century sought to impose fictitious realities on their peoples by force. They backed up propaganda with terror. They went to the far extremes of lying, of expunging reality; and yet, just *because* their propaganda played to a captive audience, it could afford to be crude, even preposterous. The political parties in the democracies, with no force at their disposal, have faced the far more difficult challenge of actually persuading voters. What is perhaps harder, they must first persuade the media-glutted voters to tear themselves away from entertainment—or, these days, "infotainment"—long enough to attend to a political message at all. (The audience for the verdict in the sensational O.J. Simpson murder trial was about 100 million people; that for the 1992 Democratic Party presidential nominating convention about seven and a half million.) For any political candidate, the battle against political apathy is easily as difficult as the battle against the rival candidate. More candidacies die of failure to achieve name-recognition than at the hands of their opponents' barbs.

An election is a choice by a people. In order to persuade the voters, each candidate now mounts a sort of multi-media pageant, costing tens of millions of dollars. Those "covering" the pageant are in fact an intrinsic part of it. At large, planned political events, they often greatly outnumber, and immensely outspend, the "participants." At the 1992 Democratic Party convention, for example, 15,000 journalists were present to 'cover' the 4,303 delegates, who in any case had very little to decide. We describe these events as gatherings of politicians that attract journalists eager to cover the events. But it would be more accurate to see them as gatherings of journalists that attract politicians eager to be voluminously covered—that is, to get days of free political advertising. (More than four thousand journalists are accredited to cover the 635 members of the Congress.) In these circumstances, it is absurd to speak any longer of campaign "events" which "the press" covers. Every candidate for office knows that, in the living rooms of the voters, where the decisions are being made, the coverage *is* the campaign. They act accordingly. All campaign events are "pseudo-events"—events, that is, whose primary *raison d'etre* is to generate a certain kind of coverage. It cannot be otherwise in a time when voters receive most of their information not from local political associations, clubs, etc., but from the news media.

As the numbers of journalists attending major political events suggest, the sheer size of the communications apparatus has increased to a point at which mere quantitative change becomes qualitative change. In 1994, the top 100 communications companies made ninety-two billion dollars. The industry regularly tops the list of major industries in earnings and by other measures. For example, in 1993, the communications industry paid out fifty-three billion dollars in wages and other compensation, beating out its closest rival, the construction industry, by about two billion. The networks spent a hundred and forty million dollars just on coverage of the Persian Gulf war. We live, it is said, in an "information age"—a phrase suggesting that the chief fact of our time is information itself, not anything that the information is *about*. There are few signs, moreover, that the voting public feels well-served by the blizzard of new technology, though in the last few years thoughtful people have been trying to devise more fruitful forms of coverage. As the machinery of communications has grown, political participation has shrunk. Like the population of Baghdad under the "smart bombs" of the information age, the electorate seems to cower under the bombardment from the satellites overhead. Whatever else the instruments of communication have achieved, they have not adequately made good the loss of the great intermediary institutions that once served to connect the people and the government—the voluntary associations so much praised by Tocqueville, trade unions, and the political parties themselves, with all their local activity and strength.

And yet are the aristocrats of the information age—the anchor-people, the owners of the great multi-media conglomerates, the political candidates and office-holders—the powerful ones of our day, presiding like lords of old over a bewildered electronic peasantry? Power is the capacity to decide great matters. However, the mighty of the information age do not so much dictate as grovel. For even as they deliver information, they also seek to glean it from the public, through polling, focus groups, and all the other instruments of market research and public opinion research. The two-way flow—of messages delivered to the public from the so-called decision-makers, and views and opinions gleaned from research from the public—is the great thoroughfare of contemporary politics. Consider the movie director who submits his film to the verdict of an audience of carefully selected target viewers who register their reactions through instruments on the arms of their chairs. If they do not like the sad ending, a happy one will be provided. Or consider the candidate or his consultant sitting behind the one-way mirror watching the focus group. When the person behind the mirror yawns, Bosnia—or all foreign policy—heads for the discard box, or banning abortion is struck off the list of promises in the Contract with America. And all of this happens *before* any vote has been cast. Or consider the political candidate surrounded by his pollster, his team of speech-writers, his propaganda experts, and his advertising director. How much of what he offers the public can he call his own? How much discretion remains to him? The danger we find in these operations is not so much the abuse of power—not the imposition by an elite of its interests and views on a mass—but the abdication of power, or perhaps one should say the disintegration of power.

It's not easy, even in theory, to imagine how to curb the misuse of the new techniques and seize the opportunities they offer. The instruments of publicity on the one hand and of market and opinion research on the other are today the high cards in the games whose winnings are wealth (for example, market-share) and high station (for example, elected office). Banning either is inconceivable; even restricting either is hard to conceive. Poll results, for example, are the gold standard of the political realm today. They have become the axle around which the political world—campaign strategies and coverage alike—turns. That this is so is a tribute to their general accuracy, even, when used judiciously, their predictive value.

All we can be sure of for now is that they and the other new techniques of communication have opened up a wide, hitherto unknown field of political maneuver and action—a field that is constantly the breeding ground of new shapes and forms of politics. In a series of pieces, of which this is the first, on the 1996 presidential campaign, I hope to chronicle and analyze these new forms as they are born and grow in the new environment. Just this year, for example, we have had such novelties as the book-tour as proto-presidential campaign (courtesy of General Colin Powell) in which it was never quite clear whether the book was being used to promote the possible candidacy or the candidacy was being used to sell the book; the electronically disseminated "college course" as election plan (courtesy of the Speaker of the House and former college professor Newt Gingrich), in which the dissemination of "educational" materials was intertwined with a powerful, brilliantly organized, successful campaign of the Republican party to take control of the House of Representatives; the radio talk-show (courtesy of the hugely popular right-wing talk show host Rush Limbaugh) as right arm of a legislative strategy in that House; the virtually single-handed campaign launched by the sheer power of a private fortune and consisting chiefly of paid advertising (courtesy of the multi-millionaire candidates Ross Perot and Steve Forbes); and the federal government budget negotiation (including government shutdowns) as campaign strategy, in which the two main political parties, aided by daily reference to polls and other expressions of public opinion, maneuver to either sign a budget deal or fail to do so in a way that creates the most advantageous possible *appearances* for the election.

All that has happened before the first vote was cast. And now the real, formal contest begins.

FEBRUARY 4, 1996

THE FLAT TAX BOOM

HOW DO THINGS HAPPEN THESE DAYS IN ELECTORAL politics in the United States? How is the agenda of issues that we are invited to consider set?

The recent prominence of the idea of the flat tax offers an outstanding case history. In the third week of January, very suddenly, all the instruments of media publicity were turned, like iron filings drawn by some great invisible magnet, to the flat tax, which was being championed by Steve Forbes, the multi-millionaire magazine publisher who is running for President in the Republican primaries. The idea, scarcely visible among the welter of other issues just a few weeks before, abruptly became virtually inescapable. *Time* and *Newsweek* put the idea and its champion Forbes on their covers. (Twin covers on the two newsweeklies are always a good sign that the zeitgeist has spoken up loud and clear that week.) *Time* dubbed Forbes with the coveted title "hot candidate." *Newsweek* announced "Forbes Frenzy." On Sunday morning, both CBS's "Face the Nation" and ABC's "This Week with David Brinkley" were devoted to the flat tax. On CNN's "Inside Politics," the flat tax was made "The Play of the Week." Newspapers all over the country ran articles on the idea. On public television, "Washington Week in Review" and "The NewsHour with Jim Lehrer" devoted lengthy discussion to it. In short, we were dealing with one of those booms in the media that today are the stock-in-trade of the news business.

In his stump speech, Forbes says that if the flat tax is adopted, the prestige of the United States in the world will soar, American families at all income levels will have lower tax bills, interest rates will fall, housing will boom, jobs will increase, the economy will roar ahead, American families will grow stronger, charitable giving will increase, and, in general, "Life in these United States would be better." However, this column is not about the flat tax. It is about the process whereby this unlikely issue moved, for a moment, at least, to the center of political discussion in the United States.

1. *The background: A story vacuum.* It was a year in which political surprises, on the order of Ross Perot's success in 1992, were anticipated, but none, somehow, had been provided. General Colin Powell, after rocketing upward in the opinion polls (itself a major media boom), had refused to enter the presidential race. President Clinton turned out to have no challengers for the Democratic nomination, and in the Republican contest Senate Majority Leader Bob Dole, a fixture of Washington for three decades, retained his huge lead in the public opinion polls while the rest of the field trudged along dully in single digits. Like nature herself, the virtual nature of the media world abhors a vacuum.

2. *Preparation: What does the public want?* Forbes, like the other candidates, used polls and focus groups to test in depth the ideas he would use in the campaign. According to his advisers, the flat tax tested well.

3. *The means: money.* Forbes possessed one asset that the other challengers to Dole lacked: tens of millions of dollars of his own money that he was willing to spend on his bid. He poured it—some fifteen million dollars' worth by the third week in January—into his campaign.

4. *The instrument: television.* Forbes spent his money on television advertising, single-mindedly promoting his theme. Forbes had very little organization on the ground. As he proudly and tellingly declared, "This is the first presidential campaign of the information age." He derided "bureaucracy and infrastructure" in campaigns (presumably, endorsements, get-out-the-vote drives, and other traditional grass-roots techniques of campaigning) and said that he alone was "going directly to the voter" (presumably, through television advertising). In other words, like the American commanders in the Persian Gulf, he preferred an air war to a ground war. Forbes has joined the lengthening list of characters around the world—in Poland, Stanislaw Tyminsky; in the United States, Ross Perot; in Italy, Silvio Berlusconi—who have reached for or achieved power by buying media time with their personal fortunes.

5. *The result: a bump in the polls.* In its cover story, *Time*, evidently a little surprised at itself for putting Forbes on its cover, indulged in a moment of introspection. "The fact that Steve Forbes finds himself on the cover of TIME magazine this week says a little about Forbes and a lot about American politics," *Time* observed in its opening sentence. The sentence, in which the observer becomes the observed and vice versa, makes itself come true, as did *Time*'s

further comment that Forbes was now "surrounded by reporters." ("The media horde had descended," was *Newsweek*'s version.) It's clear that when the press's own coverage becomes the subject matter of its stories, then any particle of substance—any actual object that is placed between the two mirrors—will be subjected to a multiplier effect.

Was there such a speck this time? There was. It was Forbes's rise in the public opinion polls from single to double digits. For example, in a *Times*/CBS poll, Forbes rose by seven percentage points from five to twelve percent. A poll by the Iowa Project of 300 caucus-goers showed Forbes at eighteen percent. Other polls showed similar results. This is not nothing. Yet when we remember that those who call themselves Republicans represent only about forty percent of the population, that less than half are likely to vote, and that of these by no means had all yet focused their attention on the primaries, which remained a month away, then we see that the rise in Forbes's support that is the factual basis for the "Forbes Frenzy" represents a strikingly small number of flat tax enthusiasts. . . .

Nevertheless, the bump in the polls was the probable critical fact in the rush of the media to suddenly cover the flat tax. The flat tax boomlet thus illustrated a law of American politics: In the period before any vote has been cast, public opinion polls are the raw stuff of political power. Their slightest motion can dictate not only the behavior of candidates but the direction and extent of coverage. They do not decide what people will think about an issue but they do decide what issue people will think about.

8. *The substance within the result.* However hyperbolic the claim may be that there is any "Forbes Frenzy," it's impossible to deny that in the blizzard of coverage there was the glint of some authentic public reaction. Even as slight a rise in the polls as six or

seven percent cannot be dismissed as meaningless. Asked about the *Time* cover, the managing editor, Walter Isaacson, said, "The flat tax is an interesting idea that's appealing on the surface but complex once you delve in, which makes it a perfect topic for what *Time* magazine ought to be doing. We wanted to look at the idea behind the flat tax and not just the horse race for the nomination. One thing I find exciting about politics is that it brings ideas to the surface. . . . You balance whether an idea is catching on and how interesting it is, and if it's both you do it."

Media bubbles, of course, have a way of bursting. Indeed, it is almost their nature to burst, for it is something like a rule of media coverage that whatever is raised up by a media boom must next be torn down, thereby making two stories of one. (1: Rise; 2: Fall.) And indeed volumes of critical fire were almost instantly fired at the flat tax. As it happened, however, in one of those accidents of timing that are as much a feature of the new, electronic politics of the old, the front-runner, Bob Dole, followed the President's State of the Union speech with a rejoinder almost universally seen as weak, and his rivals in the Republican primaries branded him unable to compete with Clinton in the general election. He had suffered two blows to his candidacy in as many weeks, and he was "in trouble." Of such stuff are media booms—and some of the most important decisions that the United States faces about its future—made.

PRESENT AT THE DISSOLUTION
MANCHESTER, NEW HAMPSHIRE

THE WEEK AND A DAY BETWEEN THE PRESIDENTIAL election caucuses in the state of Iowa and presidential primary in the state of New Hampshire was like no other period in the history of presidential primaries. This year's contest in New Hampshire, the political analyst William Schneider said on the Manchester television station WMUR, was going to be "a defining moment," but just the opposite turned out to be the case. It was, rather, a blurring moment—indeed, a disintegrating moment. In the words a few days before the vote of the executive director of New Hampshire State Republican Party, Charles Arlinghaus, "undecided" was much too weak a word to describe the inchoate, fluctuating state of voters' minds during that crucial week. So many people were saying, "I have no *idea* who to vote for," he observed. "The Republican Party is Reaganite," Arlinghaus explained. "But no one's been able to hold all the elements of Reagan's coalition elements together." Later, exit polls showed that four out of ten voters had in fact made up their minds during the week. In fact, repulsion toward all the candidates and their ill-mannered campaigns was much more evident than attraction to any of them. In the words of one Republican voter, "We used to be offered the least of two evils; now we aren't even given those any more."

The immediate thing that was coming apart was the Republican Party's ideological underpinnings, including, especially, their all-important economic component. That disintegration, however, showed every sign of being the beginning of a larger event: the belated breakup of an entire framework of political debate that was part and parcel of the Cold War, and which through sheer inertia has stayed intact for a half decade beyond the Cold War's end. In the camp of the defeated party, the Soviet Union, *perestroika* preceded the end of the Cold War. Here, in the camp of the victor, *perestroika* is only now beginning.

The election night parties in and around New Hampshire told the story of the Republicans' disarray. The principal loser, the former Republican front-runner Senator Bob Dole, did not even acknowledge the victory of the winner, Patrick Buchanan. The third-place finisher, former governor of Tennessee Lamar Alexander, tried first to pretend that Dole didn't exist, defining the contest as a race between himself and Buchanan, and then had the effrontery to suggest that Dole "should move out of the way and let Patrick Buchanan and me have a debate about where our country should go." Even Steve Forbes, with a mere twelve percent of the vote, seemed positively energized by his defeat, and, in a speech in which the name "Buchanan" was not mentioned, gave a recital of his campaign themes to delighted supporters. Former New Hampshire Senator Gordon Humphrey, who was by Forbes's side almost every day in the last weeks of the primary, was still spinning victory scenarios for Forbes. "Dole is going to fade out soon," he predicted after the speech. "It could come to an Alexander versus Forbes race. There's something marvelous, naive, and inspiring about this campaign. Steve is too naive to know it's an uphill fight. He could go all the way." The "Buchanan brigade," meanwhile, was showing every sign of coalescing into a compact, energetic mass with a momentum and a fervor quite independent of the party at large, which it now regarded as a "dying establishment" it means to overthrow.

For by week's end, the Party was virtually being drawn and

quartered by four tribes pulling in four irreconcilable directions. One tribe was the new generation of Republicans that had taken control of the House of Representatives in 1994, under the leadership of Speaker of the House Newt Gingrich. Their guiding star was balancing the budget. Not the least peculiar aspect of this election season is that it comes on the heels of an immense struggle, which included two shutdowns of the government, between these Republicans and the Clinton White House—a struggle that almost all observers say was won politically by Clinton. Most elections initiate great struggles between the parties. This election began at the tail end of one, and therein lay a great difficulty for the Republican candidates. By the time the primary season began in earnest, Gingrich was the least popular major politician in the country, and his revolution offered poor material for the campaign platforms of his party's presidential hopefuls.

Something new was needed. It soon arose. The candidate was Steve Forbes, and the issue was the flat tax. The movement for a flat tax was the second of the tribes pulling the Republican Party apart. The flat tax at the rate of seventeen percent proposed by Forbes was, in the short term at least, diametrically opposed to budget balancing. The immediate consequence of its adoption would be an increase in the deficit by some two hundred billion dollars. Forbes, however, had an answer to the objection: The decline in the tax rate would stimulate the economy as a whole to such an extent that net taxes even at the lower rate would increase, thus closing the deficit. The answer revealed the philosophical underpinning of the flat tax. It was supply-side economics, which had long taught that tax cuts could paradoxically increase tax revenues. In the opinion of many, though, it was the application of just this doctrine that had created the budget deficit in the first place.

It was not surprising, then, that Gingrich, whose revolution promised a balanced budget as its centerpiece, called the flat tax "nonsense." The progenies of the Reagan "revolution" and the Gingrich "revolution" were in collision.

The third tribe, of course, was that of the extreme right-wing populist Buchanan, championing a fundamentalist nationalistic isolationism, both economic and military. (In Russia, Zhirinovsky congratulated Buchanan, and called him his "brother in arms.") His opposition to free trade, and to international trade agreements such as GATT and NAFTA, cut to the core of the traditional belief of the Republican Party, including its most conservative wing, in the unfettered working of the free market. Buchanan appears fully aware of this. In the closing days of the campaign, he attacked the establishment of his own party with abandoned fury. It was "shaking in its boots," he said at a boisterous rally I attended in Nashua on Sunday. The "peasants" (his unflattering term for his own supporters) are "coming with pitchforks," he said, in words that became instantly famous. "We're going to take this over the top." Just minutes before the rally, George Will, a champion of that Republican establishment, had assailed him on ABC television's "This Week" with David Brinkley for his continued backing of his campaign's co-chairman Larry Pratt, who had been appearing on speaking platforms with advocates of white supremacy. Now Buchanan called Will "a yapping poodle" whom he'd had to "hit with a newspaper." After these words and many others of equal brutality, can Buchanan, if he does not win the Republican nomination, long remain within the Republican Party?

The fourth tribe is the traditional establishment, devoted to unfettered business and free trade. It has been stirred to new life by Buchanan's attacks. That establishment, it's widely said, "will not let" Buchanan get the nomination. The question, though, is whether it's in the power of any establishment to control either him or his pitch-fork-toting supporters—or, failing that, to prevent him from founding another party. Buchanan's natural constituency is the "Reagan Democrats"—the working people who voted for Reagan. Arlinghaus surmised that there might now exist a white-collar counterpart of these-seeming "yuppies" in the lower reaches of corporate life who think like the Reagan Democrats and, furthermore, are the very ones most threatened by the corporate down-sizing against which Buchanan rails.

As if all this were not division enough, the Republicans are further divided between, on the one hand, the fractured "economic conservatives," and the "social conservatives," who believe the ills of the country are not economic at all but chiefly moral, and want, above all, to ban abortion, permit prayer in schools, and strengthen the family.

Nor can the Republicans turn to foreign affairs for the "vision" that escapes them in domestic affairs. Half support the dispatch of troops to Bosnia; half deplore it. Half are internationalist; half quasi-isolationist, or entirely so. At the beginning of the week, the question the Republicans were asking themselves was *who* is a conservative (no other label being acceptable among Republicans today). By the end of the week the question was *what* is a conservative.

Yet behind the identity crisis of the Republican Party, it's clear, there stands the much deeper question of the nation's political identity. Starting in about 1948, when the hostility between the Soviet Union and the United States eclipsed earlier attempts at cooperation, until 1991, when the Soviet Union died, the Cold War provided the overarching framework in which political discussion and debate took place. The creation of this framework was, for better or worse, not merely accidental. Though created in response to events, it was, in good measure, an intentional and a bi-partisan act, undertaken by President Truman, a Democrat, in concert with Republican leaders in Congress, of whom Senator Arthur Vanderberg was perhaps the most important. An awareness that they were founding not just a policy but a framework in which future policies would be debated was expressed in the title of Secretary of State Acheson's memoir *Present at the Creation.*

This framework passed into oblivion with the death of the Soviet Union. Our generation has been present at the dissolution. Since then, no succeeding framework for political debate has replaced the one whose underpinnings history has removed. Rather, each party has made do as best it could with bits and pieces of its former position in the old order of things, hoping with improvisation and makeshift to patch something together that would appear to make sense and pass for a "vision." Lacking the glue of anti-communism, the Republicans have found nothing else to unite them, not even belief in the global triumph of the free market. The Democrats, faced with that same triumph, and with the decline in popularity of governmental social programs, have been forced to retreat from their traditional support of many elements of the welfare state. President Clinton, however, has proved especially adept at his task. He has been the most *elastic* president in recent memory—capable of sheltering the most widely disparate elements under his political tent. So capacious is his embrace that, as his recent State of the Union address announcing "the end of the era big government" shows, he is not content with the diversity of his own party and reaches out voraciously to absorb Republican ideas as well. It's a performance that leaves his countrymen uneasy, at best. In the words of a voter I spoke to here, "The problem with Clinton is not that he doesn't believe in anything but that he believes in *everything*." Yet in the interrugnum of two ages, when the coherence of the old order is gone but nothing new has risen to take its place, Clinton's talent for papering over differences, though hardly inspiring, is at least politically useful.

Senator Patrick Moynihan, asked on CNN's "Sunday Journal" what the Democratic Party stood for, replied, "Come back and ask me in a year . . . we're going to have to define ourselves in this election year." Nothing of the sort has even begun to happen. While the Republicans have been at each others' throats, Clinton has sailed through New Hampshire twice. Last week, in a rally attended by 10,000 people in the town of Keene, he made no mention of his opponents but claimed that he did nevertheless have "an opponent" in the race. The opponent was "cynicism"—an avowal that might be called, well, a little cynical, since its obvious unstated purpose was to increase Democratic turnout in the uncontested Democratic primary.

It has been enough for the Democrats, politically speaking, to observe with satisfaction the disarray of the Republicans. "Make no mistake: The Democratic Party is united this year," Rick Twombly, the leader of the Democratic Minority in the New Hampshire assembly told me last week. "Since the Republican freshmen took over the House, and began to try to cut things like medicare and fuel assistance, they have been merely acting like true Republicans. That's why they were out of power in Congress for forty-six years. These new freshmen Republicans don't remember that, but the people do. Since the time of F.D.R., the Democrats have built the great middle class. But the people who benefitted most—the children of the children of those who sweated and sacrificed to achieve these things—forgot what the price was. 'I want it but I don't want to pay for it,' they said. They didn't want to remember what their parents had given up. Now the

Republicans have reminded them. Democrats now know why they are Democrats."

No Clinton-like embrace of opposites appears possible now for the Republicans. Holding the presidency gives the Democrats an appearance of unity where there is in fact little, except in the negative sense defined by Twombly. The Republicans, seeking the presidency, must forge a "vision" that will lift them into it. Their problem, though, is not to discover the "positions" their party should take on "the issues"; it is, in the landscape of our new, as yet scarcely explored world, to discover what the issues are on which their party or any other should now be taking positions.

Their only achievement so far has been to complete the ideological dismantlement of their party. The decks are cleared for them to discover, if they are able, the principles that will define the new age. It's a challenge they might well have preferred to forego but that events, it seems, have doomed them to grapple with.

JUNE 9, 1996

RAPID REACTION

WHEN THE FOUNDING FATHERS WERE CONSIDERING what form of government to give the United States, they chose representative democracy over direct democracy. Direct democracy, they believed, was possible only in small countries in which the whole voting public could assemble in one place. Direct democracy was impossible in a large republic for the simple reason that, in the words of John Selden, "the room will not hold all."

With the rise of the electronic media, however, suddenly the room—an electronic room—*can* hold all. TV united the public as spectators and now the Internet may be on its way to uniting it as participants as well. But it is not only space that the electronic revolution has shrunk; it is time as well.

We have to picture not only that everyone is in the same room but that none ever leaves the room. In that room, action can be taken 24 hours a day, and a candidate who fails to respond can find himself in trouble. Hence the rise of what's now called "rapid response"—the organized effort to rebut instantly statements by the opposing candidate or otherwise immediately spoil his campaign initiatives.

A case in point is the recent gambit by the Clinton administration on the welfare issue. Having learned that Bob Dole was about to give a speech on the subject in Wisconsin, which is considering a radical Republican reform program, Clinton suddenly praised the Wisconsin plan and suggested that the federal government would issue a waiver of federal rules permitting the plan to be enacted. And when Dole made a campaign appearance in Chicago to address the crime issue, not only were Democratic Party staff members and activists opposed to domestic violence there to picket him but Sen. Carol Moseley-Braun held a press conference the same day attacking Dole's positions.

A decade ago, political debate in a presidential campaign still moved at a stately pace. Michael Deaver was chief of public relations for Ronald Reagan's campaign of 1984—which featured the legendary "Morning in America" political ads (showing uplifting, softly focused shots of happy events such as weddings and the like in an ideal America). Now Deaver is working on "communications oversight" for the Republican convention and he remarks of rapid response: "We never operated that way, I can tell you. In fact, the 1984 Reagan campaign, which the press says is the model the Clinton campaign is now using, didn't have to have rapid response, because there wasn't anything generated by the Mondale campaign to respond to." He goes on to note that the campaign proved to be astonishingly static. "When we generated the Morning in America theme, we thought it would be a scene-setter, but instead it ran throughout the whole campaign."

Such passivity is unthinkable in Bill Clinton's administration. If the technical origins of rapid response lie in the use of satellite transmission and round-the-clock news reporting, its political origins lie in the presidential campaign of Democratic candidate Michael Dukakis in 1988. "There are a bunch of us now in the Clinton campaign who were involved in the Dukakis campaign, which made no response to President Bush's negative ads," said John Lockhart, the Clinton campaign's national press secretary. "Intellectually, the decision was made that you shouldn't respond to a baseless and silly charge." In fact, though, the charges stick, if only because the media doesn't bother to rebut them and for the simple reason that "people are busy." Thus the public came to believe that Dukakis "had psychic problems," devoted his governorship to opposing the pledge of allegiance in school, to getting the murderer Willy Horton released on parole from prison and "personally polluted Boston harbor."

Now, Lockhart says, the Clinton campaign is geared up to "set the record straight, and set it straight in what I call real time." That, he adds, "means not two days later, when people's attention has moved on, and forgotten about it. People don't say, 'All right, I have heard one side's case, and now I am going to wait to hear from the other side two days later.'" Rather, "Responding means responding immediately." Lockhart declined to discuss the mechanics of the operation, but he commented that in such an operation "you have to have tight and clear lines of authority—you can't have seven people deciding or require a decision from the chief of staff."

Lockhart says rapid response is beneficial to campaigns. "It makes people accountable, and that has to be good," he says. Someone whose inaccurate or distorted charges have been publicly refuted, he says, will be less likely to repeat the performance.

Unsurprisingly, Deaver takes a dimmer view of the innovation. He sees a "danger" that the Clinton campaign will become "overexposed and lose all credibility." Rapid response, he notes, can be used not just for rebuttal but to switch positions abruptly on issues, as Clinton did on the welfare issue.

"At some point you have to stand for something," he remarks. "To just simply adopt the Contract with America as a whole or adopt Dole's position on taxes at some point hurts the credibility of the president," Deaver says. He further notes that "no one has done a real analysis of people's real response to news. Do we just hear one thing one day, and accept something different the next, because it's on television?" (It's worth noting that Democrats, who used to specialize in "thoughtful" criticisms of the arts of political public relations, at which the Republicans were the acknowledged masters, now seem to be the public-relations innovators while the Republicans are left to muse about debasement of the political world.)

For some, though, "rapid" response is not fast enough. They don't want merely to speed up campaigning; they want to reverse the order of the tenses to respond to proposals even before they have been made. They want to launch what Republican National Chairman Haley Barbour calls "not reaction but pre-action" and Vice President Al Gore, among others, has called "pre-buttals." Larry McCarthy, who is working on the strategy and advertising of several Republican congressional races, gives an example from the

Senate campaign of Michael Huffington in 1994. "Our opponent, Diane Feinstein, released the text of an ad for June the day before the ad was to air," he relates. "We put together a response that afternoon, and were on the air before she was." With the rise of the pre-action and the pre-buttal we seem to leave behind politics-as-usual and to enter an Alice-in-Wonderland world, in which people "react" to events that haven't happened, "rebut" arguments that haven't been made, and the future, generally speaking, comes before the past.

It is rude, our parents taught us, to interrupt. "Pre-buttal," then, is the ultimate rudeness for it is a sort of interruption even before the other person has opened his mouth. Pre-buttal, in fact, may be more important than the techniques of rapid response out of which it developed. Indeed, the better part of the Clinton campaign, not to mention his plan for governing, can be seen as a "pre-action" and the main themes of his State of the Union speech can be seen as "pre-buttal"—including the message that the "era of big government is over."

As so many observers have pointed out, his election-year strategy, inspired in part by pollster Richard Morris, who has ambidextrously worked for Republican and Democratic candidates alike, has been to head off the Republican challenge by adopting their message. (As an adviser to both parties, Morris is, of course, in an ideal position to fashion pre-buttals for either one.) The problem lies deeper than confusion among voters. The aim of a representative system is to place choices before the voters. But in a world of pre-action and pre-buttal, in which each party may be masquerading in the clothes of the other, the debates seem to be over before they have even begun. The people's choice has been spoiled not because the people are unable to choose but because the alternatives between which they are invited to choose are discredited before they are presented.

JUNE 30, 1996

THE POLITICS OF DIVORCE

IT'S OFTEN SAID THAT YOU CAN'T LEGISLATE morality. Nevertheless, this year's presidential campaign has often been roiled by issues that come under the heading of "family values." The latest is the so-called Defense of Marriage Act, which seeks to strengthen the right of states to refuse to acknowledge same-sex marriages legalized in other states. The legislation is oddly named, for it does not directly defend or support any marriages; in fact, it forbids marriages—those between people of the same sex. The states already possess a power to disallow on their territory the laws of other states that conflict with their own, but no matter. The legislation creates the appearance, if not the reality, of federal action.

This paradox and others got an airing one evening recently on the "The NewsHour with Jim Lehrer." Rep. Bob Barr (R-Ga.) spoke in defense of the Defense of Marriage Act. Elizabeth Birch, the executive director of the Human Rights Campaign, a gay rights group, spoke against it. At one point she turned to Barr, who is thrice-married, and remarked, "We've always been unclear about which marriage of his he's defending, his first, his second, or his third."

"These are arguments *ad hominem*," Barr quite rightly protested. Birch's jibe nevertheless did point to a conspicuous omission at the heart of the "family values" issue. If the cause of family values is to have any meaning, it must stand in opposition to the deed that, almost by definition, is more destructive to families than any other, namely divorce. Between 1960 and 1980, U.S. divorce rates increased by 250 percent. Today, it is estimated that about half of marriages will end in divorce—up from 16 percent in 1960.

To speak in present circumstances of defending the family or marriage without mentioning divorce would be something like trying to speak of unemployment without admitting loss of jobs, or of declaring war without mentioning who the enemy is. Nevertheless, it is just this feat that most politicians manage quite simply. The reasons are easy to understand. In the first place, a casual glance at our candidates for high office suggests that the statistics on marriage and divorce hold as true for them as for the rest of the public. (Bob Dole, for example, has divorced and remarried, and the Clintons have publicly confessed to difficulties in their marriage.) Those who have experienced divorce are, of course, in a poor position to crusade against it. What's more important, though, is that the fifty percent of married Americans who get divorced—not to mention the unknown percentage of those who have considered it but not gone through with it—is a formidable demographic group, more than enough to catch the eye of a politician. A case in point was Vice President Dan Quayle's speech during the 1992 campaign assailing the fictional television character Murphy Brown for having a baby out of wedlock. He was careful to add, "I'm not talking now about some people who may have had a divorce."

The rise in divorce is only the most easily measured feature of a cultural revolution that has affected every area of life. It seems clear that the troubled fortunes of marriage are closely related to a profound shift somewhere in the depths of people's souls. The balance between self-gratification and obligation, of self-love and love of others, is tilting distinctly away from the rigors exacted by the vows of marriage.

Another sign of this shift is evident throughout the popular culture, where the dam that once held back the dissemination of sexually explicit material has seemed not merely to erode but simply to have been washed away. Parents who compare the experience of their children today to their own experiences as children are dizzied by the onslaught of what the young are now exposed to on television, in the movies, in songs, and on videotapes. At the same time, it's become increasingly clear that a host of other social ills, including crime, welfare dependency and poor educational performance, are closely related to the breakup of families.

The group reacting most sharply to this cultural revolution is the religious right, on which the Republican Party relied so heavily for its takeover of Congress in 1994. Patrick Buchanan spoke for this constituency when he declared "cultural war" at the 1992 Republican convention, and he continued to champion that cause in the recent primaries. But his position was rejected by a majority, including a majority of Republicans. Buchanan's position indeed promises a certain coherence, for he also rails against corporate power, and it is the corporate communications giants, more than anyone else, that are at the leading edge of the tidal wave breaking down the old proprieties. Yet the Republican Party has traditionally been a defender of corporations and of the free market in which they operate. This split is one of the many fissures that divides the Republicans as their convention in San Diego approaches.

The opposition to the cultural war of the religious right—a curious assortment of feminists, conservatives, libertarians, gay groups, free-market enthusiasts and civil libertarians—is anything but monolithic. There is, of course, no divorce lobby. There are, however, millions of people who have been through this protracted, painful, bewildering, personal disaster and who probably would react badly to political lectures on the subject. Thus, even the religious right has been muted on the subject—preferring to campaign against abortion, homosexuality, and the like.

A few conservatives have nevertheless directly taken their brethren to task for the omission. One is former Secretary of Education William J. Bennett, who has delivered a biting lecture on the subject to the Christian Coalition. "Some may wish to focus and obsess on homosexuality because it's so far from them," he said. "Divorce and infidelity are something much more familiar to people." But, he adds, the example that the middle class sets in its decisions about marriage is more important than any lectures it might deliver, for "[w]hen [divorce] starts with people who are supposed to be the model for other people, then the whole thing spreads as a conflagration through the society."

Another is Maggie Gallagher, author of *The Abolition of Marriage*, in which she observes, "Even the political Right, though willing to fiddle with welfare formulas to discourage, however moderately, illegitimacy among the underclass, refuses to take on the decline of marriage more directly." She watches the current election with interest. "The Democrats have rather brilliantly called the Republicans' bluff," she said in a recent conversation. "What they've noticed is that 'family values' is little more than a slogan. So there's no reason why they can't use the right words, too. I think it's healthy that the two parties are saying commonsense things, such as that having two parents is good for children. My hope is that this will move Republicans to do the serious things that need to be done to halt the undermining of marriage."

In fact, a number of advocates, in both the Republican and Democratic Parties, are proposing modest changes in divorce law. One is William A. Galston, until recently deputy assistant to President Bill Clinton for domestic policy. He proposes, among other things, that no-fault divorce be promptly granted only to couples that mutually request it.

Another school of thought, which also includes both Republicans and Democrats, holds that government can do little to affect a decision as personal as divorce. These observers would turn to other institutions for help. However, these institutions—including churches—are either inactive or ineffective in the matter. Maggie Gallagher comments that the Catholic church she attends has not offered a sermon about marriage for several years. "The leaders of the church are afraid of offending their parishioners," she says.

Certainly, nothing of use has been offered on the campaign trail. The politicians say they have leaped to our defense. They stand ready to defend marriage against the enemies that attack it, such as homosexuals—by preventing their marriages. The Republican Congress has proposed the ban on gay marriage (evidently hoping to create a campaign issue for themselves) and the Democratic president has agreed to it (adroitly taking the campaign issue away again). True, the law's mischief is undercut by its ineffectuality, and so, strictly speaking, it may be that nothing worse—or better—than political posturing has occurred.

Are the empty sermons of the campaign trail the most that can be expected? A sort of revolution in manners and morals has occurred, and it's clear by now that its social and even its economic effects are deep. Is there nothing of value for politicians or other members of the community to say or do about it? Those who, like Bennett, are willing to address the subject head-on and those who honestly believe that government has no role to play in decisions as personal as these have at least one thing in common: They give an honest answer to honest questions. Perhaps they offer the first step in a discussion that, if it is to continue to be honest, will be conducted more in doubt, introspection, and sorrow than in easy indignation and blame.

THE UNCERTAIN LEVIATHAN*

THE PRESIDENTIAL ELECTION OF 1996 PLACES A paradox before us. Polls and other reports show that the public is disillusioned with politics. With one era—the era of the Cold War—having ended, and another, undefined era before us, the voters clearly want to turn a new page in political life. Yet the two major parties have chosen two quintessential Washington politicians, President Bill Clinton and the former Senate Majority Leader Bob Dole, as their candidates. Have the voters somehow been disenfranchised? Has a mighty establishment suffocated the popular will, as so many voters now believe? The answers to these questions may lie in deep changes that have occurred in the structure of the electoral system.

Since the New Hampshire primary, in February, I have been following the presidential campaign for *Newsday*. It has often been said this year that the erosion of the middle class threatens to divide us into two Americas, one rich and one poor. On the campaign trail, however, I noticed a slightly different division—one that runs down the center not of the economic but of the political realm. On one side is the America of those who are political professionals. It comprises politicians, their advisers and employees, and the news media. Politicians waste little love on the newspeople who cover them, and the newspeople display a surly skepticism toward politicians as a badge of honor. Yet if the voters I met on the campaign trail are any indication (and poll data suggest that they are), much

*This article ran in the September issue of *The Atlantic Monthly*.

of the public has lumped newspeople and politicians together into a single class, which, increasingly, it despises. Respect for the government and respect for the news media have declined in tandem. More and more the two appear to the public to be an undifferentiated establishment—a new Leviathan—composed of rich, famous, powerful people who are divorced from the lives of ordinary people and indifferent to their concerns.

On the other side of the division is the America of political amateurs: ordinary voters. They are above all a class of spectators—except, of course, on Election Day. This division of American politics into two worlds is in one sense as old as the Constitution, which by founding a representative democracy established a class of people who, as elected officials, would participate fully in political life, and a much larger class of people who, whatever else they might do as citizens, would participate in the formal political system only during elections. The search for intermediate institutions to span the yawning gulf between these two classes has always been a central problem of American democracy. Thomas Jefferson worried that "the abstract political system of democracy lacked concrete organs." He tirelessly but unsuccessfully advocated the formation of "ward" councils as local participatory bodies. In the mid-nineteenth century Alexis de Tocqueville famously noted the countless civic associations that had grown up to bridge the gap. The political parties, with their vast, often corrupt local machines, have perhaps been the most important and enduring bridge. Today, however, all the traditional intermediate institutions, including the parties, are in sharp decline, and their place is being taken by professional campaigns and the news media.

Thus the *activity* of politics has increasingly become an interaction, at once antagonistic and incestuous, between the media and the people running the campaigns. Everyone else is an onlooker. The line that separates newspeople from politicians is one that both groups seek to sharpen but that in fact is increasingly blurred, while the line that separates both from the public is one that politicians and press would like to erase but in fact grows steadily sharper. Indeed, rarely has there been a line of separation between classes as sharp and clear as the line that divides the new class of political participants from the larger class of political spectators: it is as sharp as the line that divides a person being photographed from the photographer, or the people in a focus group from the pollster watching them from behind a one-way mirror, or the people who glow on the television screen from the mass of anonymous viewers in the dimness of their living rooms. By comparison, the lord on his estate was as one with the peasants in his fields, to whom he was tied by innumerable social bonds. Even the divide between fame and anonymity has grown sharper. Television, one might say, has given tangible reality to the aura of brightness that has always seemed to surround the famous, while the anonymous—the mere viewers of television—seem to sink into a deeper obscurity.

In most primary states the gulf between these two Americas is immutably fixed. Few citizens are likely to have much firsthand experience of either politicians or the news media. However, in the small states with early caucuses or primaries, such as Iowa and New Hampshire, personal contact between the two Americas is possible for a considerable proportion of the voters. The encounters I saw in these states fairly crackled with tension. To begin with, at almost every campaign stop there appeared a beast that rarely failed to astonish the uninitiated citizen. A sort of many-footed, many-eyed, many-tongued land octopus held together by cords and wires and jutting electronic equipment of all descriptions, the beast was the media scrum that instantly clusters around candidates when they move from one place to another. At many events this ungainly clump outnumbered the citizenry, who sometimes had a hard time getting anywhere near the candidate. Such moments illustrated a feature of the relationship between the participating political class and the passive voting class: the severance of direct human contact, once thought to be the very glue of politics, between the two worlds into which the political United States has now been sundered.

Few of the voters I spoke to had any interest in the poll results and political strategies that so absorbed the professional political class; on the other hand, certain words and phrases, and what the political consultants call "themes," were often on the voters' lips. When they said that Clinton lacked character, or that Dole was too old, or even that there were too many negative ads, they were repeating ideas that had been tirelessly reiterated on television, both in interviews with voters and by analysts. Comments to the effect that the candidates were tearing each other down too much and not "discussing the issues" enough were almost a litany among voters. Just as each candidate had a speech, complete with laugh lines, that he gave many times every day, the voters seemed to have developed a kind of very short campaign speech of their own.

Sometimes in my talks with voters the reflection of the television messages was uncannily exact. Evidently, the voters' reported disgust with the campaigns didn't prevent the campaign messages from getting through. (This fact is, of course, the reason for negative advertising.) How else were the voters to form their opinions? They had no private channels of information. Were they being brainwashed by the very techniques they despised? Had the new Leviathan attained by propaganda the control that older, cruder Leviathans achieved by force?

Such a conclusion overlooks at least one cardinal fact that stands at the very center of the political process today. Neither the campaigns nor the news media are free to spin their messages out of thin air. Quite the opposite. The entire apparatus is doggedly devoted to ascertaining and satisfying the desires of the voters. The candidates have long since learned that the path to power is far smoother if one gives the people what they already believe they want than if one undertakes the arduous business of persuading them to want something else. Instruments of the utmost refinement have been designed to detect the faintest ripple in the public mood. No news in a campaign season is more significant than the polls on candidates' standing with the voters. These numbers, indeed, have been the axis on which both the campaigns and coverage of them—and even, to an extent, the intentions of the voters themselves—have turned. First came opinion polls. Then focus groups. Now there is "deliberate polling" (polling done after the respondent has been given a chance to discuss an issue) and "push polling" (a deceptive campaign technique by which a caller pretends to be seeking opinions but is in fact covertly delivering negative information, real or factitious, about an opposition candidate). The analysis of exit polls has become an obsession among the professional political class. Like a team of interns examining a patient strapped to a hospital table, the political professionals have wired the electorate to examine every flutter and twitch of public opinion. Examination of the public mind has become so intrusive that in the early primaries, in which backlash against negative ads became a potent political force, the patient was crying out for relief—to have the cardiograph sensors removed, the intravenous tubes withdrawn. Sometimes it is said that Washington has lost contact with the people. If that's so, it is in spite of relentless, assiduous, hugely expensive state-of-the-art efforts to be *in* touch.

In that sense the new Leviathan is a very accommodating Leviathan, a very meek Leviathan, a very nice Leviathan.

Is it possible, then, that the brainwashing is going in the opposite direction—that the establishment, for all its wealth, fame, and seeming power, in fact slavishly dances to the tune of popular opinion? If so, the problem is not anti-democratic tendencies, not exploitation of the people by an arrogant elite, but hyper-democracy—a systematized obedience of the elite to every passing gust of public opinion. And yet although it's undeniable that campaign strategists and the press both are sniffing like bloodhounds for every change in existing opinion, it's also true that opinion is formed in an atmosphere permeated by the media. . . . Once, it may have been possible for a large popular movement to take shape in the hinterlands, unnoticed and uninfluenced by the established powers, whom it then arose to challenge. The Populist movement of the 1890s, regarded by many historians as an insurrection by common people, mostly in rural areas, against the rising power of big business and big finance, was such a movement. Today, however, the first flicker of change in the popular mood shows up instantly on the pollsters' charts, and becomes the subject of immediate nonstop discussion on ABC's "Nightline," CNN's "Inside Politics," PBS's "Washington Week in Review," and so forth. Neither the news analysts nor the campaign strategists have the will or the capacity to do anything as ambitious as engineer public opinion, and certainly the last thing they'd want to do is to defy it. But they can and do detect changes that are under way, and they rapidly and gigantically inflate them, usually without meaning to. Almost any tendency that sprouts in this political incubator is subjected, like a bacterium in a petri dish, to a forced acceleration in growth. The day-to-day results of this process are the instant orthodoxies, highly perishable but ubiquitous, that spring up each week and become for their brief life the stock phrases of political discussion. Passed swiftly from commentator to commentator, and from the commentators to the public, they are more than mere phrases yet not quite ideas. All discourse needs a vocabulary. The ever-changing vocabulary of American politics is born in the loop that links voters to pollsters, poll results to television ads and commentary, and television ads and commentary back to voters.

All of that, however, leaves a large question unanswered. If "Washington"—the class of professional political participants—seeks nothing more assiduously than to please the voters, why do the voters feel so estranged from and dissatisfied with Washington? Why do so many people regard politicians as distant and indifferent autocrats, bent on thwarting or even subverting the will of the people? Why did eyes glow when Steve Forbes spoke of the "corrupt Washington establishment"? Why were Patrick Buchanan's legions hoarse with enthusiasm when he promised to overthrow the "New World Order," and why have so many polls shown that a majority of the voters wish that someone other than the present candidates were running?

The complaint that politicians tailor their views to match poll results was one I heard often, especially regarding Dole and Clinton, each an epitome of the "inside politician" whom voters distrust so much. Yet it might seem strange that the voters would be displeased that a politician goes to extravagant lengths to find out what they want and to give it to them. Don't the voters believe their own words when they say they want politicians to be in touch with the people? One answer, certainly, is that they have learned that politicians do not keep their promises. The unfulfilled promises of candidate George Bush not to raise taxes and of candidate Bill Clinton to cut them are only two notable examples. Another reason is that the voters sense that the systematic pursuit of agreement with public opinion undermines politicians' integrity, which can be defined as acting according to one's *own* beliefs, not those of others—even if the others are a majority. For example, in 1992, when, in a tour de force of public relations Clinton "repositioned" the Democrats as New Democrats, no one doubted that the prime motive was to bring the Democratic Party back into the "mainstream"—to where the votes are. It was "Slick Willie's" slickest performance by far, and the voters rewarded him for it with the presidency. Likewise, no one can doubt that in the primary season, when Bob Dole had to take into account only Republican voters, he moved sharply to the right, whereas after the primaries, when he faced the electorate at large, he began to move back to the center. Nor can anyone imagine that when Clinton, following the advice of the pollster Dick Morris, who has worked for many Republicans, announced in his State of the Union address that "the era of big government" was over, he was not acting politically. The candidates have discovered that the royal road to high station is self-abasement. The public is left in confusion and ambivalence. On the one hand, it is appreciative that the candidates agree with it. On the other hand, it feels disgusted that these same candidates have tailored their views to serve their ambition. The candidates calculate that the voters will be more pleased with a popular view than disgusted with an unprincipled performance—and so they usually have been. Yet the voters are left longing for a person of integrity—a longing that for many has been satisfied, however temporarily, by a Ross Perot, a Colin Powell, a Steve Forbes, a Patrick Buchanan ("I mean what I say, and I say what I mean"), or some other "outsider" supposedly untainted by the ways of Washington culture. The truth appears to be that the tainted ways are not only Washington's but America's, and they involve the voters as well as the politicians.

A second reason that the voters may come to despise the representatives they have chosen is more complex. When I asked one New Hampshire voter for his opinion of Newt Gingrich and his revolution, he answered, "At first he impressed the hell out of me. He promised to cut waste and balance the budget, and I liked that. But—I don't know—I guess he oversold it. He's just lost all credibility with me. I can't put my thumb on it, but when I look at him now, I see a sick politician. He overshot—went right through the tube and out the other side." In other words, Gingrich had been corrupted by the Washington culture he supposedly sought to reform. However, another interpretation is possible. Gingrich became speaker of the House promising, above all, to balance the budget and to cut taxes—perhaps the two most important promises in his Contract With America. There was nothing in the contract about cutting Medicare and Medicaid. But when it came time to make good on the promises, it turned out that cuts in those two programs would be necessary. Only in the land of promises could the budget be balanced without cutting them.

In one interpretation a politician has gone to Washington promising reform and has been corrupted by the Washington culture, disappointing his supporters. In the other interpretation the candidate has made popular promises of reform that were either self-deluding or deceptive, and has been blocked by obdurate realities. In the first case the fault lies with a rotten, seductive establishment. In the second it is a *folie à deux* of the candidate and the voters. And nothing, indeed, is so easy as such collusion in a system that eagerly vacuums up the voters' every opinion, whether well or ill founded, and then broadcasts it back to them with music in millions of dollars' worth of thirty-second ads. The problem, then, is not that the politicians have lost touch with voters but that both groups have lost touch with reality.

When reporters seek to interview voters, they naturally prefer people who are interested in the campaign and have clear views on the issues of the day. But the plain truth is that such people are a minority. For one thing, most people don't vote in primaries. A typical turnout is roughly 10 percent of the voting-age population. In the past decade almost half of eligible voters have been staying home even in general elections. The views of these nonvoters, or lack of such, are, for obvious reasons, underreported. Pollsters often try to gauge how the nonvoters *would* have voted had they bothered. But the more significant fact is precisely that they didn't vote—that they were indifferent. Everywhere I have gone I have met these people. Our conversations tended to be short. Again and again I heard the self-justifying refrains: "Why bother? It makes no difference." "All the politicians are the same." "They never do anything anyway."

It's possible, of course, that these people are ravenous for more serious discussion of the issues, as so many of those willing to give a brief interview claim, but it's also possible that for one reason or another they simply have not bothered to inform themselves about the campaign, and that their anger to some extent masks ignorance. The decline of the intermediate institutions—political parties, trade unions, civic associations, and so forth—has dissolved many of the links that once existed between citizens and the electoral process. But hasn't the arrival of the information age more than made good the loss? Don't citizens now get from television or talk radio or the Internet or any of the other proliferating media of our time the information they once got from the precinct captain, union officials, and the like? Surveys suggest not. It's a paradox of our time that the increase in information has been paralleled by an increase in ignorance. We may live in an information age, but that information, it appears, resides elsewhere than in the minds of citizens—as if while computers were being stuffed with information, brains were emptying. One reason, surely, is that even as information is more readily available than ever, it is also more easily avoided. It's easier not to read a newspaper or watch "Nightline" than it was to avoid a visit by a union organizer or a precinct captain. It's remarkable, in fact, how easy it is in the United States today to lead a life undisturbed by politics. I often asked people if they were given to discussing politics. A common answer was the old saying that they never talked about religion or politics.

In a world in which both daily life and daily conversation are largely devoid of politics, the politics that survives takes the form of a schoolroom, in which the political professionals, in the campaigns and the media, are purveying information that the voters are supposed to absorb. But adults are hardly more fond of school than schoolchildren are, and these classrooms are noncompulsory. Depoliticization is as simple as changing the channel from C-SPAN to Fox5. In these circumstances, when armies of reporters push microphones in voters' faces, they are likely to be received like teachers asking reluctant students questions about homework they have not done.

Even among those in the spectator class who choose to keep watching, there are many in whom the pulse of interest in politics is weak. Such was the case with a voter in New Hampshire whom

I'll call Dave. He described himself as a part-time farmer. I asked him what he thought of the candidates, and he said, "Oh, they all say different things at different times." Then he fell silent. Later he said of Dole, "He does have the experience. But he's too much of a typical Washington politician. There's been some comment on his age." Of Forbes: "He's come up with a different idea. I'll give him that. But I don't necessarily agree with it. By the time Congress got done with it, it wouldn't come out the way he says." Of Lamar Alexander: "He looks like a class act. He says he's different. Whether that's good or not, I'm not so sure. And I'm not sure how different he is."

Listening to Dave, I experienced a moment of irritation. As a journalist, I am conditioned to challenge the statements of politicians. Indeed, a readiness to find the utterances of the powerful absurd or contemptible has become almost a qualification for the job of journalist. The statements of voters, on the other hand, are usually received with near reverence. And yet the fact is that in the American system the voters, too, are powerful—they are the ultimate power in the land. What good is a system in which all the subordinate powers are rigorously held accountable but the sovereign is above criticism? Perhaps, I thought, I should lean forward aggressively and, Sam Donaldson-like, fire "tough" questions at him. For instance: "Dave, you said, with apparent approval, that Dole has 'experience.' But then you complained that he is a 'Washington politician.' How could he have gotten that experience without being a Washington politician?"

Or: "If you don't agree with Forbes's one idea—and I assume you mean the flat tax—then why should you care that in the event that Forbes becomes President, Congress might gut it? You should be glad."

Or: "Well, Dave, is Alexander different or not? You're going to be deciding in a few days whether he's the Republican nominee for President of the United States. Don't you think you should know by now? Your're the King. Don't you think you should take your responsibilities a little more seriously?"

In fact I engaged in no such ill-mannered inquisition of Dave, who had been kind enough to let me, a stranger, intrude on his breakfast. The mind of Dave was the target of all the high-powered manipulations I had seen in the media and on the campaign trail. The polling and the push polling, the focus groups, the exit polling, the negative ads and the positive ads, the satellite feeds, the discussion programs, the sound bites on the news programs, were all aimed at either fathoming or directing the vague trend of his thoughts, in the hope that some current taking shape there and in the thoughts of others like him would furnish a glide path to power.

"The voters are not fools," the renowned scholar of elections V. O. Key wrote in *The Responsible Electorate* (1966). But whether stupid or smart, they have become by the mid-1990s more strangers to the political system than participants in it. Isn't there something grotesquely unbalanced, even farcical, about a system in which tens of thousands of highly paid, highly trained, hyperactive, technically over-equipped professional courtiers are trying with all the vast means of modern communications to provoke a response from a sovereign who is at best half asleep with boredom and at worst turned wholly away in an angry sulk?

In civics texts American democracy renews itself according to something like the following procedure: As time passes, the nation experiences new problems. Candidates for public office ponder the problems and propose legislative plans to deal with them. Because political philosophies and analyses of the problems differ, the public is presented with a number of alternative programs. Then the public goes to the polls, chooses the candidates it thinks best, and sends them to Washington. Now they are the people's representatives. Therefore, when they enact the programs they have proposed, the people are ready to pay whatever costs are involved—in taxes, for example, or even, in the case of war, in lives. That is what it means to confer a popular mandate. Then comes the test of reality. Either the plans solve the problems or they do not. If they do, the representatives may well be re-elected; if not, they are likely to lose their offices, and new representatives, proposing different programs, will be elected.

It's perfectly obvious that in recent years the political system has not operated according to this procedure. New problems have arisen, as always, but now the candidates, instead of pondering them and asking what needs to be done to solve them, are likely to read polling data to discover what the people would like to see done. Yet most people probably have not thought deeply about the problems, and their answers are likely to reflect casual wishes instead of serious proposals. When the wishes are granted, they bring unwanted consequences.

The long story of the budget deficit offers the best example. Polls have for many years shown that the public wishes to balance the budget but does not wish to pay more taxes or endure steep cuts in government spending. In the realm of reality it's not possible to balance the budget without raising taxes or cutting spending. However, modern campaigns have at their disposal a richly variegated, compelling alternative to reality: the pseudo-reality of television, in which the feat can be accomplished several times a day. . . . Reality, though unconsulted, nevertheless imposes its price, and the bill has to be presented. Then a startled public feels either betrayed (as it did when Bush broke his no-taxes pledge and when Clinton failed to deliver the tax cut he had promised) or aggrieved (as it did when Gingrich revealed the spending cuts that would pay for his balanced budget and tax cuts). Either way, faith in the political process is undermined, and paralysis is the result. The public reacts angrily—a fact immediately registered by the polls and the media—and quickly steps in to punish the betrayer, as it did Clinton by turning both houses of Congress over to the Republicans in 1994, and as it did Gingrich when, reacting even more promptly, it stopped the hated legislation from being passed.

Hence, whereas in the civics texts representatives are at least given a chance to carry out what they have promised to do in the election, and then are judged by the results, action today is short-circuited before it can be tried, and the test of reality never comes at all. Technically, the system appears to be in working order. Candidates are running, voters are voting, representatives are being sent to Washington. No one seems to interfere at any point. And yet no mandate is produced, and, usually, no legislation either. The government—if not actually shut down, as it was this winter—is paralyzed.

Paralysis, of course, breeds disillusionment with "Washington" and "the politicians." The politicians have been sent to Washington to solve problems. Why don't they do so? Why don't they put their heads under the hood of the car, as Ross Perot said he would do, and fix the engine? And why vote if the politicians never do anything? The conclusion the voters draw is that at the center of a sound and healthy country the Washington culture must somehow have grown corrupt, as Steve Forbes said. Or perhaps the government has forgotten its responsibility to the people of the United States, as Buchanan says, and now serves an unaccountable New World Order that he would bring "crashing down" the day he took office. Instead of being the people's instrument for the solution of their problems, the government appears to be the problem.

Thus arises the whole pathos of the "outsider." The problem, it now appears, is a group of "insiders," and the solution is one outsider or another. But where is it that the outsiders wish to go if they are chosen? To that same corrupt Washington, where there is every likelihood that they will become insiders, and need replacing in turn. The Populists of the 1890s believed that the representatives in Washington had been taken over by powerful economic interests—the Money Power. They did not imagine that the people's representatives had gratuitously and independently subverted the purposes of democratic government—that the elected representatives all by themselves were the source of corruption. This belief was reserved for our time. It is the premise, for example, of one of the favorite tenets of the outsider faith: term limits. The belief that there is a need for a means other than elections for throwing the scoundrels out contains an implicit denial that it was the country at large that sent the scoundrels to Washington in the first place. The voters who attribute all the country's ills to the government in fact pay that institution an unintended compliment. They attribute to Washington ills that are in fact mostly created by history—by the collapse of the Soviet Union, the rise of the global economy, the arrival of the information age, the fraying of the natural environment.

To the extent that the electorate is in the grip of these ideas, it is not surprising that voters' behavior veers wildly. It is tempting to see the shifts of the nineties as a speeded-up version of a normal seesawing between right and left. A better metaphor, however, would be a pendulum with a wrecking ball at the end. For each time the public tries something out—now swinging right, now left—and is disillusioned, another piece of its confidence in politics as a whole is knocked down. In this atmosphere only negative enthusiasm remains possible. It's small wonder, then, that campaigns should revolve around negative ads, for the public can agree only on what it dislikes, not on what it likes or wants to see done. Nor should the fact that negative ads were so unpopular early in the campaign season be seen as very encouraging. From time to time a candidate will try to fuel his campaign with attacks on negative ads. But in politics, if not in math, the negative of a negative is not a positive—it's another negative. In fact, the unpopularity of negative ads only announces a deeper vacuum.

"As our case is new, so we must think anew and act anew," Abraham Lincoln said. Today our case is again new, but our thoughts are stale. We have lost the very framework in which political life in the Cold War years unfolded, but scant effort is being made to fashion another. The principal reason, it would appear, is that the electoral system, instead of offering new ideas suitable to the time, devotes the amazing new instruments of the information age to discovering what the public already believes and offering that. And even these offers are not honest, because only their benefits and not their costs are advertised at election time. The procedure is a formula for stagnation. In times when change is modest and slow (if such times can still be imagined), the disadvantages of the system are perhaps not great. But when, as at present, change is swift, deep, and fundamental, the gap between political practice and the world becomes dangerously wide. Then events race out ahead of thought and word, which stumble blindly behind in a world they cannot comprehend.

The public as a whole can be expected to feel the need for profound renewal but not to be the creator of the ideas that will build the new framework. Dave, for one, seems unlikely to come up with the necessary ideas, but democracy depends on the conviction that he is the best judge of ideas that others bring forward. The job of proposing at these times has always been the work of a minority—whether elite, as at the Constitutional Convention or in government councils at the onset of the Cold War, or popular, as in the civil-rights movement of the 1960s—while the job of disposing has been the work of all.

Supply-side economics proposed the idea that the strength of the economy depends as much on the vitality of what is created by business and offered to the consumer as it does on the consumer's demand. Whether or not the theory was sound as economics, it appears that we now need what could be called supply-side politics. Supply-side politics would pay more attention to offering ideas of adequate strength and vitality to the public than to discovering what the public already believes it wants. Now a whole new framework for political life is needed. A framework can be built only by imagination and perseverance. It requires looking less at focus groups and exit polls and more at the nation's and the world's problems. Above all, it requires that individuals, political parties, and public institutions develop the fortitude to hold fast to new convictions, even in the face of initial unpopularity and rejection. If no serious proposals are put forward, the voters' choices lose their meaning, and public opinion turns to mush.

The calm that has descended on 1996 as the election approaches should not be mistaken for the calm of contentment and stability. The public's inchoate but well-justified hunger for a new politics to fit the new age goes unfulfilled. The fact that frustration and anger have found no adequate voice does not mean that they have evaporated. The old parties and their associated ideas are built on a foundation that history has swept away. The voters, disappointed and resigned, have settled for the known faces, the known ideas. It's hard to believe that they will settle for them for long.

SEPTEMBER 1, 1996

A SENTIMENTAL EDUCATION

TODAY'S POLITICAL CONVENTIONS —A HISTORICALLY accidental, and probably temporary, hybrid in which the ghosts of the genuine nominating assemblies of the past have overlapped with the rise of the modern media—have become unprecedented festivals of political propaganda. Tens of thousands of people from the worlds of journalism and politics have assembled with no purpose but to either purvey or "cover" (a distinction that gets harder and harder to draw) a political message, or, as the Communists used to say, a political line.

The techniques are scarcely less shameless, though incomparably more subtly contrived, than those famously employed in the late totalitarian regimes of Europe and Russia. Consider, to give just one example, the fate at the Republican convention of Bob Dole's first wife, Phyllis. The elaborate presentation of Dole's life—supposedly a revelation of his heretofore concealed "soul"—proceeded without a single mention of her. His and her daughter, Robin, praised her father without any mention of her mother.

Strangest of all, Dole's second and current wife, Liddy, in her celebrated descent from the podium into the audience, met and warmly embraced the widow of the doctor who had helped Dole recover from his war wounds when he was married to his first wife. For a moment, it seemed that Liddy, not Phyllis, had helped Dole recover from his wounds in the late 1940s. Phyllis was erased from the Republican version of Dole's life as thoroughly as purged Soviets bigwigs once were airbrushed out of the photos of Soviet leaders perched atop the Kremlin wall.

More disturbing than the parties' propaganda, however, is the press's acceptance of the new techniques. Before the convention in San Diego, the conventional wisdom was that Dole's challenge at the convention was to "define himself." Only in our day, it seems fair to say, is it thinkable to ask a 73-year-old man who has spent nearly 40 years of those years in public life to recreate himself in three days.

There has been no reduction in manipulation here at the Democratic convention. If anything, the Democrats have become greater masters of the propaganda arts than the Republicans. Well aware that a newsless convention nominating a sitting president was unlikely to attract viewers, the Clinton campaign contrived Clinton's train trip from West Virginia to Chicago, creating the artificial "story" of a beloved leader approaching from afar to greet his adoring followers. It was a technique first used in Leni Riefenstal's classic propaganda film "The Triumph of the Will," in which Hitler was shown flying across Germany to the great rally of his followers at Nuremburg. In the Clinton version of the familiar device, ordinary citizens as well as sycophantic politicians were shown at the convention offering their gratitude to Clinton. "Thank you, President Clinton, for myself and for all the young people like me who are getting a chance to serve their country," said a young woman in Ameri-Corps, the social service program founded by Clinton. "Today, my family owns a new minivan. . . . Thank you, Mr. President, for helping millions of families like me," said an auto-worker who had lost her job and got it back.

Meanwhile, videos of Clinton were shown, "1984" style, on the giant screen above the podium. "What a treat it is!" simpered the master of ceremonies after one such video. Another video, produced by the Democratic National Committee and shown on the night of Clinton's acceptance speech, consisted largely of a montage of playful and tender moments in the Clintons' marriage. The producer of the video, Linda Bloodworth-Thomasson, asked by Maria Shriver of NBC News what the point was, answered that it showed the First Couple as "two people in love."

Of course, none of those who failed to join in the chorus of praise to the great leader was shot or sent to a concentration camp, and it would be ridiculous to liken Bob Dole or Bill Clinton to Stalin and Hitler. But this much, at least, was the same: The goal was getting or keeping power, and the means was unrelenting manipulation of people's thoughts and feelings.

One great saving grace in today's United States, a free country, is the right *not* to listen—the mind's first line of defense against mental insult and assault. It is a sign of the health of the American public—not of disgraceful apathy—that in record numbers it has tuned out the conventions in favor of entertainment.

It's in this context of tireless, carefully researched, deeply calculated manipulation that the most salient single technique of all the conventions, including the Reform Party convention, must be considered. This is the use of the crippled, the sick and the lately deceased for political effect.

Vice President Al Gore may well have opened the sluice-gates for this technique at the Democratic convention in 1992 when he described at length his grief over his son's serious injury in a car accident. (He repeated the performance this year with his description of his sister on her death-bed from lung cancer, presumed to have been caused by smoking.) At San Diego, the Republicans brought forward Nancy Reagan to stand in for former President Ronald Reagan, who suffers from Alzheimer's disease; a New York policeman whose spinal cord had been severed by a gunshot wound in the line of duty; and Miss Wheelchair America. At the Reform Party convention, fulsome tributes were paid to Ross Perot by a Vietnamese soldier who had aided American prisoners of war (whose agonies were described) and by a track-runner born without feet (he set a world record in the hundred-yard dash even as the convention met).

The Democrats, if anything, outdid these displays with what amounted to a full prime-time evening of presentations from wheelchairs: by Sarah Brady and her husband James Brady, the former press secretary to President Reagan who was crippled in the attack on the president's life, and by Christopher Reeve, the actor who played Superman in the movies and was crippled when he was thrown from a horse.

It is just because it is heartless to breathe any adverse word of criticism in the presence of serious individual suffering that its exploitation is not merely manipulative but almost coercive. Hence, in even raising questions about the practice, it's important to sharply draw the distinction between the suffering, which deserves respect and sympathy, and its political use, which does not. The important question from a political point of view is why, in 1996, all three of the largest political parties have traded so extensively in personal tragedy. It's certainly true, as many observers have pointed out, that the public's general boredom and disgust with politicians has forced them to turn to others to win the public's esteem.

But why, in this year, choose the terribly afflicted? The convention's response to one line in Reeve's appeal for more funds for medical research may hold the clue. His speech was warmly and sympathetically received, but the only standing ovation came at a moment in which he did not refer explicitly to physical injury. It came when he said, "America does not let its needy citizens fend for themselves." The crippled are certainly needy, yet the words "the needy" normally refer more specifically to the poor.

It was quite clear that Reeve was making an oblique, subversive commentary on the recent welfare "reform" bill, which ends the federal government's commitment to support families with dependent children. Clinton, a faithful defender of government programs for the middle classes, including the medical programs and social security, left the poor defenseless. Through its ovation for Reeve's comment the delegates showed their dissatisfaction.

The bill, probably the most important national decision of the Clinton years, was passed by a Republican Congress and signed into law by Clinton. The Reform Party has made no protest. In his acceptance speech, Clinton seemed almost indignant when he called for Congress and others to supply work for those required by the bill to go to work, as if someone else had ended welfare and now had to take responsibility for their actions. But it had not been someone else; it had been he who had signed the bill into law.

In a word, all three of the largest political parties have either supported or acquiesced in the severest blow delivered by the government to the poor in America in this century. In the mainstream of American politics, the poorest were without a voice. The buckets of tears being shed for the few spotlit on stage were blinding the weepers to the large-scale harm they were doing to millions. It's not the first time that brutality has been concealed by sentimentality.

SEPTEMBER 22, 1996

WHERE THEY STAND

NEITHER OF THE TWO MAJOR CANDIDATES FOR president stands for anything.

Now that the conventions are behind us and the election approaches, let us examine the truth of this proposition. Certainly, President Bill Clinton and Bob Dole have principles. The question, though, is whether they have any they would be unwilling to sacrifice to win the election.

And if not, what does this mean about politics in our country today? In a remarkably symmetrical display, each man prepared for his party's convention with a bold act that required abdication of a deeply held principle. In Clinton's case, that act was his signing of the Republican welfare bill, which ends the federal guarantee of income to families with dependent children, and the principle was the obligation of the government to provide assistance to the poorest among us. In Dole's case, the act was his proposal to cut taxes by fifteen percent without specifying cuts in spending, and the principle was the fiscal soundness of the federal government.

The point here is not that these policies are wrong (although I happen to think that both are) but that it is impossible to believe that they were adopted for any reason other than getting elected. The crisis, in other words, is not so much one of policy as one of integrity.

Just in case we failed to notice the pattern of abdication, the two running-mates repeated the performance on a lesser, presumably vice-presidential scale. Dole's vice-presidential choice Jack

Kemp, previously an impassioned spokesman for affirmative action, reversed his view a few days after his nomination. Vice-President Al Gore brought tears to the eyes of the Democrats at their convention by describing how his sister's death from cancer had turned him against smoking. But subsequently it had turned out that he had not only smoked himself after her death but grown tobacco and, what is more, bragged to the public about it. "I've hoed it, I've chopped it, I've shredded it, spiked it, put it in the barn, stripped it, and sold it," he had said. Gore's conversion, admittedly, was perhaps not so much an abdication of principle as merely a flip-flop. The precipitating event, it would appear, was not his sister's death but the emergence of the anti-smoking cause as a political opportunity.

Clinton's abdication is especially significant. Poverty has never been an incidental political issue—on the order, say, of regulating the Internet or forcing high-school students to wear uniforms. It is one of the fundamental, abiding issues of political life—an issue that is coeval with politics but also stands at the center of moral and spiritual teaching. The Bible's great prophetic exhortations to serve the needy, no matter how much ignored, remain one of the touchstones of Western civilization. The Democratic Party is the major party for which this tradition has the greatest importance. This is not because Democrats are more compassionate as individuals than Republicans but because they have argued that government, in the last analysis, bears responsibility for addressing poverty.

The end of the Cold War and the global triumph of the free market have posed the question with new insistence. Communism had boasted of its dedication to the poor—their good, in fact, was almost its *raison d'etre*. Now communism has collapsed. Less noticed but also significant has been the all-but universal retreat of mere socialism—non-communist "social" (that is, state) ownership of some or all of the means of production. That leaves only the welfare state—the idea that a governmental "safety net" for the poor should be stretched beneath the market's high-wire act. Now was even this to be yanked away? Were there—as some on the right had always claimed—some invisible lines of connection between the Soviet Union in the East and the welfare state in the West? And now that the one had collapsed, must the other, too? Were the poor now to be absolutely on their own?

It's noteworthy that the most important organization here that now supports the federal welfare guarantee is far older than any political party. It is the Catholic church, whose American bishops have spoken out passionately against the bi-partisan abandonment of the poor. Now that the political expression of the moral obligation to the poor is being cleared away, we reach the spiritual bedrock that may have always underlain this sense of obligation in the first place. Where politics has defaulted, faith has stepped in.

The Republicans, of course, hold in essence that a combination of the unconstrained working of the free market, individual effort, and individual charity are the best remedies of poverty. When Rep. E. Clay Shaw Jr. (R-Fla.) says that the end of the federal guarantee is "independence day" for the poor "trapped" in the welfare system, we may find this paradoxical, but it is not hypocritical.

With Democrats, it is otherwise. They abandon the poor only at the cost of their political souls. "But," they answer us, "when we stood fast for Social Security and the medical programs while the Republican Congress tried to eviscerate them—weren't we faithful to our conviction in this, at least? "You were," the answer must come, "but only when such programs serve the populous, vote-rich middle-class."

The administration might point, with better justification, to another achievement. At the beginning of his term, Clinton put through a tax increase that has contributed to an undoubted success: his halving of the budget deficit. Moreover, the Democratic Party paid in hard political coin to pass the increase, for which no Republicans voted. The price paid by Democratic representatives and senators was their loss in 1994 of both houses. If there has been a profile in courage in the Clinton years, this extremely conservative achievement was it. We must note, however, that the tax burden was placed overwhelmingly on the shoulders of tax-payers who earned $200,000 a year. In other words, the middle-class was spared. If we put this together with Clinton's record in his last two years, a political strategy emerges: Cater to the middle-class, where the votes are, at the expense of the rich, who are few, and the poor, who are many but tend not to vote.

In a candid moment on the eve of signing the bill, Clinton alluded to the underlying political realities. "When I sign my name to this bill," he said, "welfare will no longer be a political issue. The two parties cannot attack each other over it. The politicians cannot attack poor people over it." Left unsaid, of course, was the central proposition that the Republicans could no longer attack *him* over it. At the convention, Clinton challenged the Congress and businesses to provide jobs for the poor people that the bill will dispossess. It was as if one were to push someone off a building, and then loudly call out to everyone else to rush forward with a net to catch the falling person.

It's a performance that has left the Congressional leadership and the rank-and-file of the Democratic Party uneasy at best, sickened at worst. The sulfurous odor of a Faustian bargain hung over the Chicago convention. The party's "liberal" wing bit its tongue. Former Gov. Mario Cuomo and the Rev. Jesse Jackson registered their disquiet but supported the president. The surface was calm, but it was the calm of an underground nuclear test. A muffled explosion had taken place in the realm of hearts and minds. For now, the calculations were all working out as hoped, and Clinton was holding his lead over Dole, but at a terrible inner cost, whose consequences are bound to come to the surface sooner or later. The Democrats, not the Republicans, are the party of bad conscience this year.

Dole's abdication, upon examination, turns out to be a Republican companion piece to Clinton's. Until just recently, Dole had always been a fiscal conservative. That is, he has always stood for the principle that the government must pay for what it spends. For most of this century, this principle was one of the most durable of the rock-ribs of what people used to call "rock-ribbed Republicans." Then, with the presidency of Ronald Reagan, came the siren song of supply-side economics, teaching that cuts in taxes could so revivify the economy that tax revenues gathered on the greater production would actually increase. . . .

Dole, however, held fast to the traditional Republican principles of fiscal integrity. He shunned and mocked supply-side delirium. This led him to cooperate in the Senate, where he served as minority leader, with Democratic colleagues in passing several very large tax increases, earning a rebellion against him in his own party and the epithet "tax-collector for the welfare state" from Rep. Newt Gingrich. It was a low-key performance, as principled as it was pragmatic—a victory of common sense over ideological nonsense. This was the record that Dole turned his back on when he embraced the fifteen percent tax cut without setting forth comparable spending reductions. The choice of Kemp—one of the most fervent believers in supply-side economics in the country—reinforced Dole's reversal. But it remained impossible to accept that Dole believed in the supply-side gospel any more than Clinton believed in canceling the federal commitment to families with dependent children.

However, one difference between the two measures works to the disadvantage of Dole. Canceling welfare has never been tried; therefore its consequences in the real world are unknown. Supply-side economics, however, was tried some twelve years ago, and the resulting four-trillion-dollar debt and chronic budget deficit is known to all. When, a decade or so from now, the consequences of the welfare cut-off are also matters of experience—when, for instance, children are begging in the streets of our cities—that policy may be met with as much skepticism as Dole's tax cut now is. But for the time being the lessons of experience are available only to discredit Dole's bold abdication, not Clinton's.

The conventions were footnotes to the two abdications on which the campaigns are now based (though Dole, finding his tax proposals unpopular, now seems to be casting about in desperation for something else to talk about). If the "nominating" conventions any longer have a purpose, it is to disclose the philosophies and intentions of the two parties to the voters. But the conventions in San Diego and Chicago were devoted instead to concealment, obfuscation, and erasure. All views of Republicans on abortion, whether pro or con, were banned from prime time by the Dole campaign. The Gingrich "revolution" was dispatched down the same memory hole, and Gingrich himself reduced to brief, barely comprehensible remarks about beach volleyball. Only the party's platform gave voice to some of the rank-and-file's views; but Dole claimed he hadn't read the document. Obviously, he disagreed with it. But then he probably disagreed with his own newly professed views on taxes. If the Democrats were the party of bad conscience, then the Republicans were the party of insincerity.

Can we at least expect the two candidates to challenge the

flaws in the proposal of the other? This, too, is doubtful. The Republicans cannot challenge Clinton's signing of the welfare bill; they are its authors. Clinton does accuse Dole of promising tax cuts the government can't afford, but a new Clinton ad completely muddies even this issue by accusing Dole of having *raised* taxes. In other words, they hold Dole's most responsible actions against him, meanwhile leaving unmentioned Clinton's greatest contribution to the economy, which was also a tax increase. These ads are so much dust kicked in the eyes of voters. This year, it turns out the way to seek high office is to attack the other fellow's virtues while hiding your own.

Behind the fog of propaganda that governs both campaigns lurks a surprisingly simple and crude proposition. It is: Give the majority of voters—that is to say, the middle class—some money and they will vote for us. Clinton gives it in the form of medical benefits, Social Security, educational tax credits and the like, meanwhile slashing federal services to the poor and raising taxes on the rich. Clinton has cleverly redrawn the lines of class warfare. No longer is the contest simply between the rich and the poor. Rather, he pits the middle class against both the rich and poor, who, for their part, have no common interest. By taxing the rich, he spares the middle class tax increases. By jettisoning the poor, he wards off what previously were highly effective Republican accusations that he was taking the money of hard-working middle-class people to subsidize "welfare queens." Such is the shape of class warfare in the 1990s.

Meanwhile, Clinton conceals the crisis of middle-class entitlements that is the real, long-term threat to the fiscal integrity of the federal government. And he forgets to tell the beneficiaries that their benefits will be paid for by dollars pulled out of their own pockets by the IRS. Dole hands out the money in the even simpler form of a tax cut, even totalling up the sums for simple-minded voters. He forgets to tell them that their gains, if they materialize at all, will be paid for in reduced medical care and Social Security, for themselves and their children.

In this new political world, the rich, though slightly endangered by Clinton's tax policies, can defend their interests through campaign contributions. The poor, until they decide to vote, are out of luck altogether.

OCTOBER 20, 1996

AD NAUSEUM

FOR THE LAST MONTH OR SO, THE QUESTION AGITATING the political professionals in and out of the news media has been whether or not Bob Dole would "go negative"—to use the new jargon phrase for the decision to opt for overall nastiness and bad manners. The answer came in San Diego in the debate between Dole and Bill Clinton. It was in the affirmative, but the effect was distinctly muted. The voters questioning the two candidates showed no interest in either man's opinion of the character of the other. In the circumstances, Dole's attack seemed not so much to fail as never to get off the ground. Dole's putative "last chance" was over, and we were left with three more weeks of the daily fare of presidential campaigns, which is to say that we were left with political ads.

Certain tacit rules and customs seem to have developed regarding political ads. They must not be flatly false or inaccurate.

(It's fine, though, if a series of technical truths is made to add up to a *de facto* lie.) They must not simulate events. Every now and then, someone breaks one of these rules, and is slapped down by the other candidate or by ad monitors in the press and in the universities.

For example, when Bob Zimmer, who is running for the Senate in New Jersey, ran an ad simulating a newscast "reporting" the misdeeds of his opponent, a small hue and cry was raised. A bigger hue and cry was raised when an advertisement for the Republican candidate for Senate from Virginia, John Warner, employed computer graphics to stick the head of his opponent, Mark Warner, on the body of another man, who was shaking hands with Clinton and the unpopular former Virginia Gov. Douglas Wilder. These practices bent or broke the tacit rules. There also has been in effect a sort of collective frown of disapproval at so-called "negative" ads, although the definition of what is "negative" is anything but clear. Whatever it is, most candidates routinely deny that their ads are "negative."

What, then, is in these ads? Of what stuff are they made? Is it "positive" or "negative"? Let's look at one. Since we're doing this in print, we can take longer than the thirty seconds it requires to watch the ad. We can pause to scrutinize, even to think.

A voice speaks. We know this voice. It is the deep, "warm," roughened male voice, at once intimate and intimidating, that, in regular commercials, tells us that we really deserve the more expensive brand of whiskey or should repose our trust in this or that brokerage firm. Soothing nondescript music, somewhere between classical and folk, is heard. But now the voice, dwelling lovingly on each syllable, announces, "American Values." The words appear in print on the screen.

We see a youngish couple with a child, dressed in L.L. Bean-ish clothes, walking in the countryside. The man passes the child to the woman. And now the voice says, "Duty to our parents," and we see the young woman handing the child to a grandmother-like woman who appears to be in a hospital. The word "duty" appears on the screen. "President Clinton protects Medicare," says the voice, while we see—but do not hear—Clinton giving a speech with a Marine honor guard lined up behind him. All that we have seen, so far—a sort of mini-saga of life and death in America, with the president associated with life, has taken five seconds.

But then suddenly all the color is drained out of the world, and everything is black and white. We seem to be in a sort of underworld, a sort of Hades. The music—if you can call it music any longer—has changed, too. It is a deep, discordant groaning roar, as of bombers coming over the horizon. We are in the land of Republicans. We see a black-and-white House Speaker Newt Gingrich. He moves with a strange, jerky, slow, drunken-seeming motion, the way monsters moved in horror movies of the 1950s. And the voice, no longer warm, but now full of menace, refers to "Dole-Gingrich"—a composite sort of monster.

Gingrich's eyes are heavy-lidded and he is laughing. The voice says, "The Dole-Gingrich budget tried to cut Medicare by $270 billion." Once again, the spoken words are also written on the screen. We are too dull, it appears, to take in a message through our ears alone. We have to get it through sight at the same time. The words are typed across Gingrich's face; he has been grafitti-ed over—literally defaced. (Clinton had no writing on *his* face.)

But once again all changes. Color returns to the world, the music is harmonious, soothing, uplifting, and the male voice is warm and reassuring again. "The Oval Office," it says, simply, and the camera, which is panning slowly, shows that office. It seems that the Republican hell and its slow-motion monsters are only a dim and horrible memory.

It turns out, though, that we are not to be permitted this luxury. For just a moment later, a huge, sick-looking washed-out face of Bob Dole, bigger than the screen, all but blots out the pleasant view we have just been seeing. His lips are puckered, or pursed, as if he were trying to hold in false teeth. He is replaced by a newspaper headline, in which we can only read the word "patients." This in turn is replaced by a dim image of an old lady limping along with a walker in front of a bed. All of these images are superimposed on the agreeable Oval Office, producing a kind of visual seasickness. Each time the image changes, a violent sound, halfway between a ripping noise and a crash, is heard. The voice says, "If it were Bob Dole here, he would already have cut Medicare 270 billion dollars."

Now let's look at an ad by the opposing campaign. As it begins, we immediately recognize the surroundings. We are in the black-and-white Hades inhabited by clumsy, sick monsters. But look who inhabits Hades now! It is Clinton, whose drawn, weary features are seen on screen left. Our friend the seductive but bullying male voice is with us, too. And the very composer, it seems, who produced the groaning roar for the Democrats, has offered his talents to the Republicans as well. The voice is in its ominous mode. "The truth," it says. Republicans must think Americans are as slow-witted as Democrats do, for they, too, write on the screen almost everything the voice is saying. "The truth" appears, as if at the beginning of a philosophy course, all by itself against a black background. But the voice pronounces the word with an angry snarl, as if to say, "Your lying days are over." It goes on: "484 new spending proposals, costing us $432 billion in bigger government; a massive health-care bureaucracy." As the voice speaks, illustrations of each item on this litany appear on the right of Clinton. "Big spending proposals" is obviously a visual problem. How do you show that? The problem is feebly solved by showing a lot of people at desks. A lot is going on on the screen. Before each phrase uttered by the voice, the letters of the word FACT fly down on the screen one after another, like a flock of birds, and this is followed by the print rendering of the spoken phrases. In each phrase one word—for the second or so that it is on the screen—is written in blood red, and briefly expands on the screen, thus hammering in the already voiced and printed message with an additional technique.

More illustrations follow: "$2.5 million for alpine slides for Puerto Rico," "$76 million for midnight basketball" and, of course, "the largest tax increase in history." The word "largest," is the one that, self-illustrating, gets larger on the screen.

Next, the voice introduces Clinton with the words, "But Clinton says . . ." And now Clinton, who has been on screen all along, is heard and seen saying, "Yet I don't think that qualifies me as a closet liberal." The voice, in an aural counterpart of the grainy black-and-white footage, sounds as if it is coming over the phone or from the back of a cavern. The conclusion, of course both spoken and written, is: "The Real Bill Clinton? A real tax-and-spend liberal."

But what of full-color paradise? It makes a cameo appearance at the very end. A tiny postage-stamp-sized picture of a smiling Dole appears at the bottom right corner of the screen. It is in color.

Neither of these ads crosses the line of what is now considered impermissible in television advertisement. Neither would be flagged by the new breed of ad monitors. They are wholly typical of their genre, and it is for just this reason that they are of interest to us. Obviously, they take full advantage of commercial advertising techniques, but they also elaborate on these. For instance, they seem to rely on simultaneous use of hard sell and soft sell, in a sort of good-cop, bad-cop routine. On the one hand, they employ redundant means—voice, print, highlighting of print and other print-jugglery—to launch a frontal assault on the conscious mind, which is simply battered into remembering certain very simple and crude slogans. ("A real tax-and-spend liberal.") On the other hand, they seek to direct a profusion of uplifting or frightening images "below the radar" into the unconscious or semiconscious mind. (The grandmother receiving the child from its mother.) It's remarkable, upon examining these ads carefully, to see how much can be crammed into 30 seconds.

There are, we are assured, two major parties in the United States, the Democrats and the Republicans, and their philosophies, supposedly, differ sharply. And the overt messages of these ads, it is true, are as opposed as two armies engaged in combat. And yet these deliberately contrived and exaggerated differences are scarcely noticeable in the context of the remarkable sameness of method and tone. This sameness suggests that one mega-party presides over us. (Its candidate would be the composite "Clinton-Dole.") One plank of that party's platform, it appears, is that the American voters are of subnormal intelligence, and cannot grasp or even remember the simplest phrases unless, with the redundant means of the ads, it is, so to speak, branded on the cortex with a hot poker.

Another corollary plank is that the voters are susceptible only to seduction or bludgeoning—to the carrot or the stick—and never to reasonable and balanced information. A final plank is that the voters are moral children, inclined to divide the world into realms of dark and light similar to those in, say, the cartoon series "My Little Pony." The messages of this party do not so much demean rival candidates as they demean the public. Even the "positive" ads insult their viewers. They are all negative ads.

OCTOBER 27, 1996

THE PUBLIC'S VICTORIES

AS THIS YEAR'S VACUOUS, DISPIRITING, MANIPULATIVE, fundamentally dishonest presidential campaign drags to a close, let us take note of at least two good things that have happened. They have not occurred in the campaigns of either President Bill Clinton or Bob Dole. Rather, they have occurred among the public.

It's a significant fact that the press commentary on elections concentrates its criticism almost entirely on the candidates and rarely on the electorate. This seems curious when you stop to reflect that the decision-maker here—the CEO, so to speak, of the company—is the electorate, whom the candidates are merely petitioning for a job.

But does it make sense to subject the subordinate officers to the harshest criticism while never mentioning the chief? If we pundits were writing about a monarchy, would we fail to mention the king? (The question is more pertinent that it might seem at first. We might in fact fail to cover the king, and for some of the same reasons that we habitually fail to cover the public in our democratic system: We fear their power, which is a power not only to vote but to buy newspapers and watch television programs. What would be the ratings or the readership of an operation that continually wagged its finger at its customers?)

The fact is that in at least two areas in recent years, the voters' performance has been discouraging. One area is federal finances. Ever since 1980, the voters have picked candidates that made irresponsible financial promises. It began in 1980, when Ronald Reagan made a plainly untenable vow to cut taxes and raise military spending while at the same time balancing the budget. It continued at least until 1994, when a famously "angry" public managed to believe the promises of Newt Gingrich and the other Republican candidates for Congress that they could radically cut taxes without radically cutting spending on social programs that the public liked and depended on. When the "revolutionary" Republican Congress presented the bill, in the form of Medicare cuts and so on, the "angry" public became angry at its own creation: the Republican Congress.

Actually, of course, the voters should have been angry at themselves, for putting Gingrich and his revolutionaries in office. It's true that during this fourteen-year period, the public was gulled by deceiving or self-deceiving politicians, willing to peddle illusion to get themselves elected. But without the public's appetite for illusion, it seems safe to say, it never would have been supplied.

This brings us to the first piece of encouraging news. For the first time since 1980, the public is unimpressed by the offer of a wholly unrealistic promise of tax cuts that are unpaid for by specified spending cuts: the fifteen percent reduction in income taxes and $500 child credit offered by Dole. The polls and interviews with voters are in agreement: a majority of the voters reject the promise because, having been burned by the false promises of tax cuts by Bush and Clinton, or by the spending cuts that Gingrich's tax reductions would have required, they now know that the money promised in tax cuts will ultimately be supplied by them. It either will come out of their pockets as, for example, increased Medicare premiums, or will have to be borrowed, thus raising the budget deficit. In other words, after a decade and a half of self-deception, the public appears finally to have come to its fiscal senses.

The second area in which the voters' performance had been disappointing was in their initial response to "negative" advertising. Negative ads truly came of age in 1988, when George Bush overcame a seventeen-point lead by his Democratic rival Michael Dukakis in considerable measure by saturating the country with negative ads. The most famous of them, which was made on behalf of Bush (though it was not made by the Bush campaign), was the ad that showed the black criminal Willie Horton, who, while on parole, raped and killed a white woman that suggested that Dukakis would turn people like Horton loose on the streets. (It was also around this time that the great, proud word "liberal," under whose banner democracy put down its roots in this country and elsewhere, was confirmed as a fatal term of abuse in American politics.) The Bush campaign was not admired. One of its architects, the political strategist Lee Atwater (who helped pioneer the new wave of negative advertising), even repented on his death-bed his exploitation of radical issues in the campaign. The conventional wisdom, nevertheless, was that although the voters might dislike negative advertising, they were swayed by it anyway. The truth of the observation was confirmed by the victory of many negative campaigns. The public, apparently, let itself be guided by that which it despised. Voters made their decisions on the basis of what even in their own eyes were their darker instincts.

Yet in the area of political advertising, too, there is now good news. Dole's carefully meditated decision to attack Clinton's "character" in the last weeks of the campaign has, according to polls and interviews, also backfired. The public watching the television debate in which Dole unleashed the attacks awarded the victory to Clinton by margins of almost two to one in most polls. The tactic, recent polls have revealed, destroyed the public's trust in Dole, not Clinton, who now in fact is trusted more than Dole—a melancholy result, one might say, but only if your gaze is trained solely on the candidates, whose campaigns this year have indeed been dismaying. Dole actually won the Republican nomination in part by attacking Steve Forbes for advocating an irresponsible tax cut (the flat tax) and for unleashing a flood of negative advertising. Perhaps this is an additional reason that the public finds Dole's recent conversion to be both unconvincing and distasteful. If Dole could be secretly polled regarding his own campaign, one suspects that he wouldn't like it, either. Indeed, he has now largely desisted from the attacks on Clinton's character.

But candidates come and go, and it's even more important, I suggest, to keep an eye on their boss, the people. Aren't the people, after all, more important than any candidate? Didn't Montesquieu tell us that whereas a republic whose officials are corrupt can find a remedy by throwing them out, a republic whose people are corrupt is lost?

But—each of us might well ask ourselves—who am I to judge the people? The answer is: Each of us is one of those people, no more and no less, and as such both entitled and obligated to form an opinion regarding the decisions of our peers. As it turns out, indeed, we perhaps need not fear the wrath of our neighbors. In a finding that has no precedent that I know of, a poll done by the Media Studies Center in New York shows that seventy-eight percent of the public when asked the question, who is to blame if voters are not informed, passes up the opportunity to blame politicians and the press and instead blames themselves. This self-critical spirit is wholly in keeping with the electorate's new sober assessment of fiscal promises and its rejection of negative ads. Pollsters always ask how much we trust the candidates, but rarely inquire how much each of us trusts the public.

Looking at the evidence of recent weeks, I trust my fellow voters a little more.

NOVEMBER 10, 1996

HOW THE PEOPLE'S WILL IS DONE

THE GREAT DAY—ELECTION DAY—HAS COME AND gone. And when it was gone, everything was . . . the same. The same president was in the White House, the same party in control of both houses of Congress. Only one incumbent senator, the South Dakota Republican Larry Pressler, was defeated. None of the massed resources of graphics and virtual reality, set in cartoonish motion by Prospero-like television reporters, could bring the dead scene to life: Not ABCs space-age-imperium-style news room, with its massed banks of screens and computers, its ambulatory anchorman, and its deputy-anchor-people standing at attention at consoles like Star-Trek sub-commanders; not the kaleidoscopic, swirling graphics of NBC; not even the automated map of the USA on CBS (it didn't work anyway). Not since some 15,000 reporters assembled at each of the two parties' "nominating" conventions this summer without any story to cover have so many tried to make so much of so little. On the streets and in the workplaces of America, the verdict, heard again and again, was, "Thank God it's over!"

And yet the four years of Clinton's first term have been crammed with events—from the Republican "revolution" to the entire restructuring of the global market economy in the aftermath of the fall of the Soviet Union. Why did none of this seem to bring political change in its wake? Such uneventfulness in the midst of riptides of historical change cries out for an explanation.

In theory, an election is the day the people makes its will known. Old mandates are theoretically refreshed or new ones passed out to new representatives. But does this theory still correspond to political reality? Recent decades have witnessed the rise of the arts of public opinion polling, which makes the will of the people known every day of the year. One might argue that a professional survey with a large sample and a wide range of questions reveals more about the people's will than a national election. Certainly the information, gathered in reference to any number of issues, and broken down into subgroups according to income, age, ethnic group, and so forth, is more detailed than any election result. It's too late now, too, to wave around newspapers with "Dewey Defeats Truman" headlines as tokens of the unreliability of polling. Polls are sometimes misleading, but their accuracy in elections has been proven too often for anyone interested in political reality to ignore their results. And in actual fact, of course, the results are decisive not only for campaigns but for media coverage and even for the substantive decisions of government.

Some observers have suggested that polling reduces the public's influence by degrading the value of the actual vote, whose outcome is predicted in advance. The opposite, I suggest, is more nearly true. Polling results make the public's will known and influential even when there is no election. After all, politicians don't pay *less* attention to public opinion because they know *more* about it. Polls are perhaps best considered as advisory referenda on the doings and reputations of politicians, who thereby are placed under instant and unremitting pressure to adjust. This influence, indeed, is so great that it constitutes a virtual referendum system of government that now is in direct competition with the representative system. But since in fact we have both at the same time, the result is a confusing hybrid.

Let us consider, for example, the case of the House Republicans elected in 1994. By their own description they were "revolutionaries." Conservatives had pulled down the Soviet Union, House leaders reasoned; now they would pull down the liberal welfare state. They demonstrated that they meant business in 1995 when they allowed the government to partially shut down twice rather than compromise with the president on the federal budget. The public's sharply unfavorable reaction was immediate, and immediately made known in the polls. A titanic duel ensued for the high ground in public opinion between President Bill Clinton and House Speaker Newt Gingrich. The president—a sort of genius at these games—adopted a strategy of initial retreat (accepting, for example, the Republican demand for a plan to balance the federal budget in seven years) and then resisting. He won decisively, as was made known, of course, in the opinion polls, which showed his popularity beginning to steadily rise while that of Gingrich and his House sank.

But that was not the end of the story. What happened next is something very like what is supposed to happen in an election: The Republicans reversed course. The difference from the result of an election was that personnel did not change; only policy did. Thus, public opinion surveys are in effect like elections minus the opportunity to throw the bums out.

The bums, however, are free to act. They can change their stripes. . . . And that is what the Republicans did. No more did they speak of "revolution." All now were "moderates," in the "mainstream." They backed off their attacks on the environment, let a vote on an increase in the minimum wage take place (with some even voting for it), and passed a health bill co-sponsored by Massachusetts' Sen. Ted Kennedy.

But these acts of adjustment are of course open to both parties. The Republicans were indeed only following the example of the master of adjustment, Bill Clinton, who, under the guidance of his former consultant Dick Morris, had started *his* mid-term flight to the "center" a year before the Republicans. Not since Kafka's hero, Grigor Samsa, woke up a cockroach have we been treated to such a startling display of human metamorphosis. While the Republicans were dashing to the center (a vacuous, amoral place, whose sole true defining characteristic is that most of the voters are there, too) from the right, Clinton was dashing there from the left (if there is such a thing as a "left" in American politics anymore). Both made it to their destination by Election Day.

And so both were re-elected. The commotion of the television ads was the sound and fury not of two sides battling for their separate and independent party positions but of two armies trying to run away from those positions toward the sacred "center" while driving their opponents out of it into some "extreme" margin of the political landscape. The politicians had all changed themselves into what the public thought it wanted them to be before the public's very eyes.

Thus was the people's will done—not in the Great Election of 1996 but in the great metamorphosis of 1995.

DECEMBER 1, 1996

DE-DEFINITION

I FOLLOWED THE PRESIDENTIAL CAMPAIGN CLOSELY for most of the year, and from start to finish I was bothered by a feeling of dissatisfaction that I was never quite able to define or articulate. I was reminded of this by something George Will said just after the election on "This Week with David Brinkley." President Bill Clinton had just said that balancing the budget would be his number one priority, and Will pronounced that this was "the best example of how far the country has moved to the right."

Will was justified, it seemed to me, in saying that the country was more interested in balancing the budget than it had been at any time in recent years—certainly since the beginning of the 1980s, when the national debt began its rapid widening. But was balancing the budget a cause of the "right"? Hadn't the budget run out of control under President Ronald Reagan, who had set about cutting taxes without achieving corresponding spending cuts? And hadn't Bob Dole offered that same recipe to the voters this year by proposing a five percent tax cut and failing, once more, to spell out offsetting cuts in spending? And hadn't poll after poll shown that this was one of the reasons that people were rejecting Dole and voting for Clinton?

And, finally, hadn't Clinton, at the very beginning of his term, put through a budget reduction program of tax increases without a single Republican vote? Was Clinton, then, now on the "right," and were Republicans from Reagan to Dole on the "left"? Did it make sense to designate either party's position on the budget as right or left? Did these words have meaning? Do we know what we are saying any more if we say that someone, or the whole country, is moving right or moving left? If we do, do the words or deeds of either of the parties correspond to the definition? The more I thought about these questions, the more it seemed to me that they had to be answered in the negative.

To describe the blurring of words and ideas that the above questions suggest, I propose an ugly term: the de-definition of American politics. If I can give an excuse for introducing such an ugly term it is that it takes its place in a certain tradition of ugly terms. First, there is realignment. In a realignment, the voters quit one of the two major parties and give their allegiance to the other, or, more rarely, to a third party. The classic realignment of the first kind occurred in the 1930s, when a period of Republican dominance ended with the rise of the New Deal coalition founded by Franklin Roosevelt.

There has been a lot of speculation, not to say wishful thinking, in Republican circles that since the late 1960s we have been in the midst of a realignment in which the public is switching back to the Republicans. Exhibit A for this claim is invariably the switch of the south from a Democratic to a Republican stronghold. The classic realignment of the second kind occurred in 1860, when Abraham Lincoln became the candidate of the fledgling Republican Party and won the presidency. Ross Perot has been trying in our day to pull off a similar realignment in favor of his Reform Party.

The second ugly term in this tradition is dealignment. Dealignment occurs when the voters, finding neither major party to their taste, drift away from both, without finding a third. Both the word and the act of dealignment are something comparatively new. With the rise of the mass media, the voters, analysts point out, have lost such traditional ties to parties as trade unions and party machines, and choose their allegiance on the basis of presidential debates, campaign ads, and so forth. These voters are, depending on your point of view, either a class of independent thinkers who refuse to vote on the basis of a mere party label, or a sort of electronic peasantry, swayed by the large mass of manipulators of public opinion that now seems to be fully in charge of political campaigns. Voters' choices, in either case, represent no deep philosophical or ideological allegiance. These voters are independent—that is, up for grabs in each election.

Beyond dealignment is depoliticization. If the realigned voter is a one-time party switcher, and the dealigned voter has no lasting preference among parties, the depoliticized person is no voter at all. He is bored or disgusted with politics per se, and joins the fifty-one percent of the electorate that failed to vote in this last election.

None of this, however, is de-definition, the hallmark of the last election. In de-definition—the process by which familiar political terms lose their meaning—two things happen. In the first, the parties abandon their principles in pursuit of votes. In this process, it's not the voters that abandon the parties, but the parties that abandon whatever it was that they once stood for. That, plainly, was how Bob Dole, who as a legislator had been a true supporter of budgetary responsibility (and paid a political price for it), wound up proposing the fifteen percent tax cut. It's impossible to believe that Dole believed in this tax cut, but easy to believe that his advisers thought the voters would believe in it. Budget-busting tax cuts, after all, had been mightily effective in getting Republicans elected throughout the 1980s, budget responsibility be damned.

The same sort of political calculation, it seems clear, led

Clinton to abandon the traditional Democratic commitment to the poor, and sign the Republican Congress's repeal of the federal guarantee of welfare aid to families with dependent children. The difference between the two betrayals was that whereas Dole's backfired politically, Clinton's turned out to be astute. (Polls show that the welfare bill is extremely popular.)

Both parties were hell-bent for the same destination: what Clinton calls "the vital center" and Senate Majority Leader Trent Lott hails as a new Republican agenda that will not "stray too far to the right or to the left." Politicians who cash in their principles for power are, of course, no new thing under the sun, though our poll-possessed officials seem to go about it these days more systematically than anyone has before. They have turned the art of selling out into a science.

The second process involved in de-definition is perhaps harder to define but no less important. This, too, is an ancient phenomenon that, in our time, has accelerated. Put simply, it is the world's habit of changing faster than the political language and ideas we use to describe the world. In realignment and dealignment, voters are drifting (from one party to another, away from permanent allegiance to any party, away from politics altogether); and in the first phase of de-definition the parties are drifting (away from their traditional beliefs and principles). In this second stage of de-definition it is the world itself—history, if you like—that is drifting, as the world always has and always will, challenging everyone to keep up.

The greatest change, of course, was the end—as unexpected as it was abrupt—of the Cold War, which pulled the axle from the hub of almost a half-century of American foreign policy. What remained was a heap of fragments whose connection, if any, was not clear. (For example, the abstract debate, which divides both parties, pitting "interventionists" against "noninterventionists," becomes theoretical almost to the point of meaninglessness without the context of the confrontation with communism.) Nor has there been much pressure to rearrange these fragments on the part of the public, which seems to have forgotten that the United States shares the planet with other nations. The collapse of the framework of foreign policy sent the parties scurrying to domestic politics to define themselves—with the unsatisfactory results just mentioned.

But one may object that all this talk of definitions, principles and frameworks, and of their attenuated connection to political parties, voters and events, is merely academic, purely philosophical and without consequence for the real business of politics. I would answer that these matters are as politically real as poll numbers, election results and tax receipts. Let us consider, for example, the fortunes of Bob Dole. Wasn't his failure, at bottom, a failure to deal with politics under conditions of advanced de-definition? The Republicans were especially hard hit by the end of the Cold War. Opposing Communists and their supposed sympathizers had been their stock-in-trade. It has been no easy matter, in an era of public disinterest in foreign affairs, to redefine the party in terms of domestic issues alone. And yet that was the challenge the Republicans faced in the primary season.

The Republican Party, by its own description, was a "conservative" party. But what did this now mean? Steve Forbes, Patrick Buchanan, Phil Gramm, and Lamar Alexander all called themselves "conservative." Did conservative mean cutting taxes without cutting spending, according to supply-side theory, or did it mean cutting spending, too? House Speaker Newt Gingrich (R-

Ga.), leader of the Republican "revolution" of 1994, said the latter, but Steve Forbes, advocate of a flat tax, made waves early in the primary season championing the former. Was it conservative to sign free trade agreements, such as GATT and NAFTA? Getting governments out of the way of the market had been bedrock Republican principle for several generations. But now Patrick Buchanan, called an extreme "conservative" by himself and others, opposed these agreements. Should the government interfere in such "social" questions as prayer in schools, abortion, and the sexual content of movies, television and the Internet? The religious right, now a mainstay of Republican strength, said yes; the libertarian wing of the party said no.

Was it conservative to protect the environment or to oppose those protections? In 1994, the Republican revolutionaries attacked environmental regulation; but recently the highly "conservative" Sen. John McCain (R-Ariz.) advised his party that protecting the environment had not, traditionally, been only a liberal issue.

Such were the issues that roiled the early Republican primaries. If there was anything positive to say about this political brawl it is that it did represent an attempt, of sorts, by the party to redefine itself. Yet it was all to no avail. The three strong champions of particular views—Phil Gramm, who was the closest thing in the race to a representative of the Gingrich revolution; Steve Forbes, who championed supply-side economics; and Patrick Buchanan, the economic nationalist—all went down to defeat. None of these figures was able to unite the party around his new definition of what it meant to be a "conservative." The winner by default was Bob Dole. Throughout the general election, Dole was faulted, a million times over, for lacking a "vision." Pundits wagged their fingers, advisers pushed him from within the campaign, elected officials urged and prodded him, and Republican congressional candidates tore out their hair, but the best Dole could do by way of a vision was the warmed-over supply-side tax cut that he himself could not possibly believe in. The truth was that Dole was chosen as the nominee *because* he lacked a vision. He was unable single-handedly to forge the redefinition of his party that an army of rivals had failed to achieve in the early primaries.

And what of Clinton? He proved himself the very master of the political arts in an undefined political era. He offered a long series of careful adjustments, in which, on the one hand, he backed away from traditional principles of his party, such as guaranteeing the social safety net, and, on the other hand, drew a contrast between his position and the undoubtedly bold cuts in health and other social spending advocated by the "revolutionary" Gingrich. These adjustments were accompanied by a collection of carefully poll-tested mini-proposals, such as the V-chip and the proposal for school uniforms. In other words, without championing any particular vision of his own, Clinton bobbed and weaved (that is, "triangulated," in the new terminology) between two visions, one Democratic, the other Republican. It wasn't till the latter part of the campaign that observers began to note that Clinton had as little to suggest as a vision as Dole, and that they had no idea what the president might do in his second term.

Some consequences of de-definition are deeper still. E.J. Dionne has suggested in *The Washington Post* that we are perhaps too much occupied in identifying "frameworks." He has a point, yet in politics frameworks have an indispensable role to play, if only because, in a basically two-party representative system, the political world must be organized along lines of broad principle if the voters' choice is to be meaningful. We pejoratively dub as "labels" such alternatives as "right" and "left," "conservative" and "liberal." The fact is that without binary phrases such as these our binary party system fails. These are the language of the party system, and if the language becomes unintelligible, the system cannot serve its appointed end, which is to discover and enact the will of the electorate. For without a language to speak, how can the people's will be heard?

INDEX

INDEX

COLOPHON

The text of this book was set in Times New Roman PS, a typeface designed by Stanley Morrison (1889–1967). This face, designed for *The Times* of London, was the result of a criticism Morrison made to the management of the *The Times* complaining of the paper's typography. They asked him to improve it. Working for the Monotype Corporation, Morrison designed a face based on Granjon, and delivered it for use beginning in 1932. It has since become one of the most widely used faces and is often copied because of its readability.

Composed by Alabama Book Composition, Deatsville, Alabama.

The book was printed by Thomson-Shore, Inc., Dexter, Michigan on acid-free paper.

Moyer Bell
Kymbolde Way
Wakefield, RI 02879